THE BIG BEND

The

Big Bend

A History of the
Last Texas Frontier

RON C. TYLER

Texas A&M University Press
COLLEGE STATION

Third Texas A&M University Press printing, 2003

Originally published in 1975 by the National Park Service
Published in 1996 by Texas A&M University Press by arrangement
with the Big Bend Natural History Association

The paper used in this book meets the minimum requirements
of the American National Standard for Permanence
of Paper for Printed Library Materials, Z39.48-1984.
Binding materials have been chosen for durability.

Library of Congress Cataloging-in-Publication Data

Tyler, Ron C., 1941-
    The Big Bend : a history of the last Texas Frontier / Ron C.
Tyler. — 1st Texas A&M University Press ed.
        p.   cm.
    Originally published: Washington : Office of Publications,
    National Park Service, U.S. Dept. of the Interior : Supt. of
Docs., U.S. Govt. Print. Off., 1975.
    Includes bibliographical references and index.
    ISBN 0-89096-706-7
    1. Big Bend (Tex.) —History. 2. Big Bend National
Park   (Tex.)—History. I. Title.
F392.B54.T9   1996
976.4'93—dc20   95-26445
                                                                       CIP

CONTENTS

FOREWORD

The Big Bend region of Texas is one of the great wonders of the Southwest. Wild, vast, and isolated, this land of desert, river canyon, and rugged mountains is as close to the primeval as anything on this continent. Four centuries ago, Spanish explorers labeled it *el despoblado,* the uninhabited land. As late as the 1880s a traveler crossing the region saw it as a place with "no vegetation other than brambles, no view other than the immense sandy plains. . . . Words cannot convey the strangeness and supreme melancholy of the landscape."

Yet for all its remoteness and inhospitality to settlement, the Big Bend has enjoyed a rich human past. That story, from aboriginal times to events of recent memory, is the subject of this volume, which was initially published in 1975 as the joint work of the National Park Service and the Amon Carter Museum of Western Art, Fort Worth. Surveying topics as diverse as Spanish exploration, trade over the Chihuahua Trail, U.S. Army mapping expeditions, ranching, mining, bandit raids, and the establishment of the national park, the author helps us to a better understanding of a region that has touched the destinies of two nations. Included is a listing, with maps, of important surviving historic sites and an essay on the sources on which this account rests.

The author is Ron C. Tyler, former curator of history at the museum. His narrative was the first modern history of the Big Bend Country. It has since been reissued in a slightly different format but with the same purpose as before: to stimulate historical interest in a little known region and to interpret for students and travelers the human side of the last Texas frontier.

ACKNOWLEDGMENTS

Many people have assisted in the research and preparation of both the book and the accompanying exhibition: Dr. Ross A. Maxwell, former superintendent of Big Bend National Park and professor of geology at the University of Texas at Austin; Mr. and Mrs. Hart Greenwood of Alamito; W. D. Smithers of El Paso; Dr. Calhoun Harris Monroe and Floride Harris of El Paso; and W. P. Cameron of Mineral Wells consented to be interviewed. Mrs. Lee Bennett of Marfa, Dr. Clifford B. Casey of Alpine, and Frank Temple of Lubbock shared their material and research. Joe Coltharp, Curator of Photography for the Humanities Research Center at the University of Texas (Austin), Dr. Chester V. Kielman, Librarian-Archivist at the Barker Texas History Center, University of Texas (Austin); Roy Sylvan Dunn, Curator of the Southwest Collection at Texas Tech University, Lubbock; Carol Crowfoot, Curator of Photography at the Texas State Library, Austin; Elmer O. Parker and his staff, Old Military Records Division, National Archives and Records Service, Washington, D.C.; Joan Cobb and her staff in the Photography Division, National Archives; Irvil P. Schultz, librarian, U.S. Geological Survey, Denver, and Dr. Ignacio Rubio Mañe, Director, Archivo General de la Nación, México, D.F., helped me with their respective collections; Peggy Ponton of Big Bend National Park helped prepare the historical sites appendix.

I received many helpful suggestions from Dr. Sandra L. Myres, University of Texas (Arlington); Dr. Dorman Winfrey, Director, Texas State Library; Dr. Donald Everett, Trinity University, San Antonio; Peter Koch, Alpine; Prof. Miram A. Lowrance, Sul Ross State University; Steve Schuster, El Centro College, Dallas; Jane Pattie, Fort Worth; David Clary, National Park Service, Omaha; Leonard Sanders, Jr., *Fort Worth Star-Telegram;* and from my wife Paula.

Nancy G. Wynne, librarian, and Margaret McLean, former newspaper archivist of the Amon Carter Museum, helped collect materials throughout the project. Faythe Taylor typed the manuscript many times, and Karen Dewees prepared the index.

R.T. Fort Worth, Texas, April, 1975

THE BIG BEND

1 / World of the Big Bend

Although hard bread and unsalted venison did not make a holiday feast, Texas Ranger Capt. Charles L. Nevill probably enjoyed his meal as he pondered his good fortune. He was, after all, alive – a remarkable blessing, considering his recent adventures. A few days earlier, when he and four of his best rangers had set out to accompany a State land survey on a float down a section of the Rio Grande known as the Big Bend, they had thought a good deal about the dangers of traveling through an uncharted terrain. Yet such considerations had not adequately prepared them for the river's unsympathetic fury.

Nevill, his four rangers, and surveyors John T. Gano, Edward L. Gage, and E. M. Powell – "the greenest set of boatmen that ever started down any river" – had set out from Presidio del Norte on December 19, 1881, intending to navigate a previously unexplored section of the Rio Grande. Nevill was aware that other expeditions had attempted to float these canyons but had been stopped by natural obstacles – or fear. He saw more clearly the difficulties ahead when he damaged his own boat the first day, and his fears increased when his party entered the mountains. The banks rose higher around them, and the current swept them along toward the first big rapids. The men cautiously steered their boats around threatening boulders, and with the dangers temporarily behind them were able to proceed. "Everything went lovely," Nevill wrote. "The boys learned 'to boat' very fast."

But soon carelessness, deceptive currents, and whirlpools combined to teach the overconfident crew a lesson. They slammed into a rock, scattering men, supplies, and over 300 rounds of ammunition across the water. "I was carried down the river like I was shot out of a gun," Nevill recalled. "I had on my big boots, coat, pistol and belts, and of course as soon as I struck an eddy I sank. When I came up, I caught on a rock and by standing up my head and shoulders would be out of the water."

The rumors about the treacherous canyons and rapids of the Rio Grande were true. The captain no doubt swore at his carelessness as he perched precariously on the rock, clutching his favorite pipe between his teeth. While gesturing to a companion about to swim into the current, Nevill lost his balance and slipped off the rock. "I went under . . . [and] was so played I thought I would never make it out." Having "no further use for a fine pipe, . . . I spit it out."

Nevill finally pulled himself ashore and took stock. He, Gano, and a ranger had almost drowned. Besides his field glass, he lost nearly all the ammunition and most of the food. Christmas dinner consisted of fresh venison without salt. Neither coffee nor sugar survived the mishap. Nevill was sick for several days, but resumed the trip on January 2, only to face Santa Elena Canyon, the "one with a bad reputation – one that no outfit ever ventured to tackle before," he wrote. Recalling that the boundary survey team of 1852 had scouted the canyon, then sent an empty boat through but that "no two planks came out together," Nevill and his party decided that not everyone should risk a canyon that local Mexicans described as "utterly impassable." Two boatmen, in fact, deserted before reaching the canyon. Nevill took two men who could not swim and rode up on the Mesa de Anguila to watch the surveyors' progress. "I was so high above them, when they would hallow at me I could not distinguish a word said, and they could not hear me at all," he reported. The boatmen halted at the rock slide on January 4 and lost a day and a half portaging around it. Everyone finally reached the mouth on January 9.[1]

The Nevill-Gano expedition was the first documented float through Santa Elena, but Nevill's brief published report did not attract attention. What was even then acknowledged to be one of the least known and most beautiful sections of the State remained unknown. While Clarence King, John Wesley Powell, and Ferdinand V. Hayden were describing the majestic beauty of the Sierra Nevadas, the Grand Canyon, and Yellowstone National Park, Texans grew curious about the vast "Great Bend." The Mexican Boundary Survey team had wrecked its boats in Mariscal Canyon in 1852. Western artist George Catlin floated down the Rio Grande in 1855 but apparently left no journals or pictures. By 1883 curiosity had so overcome the editor of the *El Paso Daily Herald* that he appealed to other newspapers to contribute to an expedition to ex-

plore the Big Bend. Its "sublime and majestic scenery" would soon
be available to the Nation from detailed reports he would publish,
he predicted. "Texas is about to eclipse anything that has heretofore
been produced within the limits of North America." [2]

An expedition similar to the one the editor had visualized was
organized in 1899 when Robert T. Hill of the U.S. Geological Survey floated from Presidio to Langtry. Intrigued by rumors of
ghosts in the Chisos Mountains, bandits lurking along the river,
and 7,000-foot gorges, Hill and his small party left Presidio in October. Three weeks later they pulled themselves from the sandy
Rio Grande with geographical and geological data for Hill's study
and the first photographs of the region. Although Hill believed
they were in constant danger, the trip in reality was little more
than a pleasant float through one of the most scenic areas of the
Southwest. "We . . . navigated and mapped three hundred and fifty
miles of a portion of one of America's greatest rivers which hith-
erto had been considered impassable," Hill boasted. Traveling
through the "longest and least known . . . and . . . least accessible"
canyons in the country, Hill "escaped dangers which had over-

Texas Ranger Charles L. Nevill (left).
Dr. Robert T. Hill (above, second from left)
with his party shortly after leaving the
Rio Grande near Langtry, Texas, in 1899.

3

Hill's camp at Leon Rock, near Fort Davis.

whelmed those who had attempted the cañons before: and our little party dispersed contented with its success." [3]

Though Hill found no 7,000-foot deep canyons, his survey culminated years of desire and several attempts to navigate the Big Bend canyons. Hill's successful trip disproved rumors of cutthroat bandits lurking behind each cliff and corrected the fanciful tales of tricks that nature played on unsuspecting intruders.[4]

Many dangers Hill encountered were simply the products of a desert climate and an unbelievably rugged landscape. Even today the most impressive feature of the Big Bend is its vastness. Lodged squarely in the crook where the Rio Grande encounters the southern tip of the Rocky Mountains and turns abruptly from a leisurely southeastern course to the northeast – hence the name Big Bend that Lt. William H. C. Whiting applied in 1849 – the country remains in its "original chaotic state." Including the territory from Candelaria or Ruidoso on the Rio Grande 50 miles eastward to Marfa, then paralleling the Southern Pacific Railroad tracks for over 100 miles through Alpine, Marathon, Sanderson, and Dryden on the north, the Big Bend has always been an out-of-the-way place visited only by the adventurous or patient.

The cultural area encompassed in the term "Big Bend" is often larger. It includes Fort Davis, 20 miles beyond Alpine, where soldiers and Texas Rangers who patrolled the three-quarters of a million acres that now make up the National Park were stationed. Present-day Van Horn, 55 miles northwest of Fort Davis, is usually included in the region, and some think of the Big Bend and the Trans-Pecos as being practically synonymous. Writers have always considered the Big Bend in broad terms. Folklorist J. Frank Dobie researched the Trans-Pecos for several of his stories of lost Spanish treasures, wild mustangs, and cowboys. It is also the scene of untold stories that would rival Dobie's best and the legends of Pecos Bill himself. To Lt. William Echols, viewing this terrain from the back of a camel in 1860, the Bend was a "picture of barrenness and desolation," a place fit to be called the last frontier in Texas. Nor did 40 years ameliorate its ruggedness, for surveyor O. W. Williams found it so impassable in 1901 that he had to make many of his measurements by triangulation rather than by chain.[5]

Although the region is geologically complex, the Indians had a simple explanation for the unusual landscape. When the Great Creator had completed the earth and placed the stars in the sky, the fish in the sea, and the birds in the air, He had a massive heap of stony rubble left over. He hurled it into the Trans-Pecos where it landed in a pile and became known as the Big Bend. Ross A. Maxwell, a geologist and former superintendent of the national park, has offered a more scientific explanation, which relies on standard geological theories. Fossil shells, sedimentary rocks, and other evidence indicate that the Big Bend once lay under a shallow sea. As the continent heaved and shifted, various parts of the land were exposed to the air, permitting the growth of swamp vegetation and providing habitat for many animals now long extinct.

Over 100 million years ago a general shift in the continent produced the Rocky Mountains and the Sierra Madres, which extend from Canada to Mexico. The Chisos Mountains jut out of the Big Bend desert between the two, a mass of twisted and crumpled

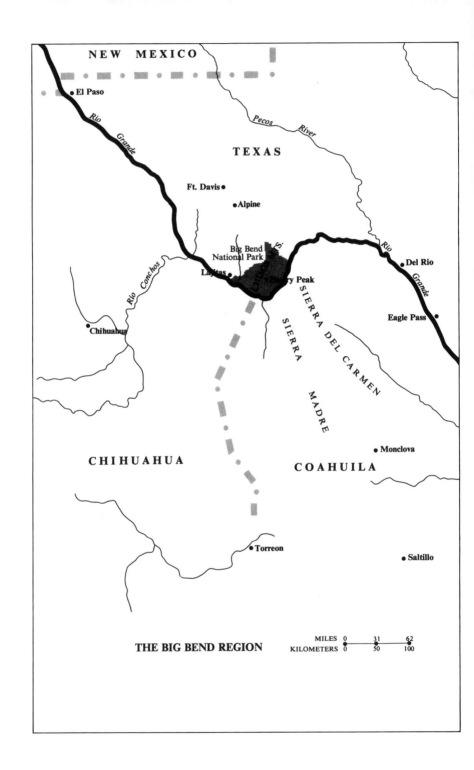

NEW MEXICO

● El Paso

Rio Grande

Pecos River

TEXAS

Ft. Davis ●

● Alpine

Big Bend
National Park

Rio Conchos

Lajitas ●

● Chihuahua

CHIHUAHUA

Torreon ●

Rio Grande

● Del Rio

Eagle Pass ●

SIERRA DEL CARMEN

SIERRA MADRE

● Monclova

COAHUILA

● Saltillo

THE BIG BEND REGION

MILES   0   31   62
KILOMETERS 0   50   100

Temple Canyon, photographed by Hill in 1899.

rock but not as high as either major range. Further shifting created
Terlingua Fault, an elongated block of the earth's crust that broke
and tilted upward. Thousands of years later the Rio Grande, aided
by the drainage patterns of the fault itself, patiently carved Santa
Elena Canyon.

The remains of this process not only explain the existence
of a complex region, but also provide some of the Big Bend's
most interesting features. Dinosaur bones, evidence of marshes,
two skulls of a crocodile-like monster, and other examples have
been found. The popular flagstone rocks of the Boquillas Formation are the remains of lime mud deposited during the early Upper
Cretaceous period 130 million years ago. Other animal remains familiar only to professional paleontologists are thought to have been
native to the Big Bend.

The ruggedness of the land is matched by the harsh climate.
The sun scorches down most of the year, and only vegetation
adapted to heat and drought flourishes. Big Bend residents endure
dry summers, broken only by 15 to 17 inches of rainfall annually
from dark clouds apparently snagged on the peaks of the towering
Chisos. The surrounding lowlands are less fortunate, receiving only
10 to 12 inches each year. Simply put, the Big Bend is a desert,

7

Maverick Mountain, at the northwest entrance
to the national park, in an evening rainstorm.

occupying the northern part of what once was the vast Chihuahuan Desert that covered two-thirds of the present Mexican state of Chihuahua, one-half of the state of Coahuila, and a large portion of western Texas. The Rio Grande, which has cut canyons through the heart of the mountains, seems at times to have its very existence threatened by this ferocious desert.

The Spaniards had a name for such an area: *despoblado,* or uninhabited land. The Big Bend is the mouth of the *despoblado,* which, on the map, appears as a funnel-shaped area bounded on the east by the road from Saltillo to San Juan Bautista, near Eagle Pass, Texas; on the west by the road from Chihuahua City to El Paso; and on the south by Parras and Torreón. It forms the northern boundary of this desolate yet impressive region. The Spaniards so feared the hostility of both Indians and the land that they traveled from El Paso to San Juan Bautista by circling southward through the frontier settlements of Mapimí, Laguna de la Leche, Cuatro Ciénegas, and Monclova, then swinging northward along one of the well-traveled routes. Only the Rio Grande penetrates the *despoblado,* although several other rivers play around it. Battered and worn smooth by wind-whipped sand, its features show the marks of a perpetual struggle—wind, rain, and sun matched against the land. Even the vegetation marks off and defends its living space. "Each plant in this land is a porcupine," wrote a 19th-century traveler. "It is nature armed to the teeth." [7]

The most recognizable feature of the Big Bend begins near Lajitas where the Rio Grande meanders through the foothills of the Mesa de Anguila and the Sierra Ponce. Santa Elena Canyon is shallow and open for the first 11 miles, with the river gathering momentum as it approaches the mesa. Steep cliffs and narrow passages mark the beginning of the deepest portion of the gorge. In the swifter current, boatmen are less sure, the margin for error considerably reduced. The canyon walls reach 1,500 feet, virtually imprisoning every creature that enters. Hill and his crew watched in sympathy as a covey of quail attempted to fly high enough to escape the rocky confines, only to fail and settle exhausted on one of the pinnacles. [8]

Santa Elena, which probably received its name from Louis

Ramírez who founded the nearby Mexican settlement of the same name, has always offered a challenge to those who would navigate the Rio Grande. About 6 miles from the mouth of the canyon is a rock slide that has troubled all canyon explorers. Arthur C. V. Schott, the draftsman with the Boundary Survey team, unimaginatively sketched the "falls" in 1852. The Nevill party took a day and a half to portage their boats over the rocks, and Hill called the spot Camp Misery. Trapping down the Rio Grande in the first decade of this century, T. M. Meler hesitated before entering the canyon. Just as the party almost decided not to risk the unknown dangers of the chasm, they spotted a message carved on the face of a large rock by Hill and the Geological Survey expedition of a few years before. "So we sed if uthers could go thro we could do it too," Meler reported. Their confidence was shaken, however, when just a mile inside the canyon they came face to face with the rock slide–20-foot boulders piled 200 to 300 feet high, with water pouring through. But Meler and his party carried their boats over and continued. "It was some haird job but wee wer haird trappers," he explained.[9]

Another well-known feature of the canyon, located just a mile below the rock slide on the Mexican side, is Smuggler's Cave, a dark opening about halfway up the wall, reportedly a hideout for cattle rustlers and outlaws. Smoke discoloration on the ceiling and tobacco and sardine cans on the ground seem to indicate a more recent resident than an Indian or a 19th-century bandit. Hill was particularly impressed with rumors of badmen on the loose in the Big Bend. He called that portion of the river below Lajitas Murderer's Canyon.[10]

The mouth of the canyon is the most spectacular sight. Flowing placidly from the 1,500-foot precipice, the river idles over a vast, fertile floodplain, as Terlingua Creek, the tributary in the Big Bend most likely to contain water, joins it at the base of the fault. The mouth of the canyon was the most often seen part of what is today the national park, even during the 18th and 19th centuries, when it was variously called the "wall" of San Damasio, the "Great Cañon San Carlos," and the "Grand Puerta." The lowlands at the mouth of the canyon were a beautiful sight to Meler and his friends, because "it taken us most of 4 days to git thrown that hole." The Geological Survey party "lingered long in contemplation of this most remarkable feature." [11]

Today the trip can be made in a day if the water is high enough. Usually it is a pleasant 2-day float, made enjoyable by the feeling that grips the traveler when night descends and the canyon

The mouth of Santa Elena Canyon.

is lighted only by moonlight reflecting off the walls and the water. Then, if not before, one is convinced of the grandeur of nature and the insignificance of a solitary man. It is only one of many places in the Big Bend where a traveler can be alone with his thoughts for a long period. Shielded from mechanical interruptions–and even radio waves – the interior of Santa Elena Canyon is an expressive reminder of what Hill and his 19th-century comrades were among the first to see.

Farther down river is Mariscal Canyon, the least accessible of the national park's three major canyons. Isolated at the southernmost tip of the Big Bend, Mariscal probably received its name from a local *jefe*, Albino Villa Alfelias, a well-known Indian fighter. The Spanish word *mariscal* can mean either marshal or blacksmith. Perhaps it also connoted an important person, or chief, such as Alfelias. Because of its proximity to the old Spanish presidio of San Vicente, Mariscal has also been known as Little San Vicente Canyon.

Carved from rugged Mariscal Mountain, the canyon contains some of the most spectacular scenery on the river. Sheer walls reach 1,600 feet. The horizon is squeezed into ribbons of light that separate the cliffs, illuminating the river as it forces its way over rock slides and boulders worn smooth. While it has no rock slide to equal the one in Santa Elena, Mariscal can be difficult to navigate if the river is high. The 1852 Boundary Survey team wrecked their boat, probably in Mariscal, and were forced to continue the journey on foot.[12] Mariscal is perhaps the most often traveled of the three major canyons, easily floated in less than a day, even when the water is low. It was inhabited until recently by a man who wanted to get away from civilization. He lived in a shallow cave on the Mexican side of the river, and dubbed his camp Dropp Knife, Mexico. A short distance upriver is the Big Bend's best known candelilla wax camp, where the candelilla plant is boiled and pure wax was recovered. It stands on the Mexican side of the river, and can be visited by almost everyone who floats through the canyon. Floaters must paddle furiously to complete the trip through Mariscal Canyon, because the winds at the canyon exit blow upriver with force.

Boquillas, the longest of the Rio Grande canyons, is carved from the massive limestone peaks of the Sierra del Carmen range. Boquillas' walls are more open than Mariscal's and reach as high as 1,500 feet. Some have suggested that the gorge is named Boquillas (a slang form of "little mouths" in Spanish) because of the canyon's narrow mouth. Perhaps it got the name from the hundreds of small erosions in the Sierra del Carmen range, which resembled little mouths. The Spanish word itself translates as the opening to a pant's leg or the mouth of an irrigation canal, either of which could be construed to be related to the mouth of a canyon. The high peak near its entrance is Schott Tower, named for Arthur Schott.

Boquillas is possibly the least known of the canyons historically. Both the American and Mexican boundary survey teams marched around it rather than risk its unknown dangers in 1851 and 1852. Col. Emilio Langberg of the Mexican team cited its length and the "many opportunities its land gives for enemy ambushes" as his reason for circling the canyon. Although Captain Nevill's party might have floated through it in 1882, they left no record that they did. The first documented passage through Boquillas was Hill's expedition of 1899, which discovered that Boquillas is probably the calmest of the three major canyons. Adventurers frequently raft or canoe through the canyon today, making a leisurely trip of 2 or 3 days. There are no rapids or dangerous spots in the canyon, and the small Mexican village at the mouth makes it one of the most frequented spots in the national park.[13]

In the midst of the Big Bend desert stands the Chisos Mountains, a legendary refuge of ghosts and spirits. They reminded Colonel Langberg of "distant figures like castles and turrets whose heights can be seen from afar; one never loses sight of this beautiful range through nearly all the expedition." Although Chisos was the name of a tribe of Indians, the term has now been inextricably associated with ghosts, an association first mentioned in print by Hill in 1901. But the old storyteller Natividad Lujan once told Judge O. W. Williams of Fort Stockton a spellbinding tale about the Apache chieftain Alsate that might explain the association of ghosts with the mountains. The warrior was betrayed to Mexican officials at San Carlos by Leonecio Castillo. The tribe was then marched off into slavery in southern Mexico, and Alsate was executed. It was soon whispered among the residents of the Big Bend that Alsate's ghost roamed his old hunting grounds. When Castillo, the informer, left the country, the ghost disappeared. Believing that the danger had passed, Castillo returned. So did the ghost.

One version of the story describes a confrontation between

Castillo and the ghost of Alsate. Castillo had stopped for the night in a cave in the Chisos when he recalled betraying the chief. Thinking of Alsate's oath of revenge, Castillo laughed out loud, then glanced up to see Alsate's face carved in the features of the mountain across the valley. He quickly turned away, seeking to blot out the vision, but he heard Alsate's soul crying out for revenge. Castillo disappeared from the Big Bend. Although the tale varies from storyteller to storyteller, the rock formation named for Alsate is easily seen in Green Gulch in the Chisos, about a mile east of the basin road junction.[14]

Others have claimed that the term "ghosts" is associated more directly with events that happen in the mountains themselves. Some have reported that the play of moonlight creates a "spooky" effect on the gray vegetation of the mountainsides. One hunter claims to have seen an entire valley illuminated as if in daylight, while Ross A. Maxwell has described a "luminous pulsating light" dancing over the mountain peaks or on the roads. Several newspapers have carried stories of strange "Marfa lights," with the usual explanation of ghosts of long-departed Indians and lost gold mines that glow at night. But Maxwell offers a more reasonable explanation: perhaps the lights are reflections of moonlight produced by tiny mineral grains or the phosphorescent glow given off by rotten wood.

Of course, there are those who insist that the mountains themselves might have been shrouded in mist—and therefore appeared "ghostly"—when seen by the Spaniards. Still, the mystery of the Chisos and the ghosts remains. "Nowhere have I found such a wildly weird country," wrote an 1896 visitor to the Chisos. "The very silence is oppressive. A man grows watchful for his own safety and becomes awe-struck by nature in her lofty moods." [15]

One of the most magnificent sights in the Big Bend is the view from the South Rim of the Chisos. Half a day's journey from the Basin, the South Rim can be reached on foot or horseback. After passing by Boot Rock, Boot Canyon, and Boot Springs, one can see on a clear day Santa Elena Canyon some 20 miles to the southwest and Schott Tower another 25 miles to the east. The visitor who watches majestic vultures soar off the rim cannot help but understand the feelings of Texas Ranger Captain E. E. Townsend as he looked out over the Big Bend from the nearby Burro Mesa:

> It was a vision of such magnitude as to stir the sluggish soul
> of a Gila Monster. It was so awe-inspiring that it did deeply
> touch the soul of a hardened human bloodhound. . . . I re-
> solved that upon the arrival of my ship I would buy the whole
> Chisos Mountains as a . . . playground for myself and friends

and that when no longer wanted, I would give it to the State. . . .[16]

The pinnacle of Emory Peak, 7,800 feet high and often enveloped by clouds, is accessible to hardy climbers over a 1-mile side trail. If anything, the vista from here is even more majestic. Only from high above the surrounding desert is the mountainous nature of the Big Bend fully apparent. The Basin lies 2,400 feet below. The massive peaks of the Sierra del Carmen, reaching miles into Mexico, where they are called the Fronteriza Range, break the view to the east, while Mariscal Mountain is visible to the southeast, and Terlingua Fault dominates the southwestern vista.

The Chisos are alpine heights in the midst of a desert. In a sense, they form a biological island. Plants and animals that once flourished throughout the region when it was wetter and cooler are now isolated in the mountains, trapped in the mild heights because they cannot survive in the desert. Completely contained within the national park, the Chisos reach almost 8,000 feet above sea level. They are located in the center of a trough formed by the Mesa de Anguila on the southwest and the Sierra del Carmen-Santiago Mountain range on the northeast.[17]

Passing Green Gulch, the highway continues through Panther Pass and into the Basin, a depression from 1,500 to 2,000 feet deep. The Basin is surrounded by the tallest peaks in the Chisos. To the southeast is Casa Grande (7,500 feet), or Big House, a sheer cliff that reflects a prism of colors in the evening sun. The highest peak in the cluster is Emory Peak (7,835 feet), named for William H. Emory, the chief surveyor of the U.S. Boundary Survey team of 1852. Between Casa Grande and Emory Peak is Toll Mountain, named for Roger W. Toll, a former superintendent of Yellowstone National Park, who was instrumental in establishing Big Bend National Park. Ward Mountain is named after Johnny Ward, a cowboy on the G4 Ranch. Carter Peak, the small mountain near the Window, or the "pour-off," as the only drainage outlet in the Basin is called, was named for Amon G. Carter, a Fort Worth newspaper publisher who lent his influence and enthusiasm to the drive to establish the park. Across the Window from Carter Peak is Vernon Bailey Peak, named after a pioneer field naturalist of the 1920's. Finally, Pulliam Peak is named for Bill Pulliam, who had a ranch at its foot for years.[18]

The view from the Chisos Basin includes other well-known features that have legends associated with them. Not far from Alsate's Face, in Green Gulch, is Lost Mine Peak. Supposedly the Spaniards stationed at Presidio San Vicente worked a mine in the mountains. An old trail leading from the presidio up Juniper Canyon encourages those who would believe the story—and has misled literally hundreds of treasure hunters—but the trail does not lead up the peak. At least, if it did, the way has now been lost. The mouth of the mine could be found, according to the legend, only by standing at the door of the old presidio on Easter morning and marking the spot where the first rays of the sun strike the Chisos. There is no record that a mine ever existed in this part of the Chisos, but if there were one, Maxwell has discredited this method of finding it. The sun's rays strike the mountains at slightly different angles each year, because Easter does not fall on the same day each year. Anyway, if the sky is clear, sunlight will strike Emory Peak first because it is the highest point in the mountains. Near Lost Mine Peak is the Watchman's House. According to the same legend, the ghost of an Indian slave, left there by the Spaniards to guard the mine, lives in a small cave on the slopes of the peak.[19]

The Chisos Basin has long been the most hospitable region. For years it was the home or hideout of Indians and badmen. Later the Civilian Conservation Corps established a camp there, followed by the headquarters of the national park. When the park's headquarters was moved to Panther Junction, the cabins, restaurant, and motel facilities for the park remained in the Basin, surely one of the most beautiful spots in the Big Bend.

The terrain and climate combine to render the Big Bend formidable to anyone traveling across it without reliable transportation. The terrain is rough, unpredictable, and hazardous. The desert is unyielding – unless one knows the secrets of extracting food and water from cacti – and unforgiving of the slightest error in judgment or conduct. The history of the Big Bend, therefore, is the story of man's efforts to overcome the natural obstacles that work in concert to defeat him. Before roads were built into the Big Bend only one race successfully lived there – the Indians.

2 / Spanish Explorers

For the peaceful, sedentary Puebloan tribes who lived at the confluence of the Rio Grande and the Río Conchos and the nomadic, aggressive Comanches and Apaches who rode from their winter abodes north of the Rio Grande to raid and plunder the frontier villages each summer, the *despoblado* was home. Its well-concealed, infrequent water holes that dried up periodically, its mapless mountains and gorges, and its haunting emptiness protected them from the slow, ill-equipped Spanish soldiers who clumsily pursued them along the northern frontier.

To the Spaniards the Big Bend was only an obstacle to their domination of other parts of the frontier. Their advance into the Bend was a slow, calculated effort required to defend their frontier settlements and to establish a direct line of communications along the frontier. Curious about the mysterious *despoblado*, the Spaniards knew no more than the 19th-century French traveler who summed up contemporary knowledge of the region all too well when he observed that "there is no vegetation other than brambles, no view other than the immense sandy plains . . . . Words cannot convey the strangeness and supreme melancholy of the landscape." [1]

The Search for Gold

The first Spanish expeditions, however, did not enter the Big Bend for either defensive reasons or out of curiosity, but for gold. The first expeditions into the Big Bend were little more than blind efforts to discover another Mexico. The Spanish quest for New World treasures met unqualified success when Hernando Cortez conquered the advanced Aztec civilization in 1521, securing wealth and thousands of Indian slaves. Montezuma's fantastic empire renewed the Spaniards' belief in such legends as the seven wealthy cities of Cibola (supposedly established by seven renegade Portuguese bishops), Queen Califia and her Amazon woman empire, and the Gran Quivira.

The Spaniards quickly established a governmental system in Mexico to control the Indians, and devoted much of their energy to exploration and treasure-hunting. The king appointed a viceroy

Indian pictographs, such as these at Hot Springs, are common in the Big Bend.

for Mexico City, who was the chief officer of the crown in the New World. He handled all civil matters, and granted commissions to adventurers and would-be explorers to search other areas for advanced civilizations or wealth. All exploration in the empire was carefully regulated by the viceroy, with the crown receiving a stipulated percentage of any discoveries. The Spanish empire was probably the most disciplined one in the New World. Its procedures were carefully thought out by the king and his council, and disobedient subjects were quickly punished.

In the decades following the conquest, Spanish adventurers fanned out along the Gulf of Mexico coast in search of another rich native kingdom, an undertaking that led to the first contact with the Big Bend. In February 1528 Pánfilo de Narváez led an expedition to Florida in search of treasure, only to suffer hostile Indian attacks and abandonment by the ships that were supposed to pick them up. The survivors constructed small boats with the intention of sailing along the coast to Mexico, following the course charted by Alonso Álvarez de Piñeda a few years before. In November 1528 the ragged survivors landed on the coast of Texas, probably on Galveston Island. They called it the Isle of Misfortune.

The first Spaniard to reach the Big Bend may have been Alvar Núñez Cabeza de Vaca, the leader of the small party. After spending 7 years with the Indians – first as a captive, then as an honored medicine man – he escaped and headed westward, hoping to find a Spanish settlement. He may have crossed the present national park, though more probably he passed north of the Chisos Mountains, perhaps nearer the Guadalupe Mountains on the Texas-New Mexico border. He eventually encountered a Spanish slave-hunting party and returned to Mexico City, where he told of the Indian civilizations to the north.[2]

Although the Spaniards finally concluded they were not interested in the Big Bend itself, it took them several expeditions and more than a century to reach the decision. The viceroy sent a small exploratory expedition northward to find out whether a more ambitious foray would be useful. Then in 1540 a major expedition under Francisco Vázquez de Coronado set out for the same country. Coronado was the first white man to see the Hopi and Zuñi

Spanish Explorers

villages of Arizona and the Pueblos of New Mexico; some of his men discovered the Grand Canyon of the Colorado River. But the Southwest was not another Mexico, and the Spaniards turned their attention elsewhere.[3]

Los Entrados

What probably was the first Spanish penetration of the Big Bend came years later as a result of the natural expansion of the frontier northward. Mining settlements had been founded, and Spaniards thrust their expeditions into unknown territory to enslave the hapless Indians. Thus they reached the Río Conchos and followed it to La Junta de los Ríos, at the confluence of the Rio Grande and the Río Conchos. They were too late to see the pre-basketmaker culture that lived at La Junta – Indians who probably combined a mixture of traits from their own hunting and gathering culture with others acquired from the Pueblos who lived up the Rio Grande – but they did encounter Indians they called the Jumanos.[4]

The first Spanish contact with the Jumanos might have been Cabeza de Vaca and his ragged party, for the Indians later reported that they vaguely remembered seeing four bearded men. The first documented contact with the Jumanos of La Junta came in 1581. One of the Indian slaves captured in 1579 told of large settlements to the north, populated by natives who raised cotton for clothing and had plenty of food.

Inspired by the prospect of converts, Fray Agustín Rodríguez, a Franciscan lay brother stationed in the mining village of San Bartolomé, received permission in 1581 from the viceroy to make the *entrada*. Fray Francisco López and Fray Juan de Santa María accompanied Rodríguez. The military commander of the party was Francisco Sánchez, known more widely as "El Chamuscado" (or, "the singed one," probably because of his red hair), who was interested only in finding riches. Following the slavers' path down the Río Conchos, the Rodríguez party encountered the Jumanos at La Junta. "The . . . people . . . are very handsome, very spirited, very active and more intelligent than the people previously met," recorded Hernán Gallegos, a member of the Chamuscado party. "They are of large stature. Their faces, arms and bodies are striped with pleasing lines. These people are cleaner and more modest than . . . [the others they had met.] They go about naked . . . [and] wear their hair in the shape of skull-caps."[5]

The Jumanos were an established civilization. In fact, the Indians were probably the fringe settlements of the Pueblos, who had migrated down the Rio Grande as far as La Junta between 1200 and 1400. By the time Rodríguez visited them, their farming cul-

23

ture extended up the Conchos a few miles. Because the Jumano culture probably had peaked and begun to decline before the Spaniards encountered it, there is much confusing information concerning its origin and civilization.[6]

Two distinct groups of Indians were called Jumanos by the Spaniards: the puebloan culture at La Junta, and a tribe of nomadic hunters in the Chisos and Davis Mountains. Since they both belonged to the Uto-Aztecan language group, some authorities speculate that they were at one time part of the same group that dispersed because of a food shortage. The Chisos Indians the Spaniards encountered in the area of the national park probably were forced to turn to hunting, but even less is known about them.[7]

After moving down the Rio Grande to La Junta (a climate change probably allowed them to cultivate more of the desert), the Jumanos then encountered difficulty. A severe drought may have disrupted their culture. The Indians Cabeza de Vaca saw were in such desperate condition that they ate their seeds instead of planting them. By the 15th century the Jumanos Rodríguez visited had dispersed their communities, probably because the land would not support large concentrations of people. The shifting, unsettled conditions continued for the Jumanos, because the Spaniards and unfriendly Indians from the north combined with the climate to drive them from their homes.[8]

After visiting the Jumanos, Rodríguez and Chamuscado turned northwestward, traveling to the upper reaches of the Rio Grande in New Mexico. Finding no riches, Chamuscado was soon ready to return to Mexico. The friars remained to minister to the Indians, although they would no longer be protected by their soldiers. Although the expedition failed to discover new wealth, Rodríguez and Chamuscado opened the route by which other parties would enter New Mexico. For years Spaniards traveling this route were the only foreigners to enter the Big Bend.[9]

Rodríguez's expedition led directly to the next *entrada*. Antonio de Espejo, a wealthy rancher in the Querétaro and Celaya districts, used the alleged threat to the friars' safety as an excuse to organize another expedition in 1582, hoping, of course, to explore further and find the fabled cities. After the Franciscan priests in

Santa Bárbara pleaded that they be allowed to go along because they had not heard from their brethren, even the viceroy agreed that such a task should be undertaken. Espejo and his companions traveled the path of Rodríguez and López. They talked with the Indians at La Junta, including some who claimed to have vague memories of Cabeza de Vaca and his friends. There they learned that Rodríguez and López were dead, but continued on to New Mexico since the real purpose of the expedition was to explore the new land.[10]

They searched New Mexico extensively without finding any mineral riches, finally reaching the Pecos River. Marching down that stream to the vicinity of present-day Toyah Lake, near the city of Pecos, they met some Jumano Indians who told them of a more direct route. The Jumanos pointed out that the expedition would save time by marching overland to La Junta and offered to guide them. Espejo thus became the second Spaniard to pass through the Big Bend. He did not find it as inhospitable as later explorers, describing the "many watering places in creeks and marshes on the way," and receiving "fish of many kinds, prickly pears and other fruits . . . buffalo hides and tanned deerskins" from the Jumanos. His good fortune probably can be credited to his Indian guides.[11]

In addition to the licensed expeditions of Rodríguez and Espejo, Gaspar Castaño de Sosa illegally passed through the Big Bend in 1589. The ambitious Gaspar, lieutenant-governor of Nuevo León, led a colonizing party northwestward from Monclova, hoping to settle in the productive lands in the north. Perhaps the party entered the Big Bend region near the present Rio Grande Village, as some authorities claim. More likely it crossed near the Pecos River and paralleled it, following closely the route that Espejo had traveled to New Mexico. The Spaniards' presence was documented in Indian pictographs in the southeastern corner of the Trans-Pecos. Although the fringes of the Big Bend had been penetrated, it still had not been explored.[12]

The Church Returns

The Indians themselves were responsible for the next expedition. Priests had visited La Junta in the past only because the Río Conchos provided a good route to New Mexico. After the Spaniards shifted the Chihuahua City-Santa Fé road westward to El Paso, La Junta was isolated. It was soon deserted. A Jumano chief, Juan de Sabeata, surprised the Spaniards when he visited El Paso in 1684 and requested that the friars come back. His request was granted by the governor, and Capt. Juan Domínguez de Mendoza organized an expedition.[13]

The venture was commercial as well as religious, like so many Spanish endeavors. In addition to helping Jumanos, the Spaniards still hoped to find the fabled cities of the north. Mendoza was instructed to travel as far as the Nueces River, where he was to search for pearls and riches.[14]

The captain provided one of the first detailed reports on the Big Bend. Leading his men down the Rio Grande, he met Fray Nicholás López and Fray Juan Zavaleta, who had come down the Conchos. The combined party journeyed northeastward across the Big Bend country, passing through much of the same land that Espejo had visited over a century before. Mendoza went down the river as far as Alamito Creek, then turned northeastward, passing by San Esteban and Antelope Spring. Continuing through Paisano Pass, the party marched to the southeast of Músquiz Canyon through Leoncito Draw to the spring, which Mendoza named San Pedro de Alcantara. A few days later he christened present-day Fort Stockton (Comanche Springs in the 19th century) San Juan del Río. Mendoza, in fact, named most of his campsites in the Big Bend, although none of them has retained the designation. He went as far as present-day Menard County before turning back in May 1684. Fathers Acevedo and Zavaleta remained at La Junta to minister to the needs of the Jumanos, while Mendoza and Father López returned to Mexico to present their memorials to the viceroy and urge that La Junta be granted a mission. All hope of the La Junta mission vanished, however, when a French expedition under command of La Salle landed on the Texas coast in January 1685, threatening Spanish control in that region, and forcing the Spaniards to recall their frontier forces. It was not until 1715 that Franciscans were able to reestablish missions at La Junta.[15]

Defense

The changing relationship with the Indians of the *despoblado* soon required the Spaniards to turn their attention from religious and financial interests to defense. The first Spanish contacts with the Indians were of a cautious but friendly nature. Coronado encountered some hostility but probably as much curiosity in New Mexico and Arizona. The Indians of La Junta had welcomed the Spaniards. "Standing on top of their houses they showed great mer-

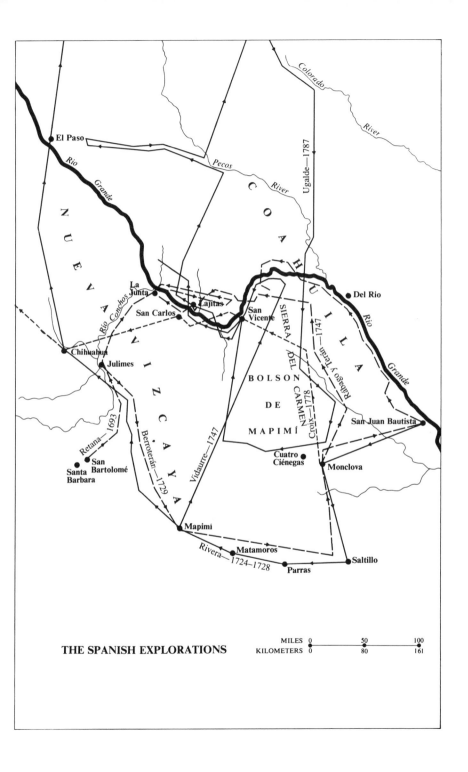

El Paso

Rio Grande

Pecos River

Colorado River

Ugalde—1787

COAHUILA

ZUEVA

La Junta

Rio Conchos

San Carlos

Lajitas

San Vicente

Del Rio

SIERRA DEL CARMEN

Rábago y Terán

Rio Grande

Chihuahua

Julimes

Retana—1693

Berroterán—1729

VIZCAYA

Vidaurre—1747

BOLSON DE MAPIMÍ

Croix—1778

Rábago y Terán—1747

San Juan Bautista

Cuatro Ciénegas

Monclova

Santa Barbara

San Bartolomé

Mapimi

Rivera—1724–1728

Matamoros

Parras

Saltillo

THE SPANISH EXPLORATIONS

MILES   0   50   100

KILOMETERS   0   80   161

riment on seeing us," Gallegos recalled. Juan de Oñate, colonizer of New Mexico, later noted that, "We were not disturbed by them, although we were in their land, nor did any Indian become impertinent." The French seem to have proved that Europeans could trade and coexist with the natives.[16]

But the Spaniards provoked hostility, and the Indians' attitude changed drastically. First, the Spaniards seized Big Bend Indians and sold them as slaves to mine operators in Mexico. Then, the Spaniards severely punished the Indians who resisted, as if to show the natives the power of the Europeans. When a group of Apaches raided Gaspar Castaño de Sosa's camp near the Pecos River, killing one friendly Indian and driving off some stock, the Spaniards pursued, killing several Apaches and capturing four. One was hanged, the other three kept for interpreters. Although the Spaniards were no doubt convinced that harsh measures were necessary, such reactions precluded any possibility of peaceful coexistence.[17]

The Indians quickly struck back. For months after the incident they raided Spanish settlements across the northern frontier with impunity, then retreated into the *despoblado* where the Spaniards could not follow. The Apaches and their neighbors, nomadic hunters and excellent warriors, proved immune to the methods that had humbled the more civilized natives of central Mexico and the upper Rio Grande. In addition to the cunning of the Indians, the Spaniards had to deal with the problems of the *despoblado* itself. The Big Bend thus assumed a negative importance to the Spaniards. There would be no reward for sacrifice in its conquest; survival depended on it.

Realizing that the Chisos Indians in the Big Bend were some of the more ardent troublemakers, Gov. Gabriel del Castillo of Nueva Vizcaya dispatched Juan Fernández de Retana to La Junta to rout them from their stronghold in 1693. An able military man, Retana closed in on the Chisos in an area south of the Rio Grande, where they had recently been involved in a struggle with another tribe and had lost their horses. He trapped them on Peñol de Santa Marta. After several assaults on the height, he convinced them to surrender. Most of the Chisos returned peacefully to La

Junta, where they had lived for years, and asked that the Spaniards again send missionaries to them. A few months later Retana conducted another foray into the Rio Grande country. Marching from La Junta toward the junction of the Pecos and the Rio Grande, apparently without crossing the Rio Grande, he encountered another hostile band of nomads and defeated them. He would have pursued them until they were dispersed, but he elected to return because the waterholes in the *despoblado* were dry.[18]

Retana's raids seemed only to aggravate the Indians. Their attacks continued. In central Mexico the Spaniards had confronted a people who controlled the area; once the dominant tribe was conquered, the land belonged to the Spaniards. On the frontier, however, one or two successes did not assure control. Victory meant only that one or two bands were now scattered. The Indians could easily regroup and raid again. When a tribe such as the Chisos was finally beaten and pacified, another tribe migrated from the north to take its place. The Indians were a continuous threat, requiring constant vigilance. The Europeans at this point must have shared the impression that the Indians soon were to have: that there was no end to the wave upon wave of enemies entering their land.[19]

Apaches in the Big Bend

The Indians who migrated southward to fill the void left when the Chisos turned to more peaceful ways were the Mescalero Apaches. Pressed from their traditional hunting grounds by the Comanches and Utes, the Apaches moved first into New Mexico, then into Texas and Mexico, raiding Spanish settlements. There are many bands of Apaches and often the same band was called different names, adding to the confusion. The Mescalero Apaches (from mescal eater) established *rancherías* in New Mexico, where they raised crops in spring and summer and roamed from southern New Mexico to northern Mexico, including the Big Bend. They historically were the most warlike of the Apaches. Their small, isolated settlements made ideal targets for the far-ranging, aggressive Comanches, who rode into village after village, pillaging, killing, and driving the Apaches even farther south. The continual pressure from the north forced the Apaches into conflict with the less-feared Spaniards, who could not penetrate the *despoblado* with the same ease.[20]

Although they led a meager existence, the Mescaleros solved the mystery of living in the Big Bend. They seldom, if ever, established permanent residences there, but did locate *rancherías* in the mountains, which they occupied seasonally. They knew how to live as they crossed the *despoblado,* which the Spaniards and later the

Americans could only do by carrying provisions with them. They knew through experience where the *tinajas,* or temporary water-holes, were located and when they would have water in them. They knew the edible plants. And they knew they could not stay long in one place without exhausting the land's scanty fare. So they traveled light and moved quickly from place to place, continually eluding their pursuers merely by fleeing into the *despoblado.* They were the only people who learned to live in harmony with the raw forces of nature in the Big Bend.

A New Policy Toward the Indians

Defeats and wasteful expeditions soon forced the Spaniards to reevaluate their frontier policy in the light of the realities of the Big Bend. The terrain ruled out a large expedition to end the Indian threat, because the Indians were much more accustomed to the desert than were the Spaniards. There was serious doubt, in fact, that an isolated Spanish force could defeat them in a pitched battle in the *despoblado.*

The presidio plan recommended in 1667 by Gov. Antonio de Oca Sarmiento of Nueva Vizcaya, therefore, received serious consideration. One of the first suggestions as to how to overcome the raiders, the presidio plan recognized that a few, widely spread Spanish troops were no match for the Indians in such a vast land. The shrewd Oca suggested to the viceroy that a line of "watchtowers" be established at vulnerable points. The watchtowers, or presidios, would be staffed with 10 soldiers and four friendly Indians each and would be spaced evenly across the frontier so they could support each other. Oca was thus the first to formulate the plan that ultimately became the backbone of the Spanish, and later the Mexican, defense of the northern frontier. "If the plan is not adopted our total desolation is daily anticipated," he concluded.[21]

Don José Francisco Marín, an agent of the viceroy, refined the plan. After viewing the disarray of the Spanish forces on the frontier, he concluded that the nomad's advantage would be difficult to overcome unless the Spanish troops took the offensive rather than waiting for the Indians to ride out of the *despoblado* and attack another defenseless village. Francisco Marín further suggested that the governor of the northern provinces be a military

The ruins of the San Vicente Chapel, which was constructed as part of a presidio-mission by the Spanish in 1774.

man, and that European colonization along the frontier be encouraged. Revealing the Spaniard's ignorance of the canyons and rapids of the Rio Grande, he suggested that it would be an easy matter for the colonists to reach sites along the river, because they could simply be transported from the gulf in boats.[22] Most of Francisco Marín's proposals were accepted, but his colonization scheme was rejected. It would be decades before the Big Bend felt the impact of the presidial system.

By the time Pedro de Rivera, an influential viceregal appointee, conducted an investigation of the frontier in 1728, the situation had changed. The Apaches were under increasing pressure from the best warriors on the plains, the Comanches, who had migrated southward in bands searching for hunting grounds not disputed by more powerful tribes. A simple people who lived off roots, insects, jack rabbits, and other wild creatures and plants, the Comanches became supreme warriors – and predators – with the acquisition of the horse. Not only were the Comanches and Apaches at war with each other; both preyed on the isolated settlements along New Spain's northern frontier.[23]

Rivera therefore resolved to follow Oca's plan and advised that the presidios along the southern rim of the *despoblado* be moved northward and located along the Rio Grande to establish a

31

line that the raiders supposedly could not penetrate. Several residents of the area recommended to Rivera that to be successful a presidio had to be located in the *despoblado* itself, preferably at La Junta de Los Ríos. Some authorities also recommended La Junta, but Rivera disagreed. He believed that a site southeast of the junction would be more advantageous. The viceroy ordered Capt. José de Berroterán of the presidio of Conchos to take 70 men, march into the *despoblado,* and find the best location for the presidio.[24]

Captain Berroterán, a cautious officer, planned his expedition carefully. Following José Antonio de Ecay Múzquiz's recommendation that the easiest route into the region was along the Rio Grande, he gathered his force at Conchos in January 1729, and circled eastward around the *despoblado* – via the frontier villages of Mapimí, Laguna de la Leche, Cuatro Ciénegas, and Monclova–to San Juan Bautista. Although their instructions called for them to divide into two groups to scout for hostile Indians as well as search for a site for the presidio, Berroterán and his council decided that they should remain together because the country was completely unknown.

Berroterán apprehensively left San Juan Bautista on March 28. Gone less than a week, he received a message from the governor of Coahuila reporting Indian raids in the Parras and Saltillo areas and requesting that he relinquish part of his force for defense of the towns. Proceeding cautiously, Berroterán feared for the success of his mission and again decided to hold his force together. His officers warned that the Indian scouts were moving too slowly, but were not sure if it was from ignorance of the land or an intentional effort to hamper the expedition. "Thus I remained in a state of confusion," reported Berroterán, "awaiting the return of the scouts, hoping that one of them might be able to extricate me from this labyrinth."

As Berroterán marched into the vicinity of present-day Langtry, he noticed that the river banks got steeper. He crossed to the left bank of the Rio Grande and followed it closely for 5 more days. They camped near present-day Dryden and held a council. Supplies were low, they had found no site that they could recommend for a presidio, and they feared that they would be lost in the desert. The council voted to discontinue the expedition. Berroterán ordered the soldiers from Monclova and San Juan Bautista to return by the outward route, while he and his troops elected to bypass La Junta and travel across the *despoblado* to the Río Conchos. Although they marched 2 days without water and had to abandon several horses and mules, they reached their presidio safely.[25]

Berroterán had been the first to cross the *despoblado,* but his mission was a failure. He had explored much new territory, yet had found neither hostile Indians nor a site for the presidio. Rivera denounced him for faintheartedness. The captain had been hesitant from the first, he claimed. "He knew nothing of the country he was to traverse, but seemed to know beforehand what was going to happen," Rivera wrote Gov. Ignacio Francisco de Barrutia of Nueva Vizcaya. Of course, "the officers and men knew nothing of the land ahead, for it is a fact that for all discovery one presupposes a lack of knowledge of the places ahead." Rivera insisted that the job should have been simple. Although he admitted that "its banks offer some difficult places," he claimed that all Berroterán had to do was follow the Rio Grande.[26]

The governor of Coahuila, meanwhile, was still interested in establishing a presidio along his northern frontier to fend off hostile raids by the Apaches. After a survey of the frontier in 1734, Gov. Blas de la Garza Falcón had asked the viceroy to permit establishment of a post at a site to be determined, then reconnoitered the banks of the Rio Grande in search of a location the following year. It was a difficult march. Reaching the Río San Diego, he learned that the terrain ahead did not improve and that his advance party had found traces of Apaches nearby. Low temperatures, snow, and dry waterholes killed several horses in January 1736. Somewhere near present-day Randale, Garza Falcón decided to turn back. Berroterán had gone farther. Garza Falcón did recommend a site for the presidio about 30 miles south of present-day Del Rio, and construction was completed in 1738. [27]

If Berroterán and Garza Falcón proved anything by their expeditions, it was that La Junta could not be approached from the southeast via the river. Several years of speculation regarding the nature and course of the river in the *despoblado* were ended, but the unfortunate answer was that the Spaniards could expect no relief from the agonies of the desert. It continued to shelter the Indians from retribution for decades.

In his report Berroterán claimed that the Apaches raided the frontier with impunity because there were no presidios between

San Juan Bautista and El Paso. He reported to the viceroy that after the Indians entered "this unpopulated, long and wide gulf," they controlled the eastern border of Nueva Vizcaya and western Coahuila and could "easily destroy and annihilate" the two provinces. He argued that the area could not be inhabited by settlers because the "gulf or pocket" – the *despoblado* – contained "steep places, dry places, few waterholes, and great distances." He recommended that the presidios of San Bartolomé and Conchos be moved to the Rio Grande frontier, where they possibly would slow the Indians who came "like waves of the sea–when one ends, another follows." Although Berroterán technically failed in his mission to find a location for the presidio, his experience on the frontier gave credence to his recommendations, and his opinion was still valued by the officials in Mexico City.[28]

Having found no better plan, the viceroy and his advisors took up Berroterán's suggestions 18 years later. The viceroy agreed that the presidios should be placed along the Rio Grande and dispatched three expeditions to explore northern Coahuila and Chihuahua for good sites. He sent Capt. Joseph de Ydoiaga from San Bartolomé to La Junta; Capt. Fermín Vidaurre was to seek another route. The new governor of Coahuila, Pedro de Rábago y Terán led the most difficult expedition, which would attempt to cross the *despoblado* from Coahuila to La Junta.[29]

Boquillas is the longest and calmest of the three major canyons of the Rio Grande.

Rábago left Monclova in November 1747 with 20 soldiers and 10 Indians. At Sacramento he picked up 45 more soldiers. He marched to the Río Escondido, then to Arroyo de la Babia. Following the Arroyo, he found an old Indian trail into the mountains. He passed the Mesa de los Fresnos (about 100 miles from present-day Santa Rosa), then marched into the Sierra del Carmen. The terrain was rough, with little water and several abandoned Indian camps. On December 2 the expedition reached the Rio Grande upriver from Rio Grande Village. "Its banks were explored and no passing area was found on account of its currents coming so close to the mountain ranges," wrote Rábago. "The rocks make a high wall along the upper and lower part: In spite of this, I ordered all of the train to pass from the other bank . . . and we camped . . . ," thus becoming the first Spanish expedition to enter what is today Big Bend National Park. This new ford, located probably below Mariscal Canyon, Rábago named Santa Rita.[30]

Rábago was not satisfied with his campground. The "sandy land, some hillocks and little grass" were inadequate to support his expedition. He sent 17 soldiers and a corporal upriver in search of rich grassland for the horses, then ordered his Indian auxiliaries to scout the mountains, probably the Chisos to the north or northwest for a pass.

After celebrating Mass on December 3, Rábago walked a short distance from camp to inspect the "banks and hilly areas" near the river, where he found "several veins" of ore. After speculating about "good mineral sources" in the Big Bend, he investigated the fertile strip that parallels the Rio Grande, concluding that there was not enough of the lowland to support farming in the immediate area. The region, in addition, was "so boxed in between mountain and mountain" that Rábago thought it impassable. The Indian scouts returned, reporting that several old Apache campgrounds were located in the Chisos Mountains.

Rábago had hoped to follow the river northwestward, but canyons and steep banks forced him to find another route. After learning of a better camping place upriver. Rábago marched in a northwesterly direction, stopping for the night without water in his haste to find the site. On December 5 he found one of the hot springs along the Rio Grande. This place he named Santa Bárbara. At another abandoned Apache camp he found three horses that the Indians had left behind in their hasty retreat. Encountering unusually cold weather for the Big Bend, Rábago continued his march northwestward to an area where squash plants grew up to the water's edge. He named it El Real de las Calabasas.

Rábago marched on, with the Chisos Mountains on his right and the Terlingua Fault, which he named the "wall" of San Damasio, on his left. He saw the jagged bluffs of the Chisos, the twin peaks that the Anglo-Americans later named Mule Ears, and on December 11 probably became the first European to see steepwalled Santa Elena Canyon, which he found too forbidding to explore. The party marched along Terlingua Creek, which they named El Arroyo, then turned westward to the Rio Grande again, probably near the modern village of Lajitas. On December 18 Rábago sighted Nuestra Señora de Guadalupe, one of the pueblos of La Junta. The Rábago expedition was the first to march across the *despoblado* and reach La Junta.[31]

Rábago remained there for several days, visiting with the mission fathers and inquiring about the conditions of the surrounding country. He spent a few days exploring the Rio Grande on either side of La Junta, then followed the Conchos upriver for a few miles. On December 29 he directed his party eastward on the return journey. They followed Indian trails to the vicinity of present-day Terlingua. Wanting to return via a different route, they circled northward around the Chisos Mountains to San Vicente. Deciding not to follow the river back to San Juan Bautista because his scouts had sighted the sheer walls of Boquillas Canyon, Rábago crossed to the right bank and divided his force. One group he directed to return to Sacramento by the path they had followed enroute, while his force attempted to find a new route to Monclova.

The other two expeditions explored better known territory. Captain Ydoiaga marched down the Río Conchos to La Junta, in the neighborhood of what its today the village of Shafter. Captain Vidaurre saw what is now the national park, but only after Rábago had already been there. Vidaurre left the Presidio of Mapimí in November 1747, following a northeasterly course until he reached the Rio Grande near present-day Del Rio. He found tracks left by Rábago's party as he marched toward La Junta.[32]

The *despoblado* was no easier to penetrate physically because of Rábago's marches, but he had crossed the breadth of the region to La Junta and had mapped new routes from both Sacramento and Monclova. The land was as harsh as ever for the unknowing, but with trails and waterholes marked, the Spaniards could now apply pressure to their enemy even in the *despoblado*.

As a result of his reconnaissance, Rábago agreed that a presidio should be located at La Junta. On his visit to Indian *rancherías* in the La Junta area he had found horses that belonged to settlers in Saltillo, Sacramento, Monclova, and Nuevo León, including some stolen from members of his expedition. Even among peaceful Indians, Rábago had found two Indian women captives from missions near San Juan Bautista. Both they and the horses had been captured by the Apaches on their wide-ranging forays and traded to the natives at La Junta. He believed that a presidio at La Junta would help decrease the number of raids. Seeing the Rio Grande as the first line of defense for the Spanish frontier, the captain also recommended that the presidio of Santa Rosa be moved closer to the river.

Never known for their hasty decisions, the Spanish officials in Mexico City requested more information. Rubín de Celís was sent in 1750 to explore the territory between El Paso and La Junta. But increased Indian raids on the Nueva Vizcaya frontier finally convinced the authorities that a La Junta presidio was necessary. Work on Nuestra Señora de Belén, or Presidio del Norte, was completed in July 1760.[33]

If the Spaniards thought that a lone presidio at La Junta would stop the incursions of the Apaches, they were mistaken. Frontier settlers could have told them of the ineffectiveness of a few troops scattered among the mountains and canyons of the Big Bend. Pushed southward by their mortal enemies, the Comanches, the Apaches continued their plundering, seemingly immune to all the official acts of the Spanish bureaucracy.

Reforms Reach the Frontier

Charles III, the new Bourbon monarch who came to the throne of Spain in 1759, is known as the reforming king. He seized power in Madrid amid great domestic difficulties and declining prestige abroad. Strict mercantile policies had led to widespread smuggling; centralized authority in the viceregal capital of Mexico City had led to neglect of the frontier. The poorly protected frontier, in fact, was one of the most vexing colonial problems. Charles decreed reorganization of the colonial administration and opened numerous colonial ports to international trade. The impact of his reforms finally reached the frontier when a trusted officer, the Marquis de Rubí, made an inspection trip covering some 7,500 miles along the entire frontier of New Spain in 1767. While Rubí was on his way to inspect the La Junta presidio, he learned that the governor of Coahuila had ordered the post evacuated and relocated at Julimes, several days journey up the Río Conchos. Rubí turned and headed for El Paso, bypassing the Big Bend because there were no settlements to be inspected. After his reconnaissance, however, he agreed with Berroterán and Rábago that the Rio Grande was a natural defense line. If the Spaniards could stop the Apaches before they entered the *despoblado,* the settlements of Nueva Vizcaya and Coahuila would be safe. He advised that the northern presidios near the *despoblado* be moved to the Rio Grande. The presidio at Julimes was to be returned to La Junta.[34]

Two important results came out of Rubí's inspection. First, Rubí's engineer and lieutenant produced one of the first maps that shows the Big Bend. Nicholás de Lafora and Joseph Urrútia, Ensign of the Regiment of America, were both with Rubí as he bypassed the Big Bend. From their own observations and by gleaning information from other maps and travel descriptions, Lafora and Urrútia mapped the entire frontier. Their map shows the Big Bend trapped between a somewhat unrealistic nook of the Rio Grande and the Pecos River, which erroneously curves abruptly to the northwest on the map. The presidios of Julimes, Cerro Gordo, and San Sabá (all of which would soon receive new names in the coming reorganization of the frontier defenses) are shown adjacent to the Rio Grande on the right bank, but somewhat out of position. Cerro Gordo is located at what would be more nearly the southernmost tip of the Bend, rather than in the location of present-day San Carlos. San Sabá appears downriver from what probably is the Pecos—much too far east for the actual site, which is present-day San Vicente. These inaccuracies would probably have been cleared away if Lafora and Urrútia had visited the sites while on their tour. The Big Bend itself is correctly shown as mountainous and occupied by Mescalero Apaches. Despite these difficulties, the Lafora-Urrútia map is a significant document for two reasons: the Big Bend is shown to be an important part of the Spanish frontier defenses, and the map is a technical achievement for Spanish mapmakers in 1771.

One of the first maps of the Southwest to
identify the Big Bend region, the 1771 Lafora
map showed Mescalero Apaches living there.

NUEVO MÉXICO

TIERRA DE LOS CUMANCHES

Apaches Xicarillas

Apaches Nuevolites

GRANDE DEL

PROVINCIA

DE COAHUI NORTE

N. REINO DE LEON

VIZCAYA

PROVINCIA

NUEVA GALICIA

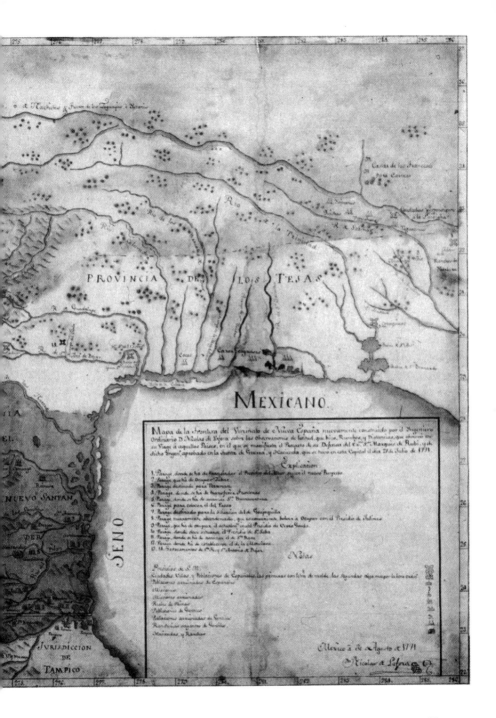

MEXICANO.

Mapa de la frontera del Virreinato de Nueva España nuevamente construido por el Ingeniero Ordinario D. Nicolas de Lafora sobre las Observaciones de latitud, que hizo, Rumbos, y Distancias, que observó en su Viaje á aquellos Parages, en el que se manifiesta el Proyecto de su Defensa del Cav.º S.r Marques de Rubí, y de dicho Inger, aprobado en la Junta de Guerra, y Hacienda, que se tuvo en esta Capital el dia 21 de Julio de 1771.

Explicacion.

1. Parage donde se ha de transferir el Presidio del Altar segun el nuevo Proyecto.
2. Parage que há de Ocupar Tubac.
3. Parage destinado para Terrenate.
4. Parage, donde se há de transferir Fronteras.
5. Parage, donde se há de avanzar S.ta Buenaventura.
6. Parage para colocar el del Passo.
7. Parage destinado para la situacion del de Guajoquilla.
8. Parage nuevamente abandonado, que se atentamente habra á Ocupar con el Presidio de Julimes.
9. Parage, que há de ocupar el actual, ó actuales en el Presidio de Cerro Gordo.
10. Parage donde deve avanzar el Presidio de S.ta Saba.
11. Parage, que há de avanzar el de S.n Xavier.
12. Parage donde há de establecerse el de la Bahia.
13. Id. Destacamiento de P.s Rey S.n Antonio de Bejar.

Notas

Presidios de S. M.
Ciudades, Villas, y Poblaciones de Españoles, las primeras con letra de molde, las segundas de letra mayor la letra usual.
Poblaciones arruinadas de Españoles
Misiones
Misiones arruinadas
Reales de Minas
Poblaciones de Gentiles
Poblaciones arruinadas de Gentiles
Rancherias vagantes de Gentiles
Haciendas, y Ranchos

México á de Agosto de 1771.
Nicolas de Lafora

PROVINCIA DE LOS TEJAS

SENO

NUEVO SANTAN.

JURISDICCION DE TAMPICO

Rio de la Trinidad

Casas de los Franceses para Carros

The second result of the Rubí expedition was that the king issued the New Regulations of 1772, which embodied, among other things, Rubí's plan to relocate the presidios along the Rio Grande frontier. Viceroy Antonio María Bucareli appointed one of his favorites, Hugo Oconor, to carry out Rubí's recommendations.[35]

As a part of his frontier reorganization, Oconor made a thorough tour of the Big Bend. Before leaving on his inspection, he studied the diaries of Berroterán and Rábago. Then he headed for the frontier to supervise the moving of the presidios. Leaving from San Fernando de Austria in April 1773, he camped several miles upriver from San Juan Bautista, searching for a new site for the presidio of Monclova. He finally decided on the Río San Rodrigo. Leaving men there to build that presidio, Oconor moved upriver to the Arroyo de Agua Verde, about 20 miles south of Del Rio. There he ordered the presidio of Santa Rosa established. With the assistance of Lipan guides, Oconor rode into the Big Bend, probably following Rábago's route, where he located a site for the presidio of San Vicente. He positioned the fort near the Rio Grande, next to a well-known Indian ford. He ordered the presidio of San Sabá moved from the Río San Sabá in present-day Menard County, where it was exposed to attack and useless to a frontier defense line, to San Vicente. To cover the 100 miles of desert between Agua Verde and San Vicente, Oconor proposed that another presidio be established at La Babia, south of the Rio Grande and almost directly between Santa Rosa and San Sabá. The Big Bend country could not be left unprotected, he argued, because it was the main trail for Indians raiding the frontier settlements farther south.

Oconor then moved upriver to the Arroyo de San Carlos. He ordered the presidio of Cerro Gordo relocated to a small mesa about 15 miles south of the Rio Grande, believing that the new Presidio de San Carlos would benefit from the nearby water, farming land, wood, stone, and other resources. Oconor finally reached La Junta, which had been abandoned in 1751, because of the uncooperative attitudes of various frontier officials. He was dismayed to find only the ruins of the old presidio. Indians had burned the buildings, leaving only the parched adobe structure.

Oconor marched up the Río Conchos to investigate the presidio at Julimes, ordering it moved back to La Junta. He continued his tour of the frontier, relocating presidios as he went. He returned in 1774 to check construction and found that San Carlos was almost finished, but that San Vicente was behind schedule.[36]

Oconor's plan, however, was destined to fail. As a result of his journey, San Vicente and San Carlos were established in the Big Bend country south of the Rio Grande. But the plan was based on theory and on a similar project – the Roman military colonies – that had been successfully carried out, but under significantly different circumstances. Oconor had not considered the realities in the Big Bend in making his plans. A line of posts that proved convincing on a map in bureaucratic discussions simply did not provide the promised impenetrable wall or even offer adequate protection for nearby settlers. Despite an aggressive campaign carried out under Oconor's instructions against the Indians of the Big Bend, another investigation soon proved that the frontier could not be guarded by widely separated posts or so few troops.[37]

Las Provincias Internas

In 1776 the northern provinces of New Spain were reorganized. According to the reforms instituted by Charles III, the entire frontier was included in one administrative unit called the Provincias Internas. Charles named Teodoro de Croix, one of his ablest military men, commander general of the provinces. Croix arrived in Mexico City in December and remained there almost a year studying the reports of frontier governors and captains. He found a dismal scene, and decided that Oconor's reorganization was a mistake. The governor of Coahuila reported that the number of raids had actually increased since construction of the new presidios. José Rubio, an experienced frontiersman, described soldiers and presidios in such miserable shape that it was difficult to tell which was a worse problem, the Indians or the soldiers. The troops' weapons were old and ineffectual, the officers were poorly prepared and corrupt, discipline was lax. Communication was slow, the soldiers' pay lagged behind schedule, and the officers extracted a percentage when it did arrive.[38]

Croix hoped to implement an aggressive policy. He immediately requested an additional 2,000 troops for the frontier, then left on an inspection trip along with his chaplain, Father Juan Agustín de Morfi, who kept a detailed diary of the trip and later wrote a history of Texas. While circling the *despoblado*, Morfi noticed the situation was so desperate that many farmers had sentry boxes in their cornfields where they could hide in case of a sudden

Indian attack. Croix and Morfi visited the Big Bend presidios of San Carlos and San Vicente in early 1778. After several conferences, Croix decided that the Rio Grande was ineffective as a defense line. Moving the presidios to the river left the settlements unprotected.[39]

Several suggestions came out of Croix's talks. The frontiersmen urged the commander general to mount a 3,000-man campaign against the Apaches. The conferees suggested that detachments from Nueva Vizcaya be instructed to march into the *despoblado,* rout the Apaches, then turn northward to the presidios of San Carlos and San Vicente and meet troops from Coahuila, who, meantime, would have swept through the Sierra del Pino, and along the Río de San Pedro, the Ojos de las Nuezes, and the Agua Amargosa. Croix's officers also hoped to .turn the Indians against each other by signing treaties with one faction or the other, thereby renewing old tribal hostilities, but they did not place as much confidence in this suggestion as in the offensive campaigns. Finally, Croix urged that the presidios again be relocated nearer the people.[40]

Croix's plans for a massive campaign against the Indians were doomed, however, when Spain entered the war against England in 1779. With all his military might sequestered for the European conflict, the king ordered Croix to employ peaceful means to overcome his enemies in New Spain. The commander general was, nevertheless, allowed to modify the frontier defenses to suit his scheme. He was convinced that placement of San Carlos and San Vicente on the Rio Grande was an error that created an artificial frontier. There was little support for either fort, communications were poor, and they were isolated, even though they had been intended to guard two important fords. Croix suggested that the garrisons be moved, but that the physical plants of the two presidios be kept to serve as bases against the Indians. Only La Junta would remain in the Big Bend area. Croix wanted to defend what he considered to be the real frontier, the area of the northernmost villages along the edge of the *despoblado,* not a false frontier created by bureaucratic decree.[41]

A More Aggressive Policy

Still, the Spaniards were not helpless. Juan de Ugalde, the governor of Coahuila, undertook a series of campaigns designed to break up the Apache concentrations in the Big Bend. The soldiers had ventured cautiously into the Bolson de Mapimí, in the heart of the *despoblado,* in 1779. A second campaign in 1780 took them to San Fernando de Austria, then to Monclova Vieja, and finally to Agua Verde. In 1781 Ugalde got as far as the Arroyo de la Babia and the deserted presidio of San Vicente before turning back. He found that the Indians had burned the presidio, destroying the roof and the main gate; it would provide little protection in a campaign. Ugalde made a third expedition into the *despoblado* in the spring of 1782, capturing or killing 50 Indians and regaining some 400 head of stock. A fourth expedition, terminating in early 1783, led him into the Big Bend country and completed his sweep of the entire Bolson region.[42]

After the close of the American Revolution and the Spanish committment of troops to Europe, the Spanish bureaucracy allowed hostilities to resume along the frontier. Ugalde's most extensive campaigns came in 1787. He set out in the snow of winter and reached San Vicente in March. After learning that the Indians were camped in the Chisos Mountains, he crossed the Rio Grande into the Big Bend National Park area and attacked the Mescalero band under chief Zapata Tuerto.

When Ugalde marched to San Carlos, he received a warning from the captain at La Junta that he was now in Nueva Vizcaya, beyond his range of authority. Ugalde angrily responded that he was in hot pursuit of Indians who had attacked his domain, but then realized that the Mescaleros who lived in this region were friendly to the Spaniards who occupied La Junta and had, in fact, signed treaties with them. It was the usual procedure for the Indians: they were friendly to the soldiers who guarded the region where they lived, and raided only in other areas.

Although Capt. Juan Bautista Elguézabal of La Junta insisted that the redmen were at peace with the Spaniards and tried to stop Ugalde, the Coahuila governor continued his assault. He raided a small *ranchería* near the Bofecillos Mountains, killing one and capturning six Indians. He turned northward, hoping to find another camp, but the Indians had been warned and had fled toward the Pecos. After further reconnaissances, Ugalde returned to Santa Rosa in August, where he met Picax-ande Ins-tinsle, the pressured Llanero leader, and concluded a treaty. Ugalde had risked a campaign into the *despoblado* and a jurisdictional conflict with his

46

Working from maps like this, Spaniards logically
concluded that the Rio Grande was navigable.
No topographic features are shown on this

"La Paz" map, which was probably made by
a cartographer who never visited the New World.

neighbor to the west, but he had achieved the desired end: peace in his domain. The viceroy approved.[43]

About 1783 an unknown Spanish mapmaker, confessedly using maps of foreign cartographers as well as travel accounts by various explorers, attempted to set down in graphic form all that the Spaniards then knew of the Big Bend. The general outline is fairly accurate. The bend in the river is recognizable, with the southernmost dip coming in Mariscal Canyon. San Carlos and San Vicente are correctly located south of the river, while the Chisos Indians are shown to be in control of the domain to the north. The Chisos Mountains are correctly positioned, and what appears to be the Basin, where the motel and cabin facilities are located today, is labeled "Basilio," which in today's usage translates as Basilian (a monk), but might have been somehow related to "basin" or "cloister" in the language of the 18th century. Dedicated to the "principe de la Paz"–hence the name "La Paz" map–the chart is probably the most accurate contemporary Spanish map of the Big Bend, even though it is the work of a cartographer who most likely never visited America.[44]

Judging from the La Paz map, the Spaniards probably knew more about the Indians than the Big Bend itself. To keep the Apaches at peace, the Spaniards had to protect them, for the warlike Comanches continued to press southward. The officials at La Junta guarded one Apache party during a buffalo hunt, and Ugalde offered protection to a group of Mescaleros who ventured into buffalo territory in late 1787. The Comanches attacked, but were repulsed by the Spaniards. The system apparently was working.[45]

During the last quarter century of Spanish rule in New Spain, the Indians were virtually at peace with the Spaniards on the frontier. Gov. Juan Bautista de Anza of New Mexico and Gov. Domingo Cabello of Texas concluded a treaty with the Comanches which called for the Comanches to aid the Spaniards in defeating the Apaches still at war. The increasing number of soldiers and location of the presidios made the raiding more difficult. Rubí's inspection along with Oconor's recommendations and Croix's visits had increased the efficiency, discipline, and training of the troops.

Oconor, Croix, and Ugalde had carried out campaigns designed to disperse the concentration of Indians throughout the *despoblado,* and Ugalde continued his forays, staying out as long as 7 months in 1789.[46]

In addition to putting military pressure on the Indians, the Spaniards also held out several inducements to peace. A friendly attitude by the commanders of the presidios made the Indians realize that the Spaniards could make their life easier. Reviving a program that had been used for over a century to help the Pueblos, the Spaniards offered the Indians food for their first year of peace and farm equipment and seed in subsequent years. The Spaniards also took advantage of the Apaches' fear of the marauding Comanches. When Viceroy Revilla Gigedo outlined a realistic program for peace in 1791 – the Spaniards would protect the Indians if they lived in peace – the Indians were quick to accept.[47]

Thus, a century of conflict came to an end. The Spaniards withdrew from the Big Bend. Their initial exploratory efforts had been failures. When it became evident that the Indians were difficult converts and that the Big Bend was not another Mexico, with gold and silver stored by the roomful, the Spaniards turned their attention elsewhere. They entered the Big Bend only because it was in the way; for years the route to New Mexico led down the Río Conchos to the Rio Grande and up that river to Santa Fe. The Big Bend finally captured the Spaniards' attention because of the nomadic and hostile Indians who hid there. It then became necessary to find a route through the *despoblado,* to locate presidios there, and finally to conduct raids of several months' duration in the heart of the present-day national park. The Spaniards were never interested in the Big Bend for any reason other than peace; it was an obstacle to overcome in establishing a secure frontier. But their peace did not last. The hostile Comanches continued their southward migration, soon presenting an even more serious threat that the Spaniards would not be around to answer.

49

3/The Chihuahua Trail

"Jack" Hays was an unusual man: respected captain of a Texas Ranger company during the Mexican War, good shot, eloquent commander, and shrewd military man, yet kind, respectful, and resourceful. For all that, he often bemused those who met him for the first time, for he was less than 5 feet tall, weighed about 150 pounds, and had a smooth, whiskerless face. A disciplined man in modest clothes, John Coffee Hays had an impenetrable countenance. His firm jaw foretold determination, and his piercing eyes betrayed nothing. "The fame of Colonel Hays rested on a substantial basis," explained one who had followed him. "It was acquired by hard fighting, by suffering privations, and by the exhibition of the high qualities adorning a citizen and soldier." [1] It was "Jack" Hays who, in 1848, led an expedition of adventurous, naive Texans into the Big Bend.

Hays' trip was not the result of a foolhardy plan. Dr. Henry Connelly, an American living in the city of Chihuahua and later Territorial Governor of New Mexico, had gathered between $200,000 and $300,000 in specie and gold bullion and organized a wagon train for such a trip in 1839. He hoped to initiate trade between Chihuahua and New Orleans, which he believed to be a more lucrative market than either Santa Fe or Independence, Mo. Leaving the Mexican city on April 3, the doctor crossed the Rio Grande at Presidio del Norte, a small village surrounding the site of La Junta de los Rios, and headed through the Big Bend along a route similar to the one Mendoza had charted over a century and a half before. Bouncing across the Texas plains, through the Cross Timbers to Fort Towson, and down the Red River and the Mississippi, he reached New Orleans a few months later with no unusual difficulties. [2]

New Orleans, unfortunately, was depleted of many goods that the merchants could have easily sold in Chihuahua, but after several weeks they obtained calicoes, prints, unbleached cottons, cloths, silks, and other items. The return trip was equally uneventful, except for a minor accident that cost them about $30,000 worth of goods when the steamboat towing them up the Red River hit a snag. The 80-wagon train cut such a swath across the Texas prairies that their trail remained visible for several years. They left an even more graphic sign of their presence when they could not find their route through the dense Cross Timbers and were forced to hack a new trail.[3]

In West Texas the traders encountered Comanches, but passed them without a fight. Finding the Pecos too deep to ford, they resorted to an "expedient characteristic of the Prairies," according to Josiah Gregg, a veteran Santa Fe trader. They emptied several barrels, tied them to the bottom of each wagon, and floated it across the river. When they reached Presidio del Norte they found that the governor with whom they had reached agreement before leaving had died. Because he had no investment in the project, the new governor was not as friendly to their endeavors and threatened to charge the full tariff. Forty-five days were required to negotiate a compromise. The caravan finally entered Chihuahua on August 27, 1840. "The delays and accumulated expenses of this expedition caused it to result so disastrously," claimed Gregg in 1844, "that no other enterprise of the kind has since been undertaken."[4]

Hays knew that the caravan had not ended satisfactorily for the investors, but it had stirred interest in a wagon route through the Big Bend. While in New Orleans, Connelly had assured the Louisianians that if their government would encourage the commerce, "the whole trade of Chihuahua, and as far west as the Pacific ocean," would be theirs. Some reporters waxed enthusiastic, claimed that Chihuahua contained the "richest gold mines in all Mexico" and that bullion would find its way to New Orleans even though the Mexican government prohibited its exportation. The distant *Western Star* of Lebanon, Ohio, believed that Americans should come to know Chihuahua better. Texans held even stronger convictions because a change in the trade pattern obviously would divert commerce to San Antonio, Houston, or Corpus Christi. The editor of the Houston *Morning Star* endorsed efforts to establish a permanent post on the Red River for the Chihuahua trade, hoping, of course, that Houston might be able to divert some of the trade because of its favorable location near the Gulf of Mexico.[5] Con-

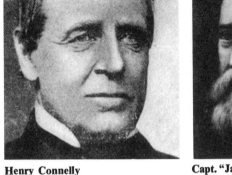

Henry Connelly   **Capt. "Jack" Hays**

nelly's expedition had proved that the trip could be made, and that the trade could be profitable under favorable conditions.

Others hesitated, however, wondering if Connelly had not been extremely fortunate in safely crossing a virtually unexplored region known to be populated with hostile Indians. Few travelers had entered the Big Bend since the Spaniards had recalled their soldiers in the face of the on-rushing Comanches. Yet Connelly's caravan encountered only routine difficulties. The Indian threat combined with the poor return on investment and the Mexican War proved sufficient to dampen for a few years whatever enthusiasm there might have been in a Chihuahua Trail.

Interest rekindled in 1847 when Maj. John Polk Campbell and 39 Mexican War veterans left Chihuahua headed for Fort Towson via Presidio del Norte. Traveling over a route that the editor of the *Western Star* claimed was superior to the Santa Fe Trail, Campbell and his party safely reached their destination several weeks later, having sighted no hostile Indians. Three other Mexican War veterans in Chihuahua, Ben Leaton, John W. Spencer, and John D. Burgess, thought the route had a good future and decided to establish a mercantile business at Presidio. After buying property in the village in 1848, they left for the United States to purchase sale goods. Upon their return they learned that the land on the left bank now belonged to the United States as a result of the Treaty of Guadalupe Hidalgo, which ended the Mexican War. They obtained land from several Mexicans on the American side and moved their operations across the river. Leaton constructed a fortification to protect his property (today a historic site). Theirs was the first American settlement in the Big Bend.[6]

53

The Hays-Highsmith Expedition

By this time "Jack" Hays had decided to lead his own party into the Big Bend. He found merchants and newspapermen throughout the State excited about the expedition; among those who signed up for the trek was Samuel Maverick, a prominent citizen of San Antonio, who was given the task of keeping a journal of the trip. The expedition was widely publicized in the State's newspapers. Expectations ran high. On August 27 the party left San Antonio and headed for El Paso. At the Llano River they joined Capt. Samuel Highsmith and his Texas Rangers, who were to protect them from Indian attack.[7]

Oblivious of the dangers, the 35 adventurers set out on September 4 up the Llano. They crossed Comanche Creek and James Creek, then proceeded to the Nueces River. At Las Moras Creek, a tributary of the Rio Grande, they met some friendly Indians who advised them to pursue a more westerly course. As they paralleled the Rio Grande, crossing creek after creek, Hays finally realized that the inaccurate map he carried was worthless. He eventually arrived at the river the Indians called "Puerco," which had steep banks and such a crooked course (Hays crossed it eight times within a mile) that he renamed it Devil's River. The march continued uneventfully into the Big Bend.

There the trouble began. Food ran short. Men turned to eating their mules, prickly pears, and whatever else they could find. The expedition's physician, a Doctor Wahm, strangely refused to eat. Two nights later he went insane, perhaps from eating some of the many alkaline plants that grow in the Big Bend, and fled into the hills. Sam Maverick noted in his journal that the men killed and ate a panther on October 2 and began eating bear grass on the 7th. Passing near Boquillas Canyon in the Sierra del Carmen, the party crossed to the Mexican side of the river near San Vicente, hoping to find food. The mountains were even more rugged on the right bank. By the time they stumbled onto the village of San Carlos, the site of the abandoned Spanish presidio, Hays and his campanions had been without food for 12 days.[8]

Rumors of their hardships quickly filtered back to San Antonio. Several adventurers had left the city a few days after Hays,

and near Devil's River they overtook the expedition. After traveling with them for a few days, however, the disheartened late-start-
ers returned to San Antonio. They reported that Hays was out of
provisions, traveling over rugged ground and already killing his
horses for food. Because the party was gone so long, many suspected a disaster. The editor of the *Corpus Christi Star,* who had
hoped that the Chihuahua Trail would one day reach as far as his
city, conceded that the expedition had encountered "more difficulties than had been anticipated." [9]

But the Hays party had endured the worst of the Big Bend.
They refreshed themselves with bread and milk in San Carlos, then
continued the journey to Presidio del Norte. While at Presidio, the
Texans provisioned themselves at Ben Leaton's ranch. They purchased mules and food from Leaton and remained there about 10
days, recovering from their near-fatal march across the Big
Bend.[10]

El Paso, their original goal, lay 150 miles farther west, but
the men physically could not continue. The leaders decided to give
up. They voted to return to San Antonio by a more northerly
route, passing by Horsehead Crossing and Live Oak Creek. This
route was not so treacherous as their outbound path, and they did
not suffer as much from either heat or lack of water. But they did
encounter Indians who stole six horses, which they recovered a
few days later. On December 12 a battered force trudged into San
Antonio, having traveled some 1,303 miles by their own
calculation.[11]

Hays gave reports of his trip to the citizens of San Antonio
who had sponsored it and to the Federal Government, which was
interested in establishing a fort in the Big Bend. His route west was
treacherous, he said. "The whole of this part of the country, from
the mouth of Devil's River up the Rio Grande, as far as San Carlos,
a town 40 miles south of Presidio del Norte, is one constant succession of high broken mountains, destitute of timber and water."
Returning by a more northerly course, he found a better trail and
more water. Had his guide been competent or the map accurate, he
might have had no problem on the way out, but the guide was "entirely ignorant of this part of the country"–few people besides Indians knew anything substantial of the Big Bend in 1848–and the
map was sketchy. His mistakes led Hays and his party into avoida-
ble hardships. After dismissing the guide, Hays took charge of the
party and led it to San Carlos by his own reckoning.

Hays characteristically minimized the Indian attack and recommended the northern route as the safe, easier one. By avoid-

ing the lower portion of the Big Bend, the wagon trains would be able to pass over "beautiful and level country," he said. The only obstacle would be the Pecos River, which could easily be forded except during seasonal crests.[12]

Travelers in the Big Bend

The discovery of gold in California drew others to the Big Bend. By 1849 literally thousands of gold seekers were traveling to California; many observers expected the Forty-Niners to find a route across Texas. "Reference to the map indicated that an overland route to the new El Dorado would . . . pass . . . not very far from Austin," wrote John S. Ford, a doctor and former Texas Ranger recently returned from Mexico. Austin citizens decided to send Ford on an exploratory trip to see whether a good road could be found between Austin and El Paso. Since the U.S. Army was also looking for a western route, Ford joined Maj. Robert S. Neighbors, Texas Indian Agent, for the jaunt. They left in March, tracing a route north of the Big Bend, by Brady's Creek, Horse-

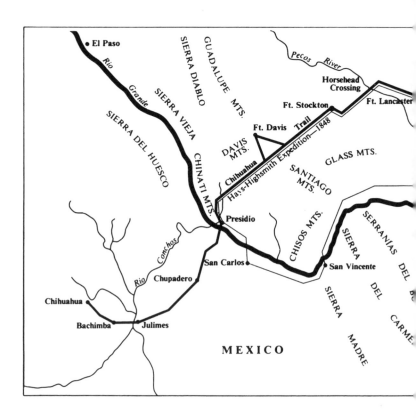

head Crossing, then west to the headwaters of the Concho River. After reaching Brady's Creek, they swung southward through Fort Mason, Fredericksburg, and San Antonio.[13]

Immigrants obviously needed an up-to-date map. So in the fall of 1848 Jacob de Cordova rushed into print with a map drawn by Robert Creuzbaur, the head draftsman of the State land office. Few details are shown for the Big Bend, but a caravan route from the Arkansas River in 1840 is depicted. If Creuzbaur intended to show Connelly's route, he probably placed it several miles too far north. For months de Cordova's map was the only one listed for sale in the advertisements of the *New York Tribune*. Using information gleaned from expeditions by Capt. John C. Frémont, Lt. Philip St. George Cooke, Lt. William H. Emory, Dr. Adolph Wislizenus, from Hays, Neighbors, and Ford following the war, and from the records of the State land office, Creuzbaur prepared his own guide book to aid the hundreds of Forty-Niners who were passing through Texas on their way to California. Entitled *Route*

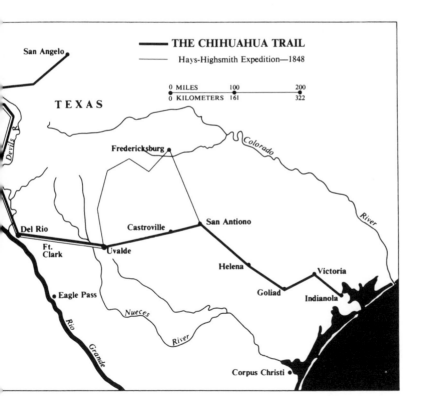

From the Gulf of Mexico and the Lower Mississippi Valley to California and the Pacific Ocean, the Creuzbaur work had a sizable national audience. On it Creuzbaur specifically drew Connelly's trail, indicating that the doctor passed closer to what is today the national park than he really did. Still, there is almost no information on the Big Bend itself, for little was known in 1849. Interest in the western route was so great that the *Texas State Gazette* also published the route of another Forty-Niner for all other "western adventurers" who were interested in where the waterholes and passes were throughout West Texas.[14]

Hays and his fellow travelers had crossed the most difficult part of the Big Bend. Their success encouraged others. Traders and Forty-Niners launched out across the plains. George W. B. Evans and a party from Ohio tried a different route. Instead of heading west from San Antonio, they journeyed through Eagle Pass and San Fernando. Hiring a Mexican guide, they then turned westward toward San Carlos, roughly along the path that Rábago had traveled a century before. It was a difficult journey through a bleak country at least as rough as the trails on the American side of the Rio Grande. "Kind reader, this is work, labor that requires the strength and exertion of every muscle of the body, and nature almost sinks under these repeated trials and privations," Evans noted in his journal. "Our limbs are sore and stiffened by this continued labor, and God only knows when we will find ourselves again upon the plains below." For an 80-mile stretch the party found no waterhole. One member of the group was lost in the desert. Evans also mistrusted the guide. Threatened by Apaches and Comanches every step of the way, he feared that the guide probably had agreed to lead the party into an ambush in return for part of the booty. The *despoblado* was so barren that they marched to within 10 miles of San Carlos without realizing it. Searching for words to "convey a perfect idea of this almost forsaken town," Evans pointed out that there were houses of "dried mud" and "upright poles plastered with mud." "There are no streets, but everything of or concerning this town is arranged in admirable confusion." The Forty-Niners continued the journey to Presidio del

Norte and Chihuahua, having crossed one of the most rugged parts of the *despoblado*.[15]

Corpus Christi merchants, in a favorable position on the Gulf of Mexico to make their city a shipping center, showed interest in the Chihuahua trade. The editor of the *Corpus Christi Star* argued with newspapermen in Houston as to which city was better located for the trade. The editor of the *Star* printed stories about the Hays expedition and was anxious to get the formal report. In September 1848 he announced plans of H. L. Kinney and other Corpus merchants to sponsor a wagon train to "open the road for permanent trade with Chihuahua." The expedition would be as "large as possible," he declared, and an "invitation is held out to all who may wish to join it." Kinney also hoped to obtain the U.S. mail contract for western Texas.[16]

While the train organized, the editor raved about the possibilities of trade over the western road. He glorified Lts. Francis T. Bryan's and Nathaniel Michler's trailblazing in early 1849. He printed letters from travelers claiming a good road existed from Corpus to Presidio del Norte. And his publicity campaign was successful. The editor of the *New Orleans Picayune* was convinced that the Hays route would divert trade from Santa Fe to Texas. "A glance at the map shows that San Antonio is the nearest from the United States to Chihuahua," he concluded, and "a trail or plank road" from San Antonio to the coast would rapidly bring the trade to New Orleans.[17]

The long train was finally ready for departure from Corpus Christi on July 17, 1849. For over a week, carts gathered in the city, and teamsters drove their wagons through the streets, a few leaving each day for the rendezvous point. Gen. William L. Cazneau, a prominent businessman, led such other well-known residents as Col. Jacob Snively in an effort to establish trading posts at Presidio del Norte and El Paso del Norte. Bearing perhaps $90,000 worth of goods for Chihuahua, the 100-man party headed westward toward Leona Creek. When they reached the Big Bend, Indians "hovered about" the 50 wagons so threateningly that the teamsters finally fired upon them. Whatever happened to the train – we have no evidence of its fate – the next trace of Cazneau has him founding a trading post at Eagle Pass the following year to foster his plans for Mexican trade.[18]

Cazneau was not the only speculator in the Chihuahua trade. In May 1849, Capt. W. W. Thompson left Fredericksburg with a party headed for El Paso. Employing Joe Robinson, the Delaware Indian who had been with Hays, the Thompson party traveled the

**Robert Creuzbaur's map was in great demand by
the argonauts en route to the California gold fields.**

AUTHORITES

1. *Fremont's Map of 1848.*
2. *Emory's Map of 1847.*
3. *Wislizenus's Map of 1847.*
4. *The Records of the Genl Land-*
   Office of the State of Texas.
        And others.

He was among the first to suggest a route
through the unknown Big Bend country.

northern route, anticipating few hardships. Robert Hunter, a member of the expedition, expressed their shock at the country in a letter to his wife. "We have travelled two hundred and forty miles without seeing any timber and at two different times we drove two days and nights without water over mountains and ravines on the route that Jack Hays said he found water so plenty, and if he had been in sight he would not have lived one minute. Our mules suffered immensely, but the men done very well as we had gourds and kegs." [19]

A Houston editor predicted a "snug little fortune" for the Bayou City merchant who left the city with his goods and declared that he would "not unload them till his wagon arrived at the public square" in El Paso. Persons who made the trip with Neighbors in 1850 reported that common products such as tobacco, domestics, and coffee were selling at seven or eight times their price in Houston. Although the Houston merchant intended to continue on to California to hunt for gold, the editor predicted that "we should not be surprised to hear that this adventurer should conclude to forego his journey to California and return to Houston for another stock of goods for the Chihuahua market. . . ." Such was the optimism that awaited the trade. [20]

An expedition under a Major Sprague was organized in San Antonio to start in April 1850 for El Paso. The caravan consisted of 200 Mexican carts and two companies of mounted troops. A local editor reported that other Alamo City merchants had departed for New Orleans and New York to purchase trade goods. Newspapers quickly reported journeys across the Trans-Pecos, emphasizing the ever-decreasing amount of time required to make the journey and the fact that difficulties were minor. One Robert Hays made the trek in just 31 days, and two merchants named Durand and Holliday made it in less than 20 days, according to the editor of the *San Antonio Ledger*. [21]

But merchants were more interested in the trip made by Maj. W. S. Henry, of the 3d Infantry Regiment in the summer of 1850, because he carried many goods and wagons. Departing El Paso on August 26, Henry, along with 18 persons, three wagons with mules, and one ambulance, arrived in San Antonio on September 13, causing the *Western Texan* to think it was the "quickest trip ever made with wagons." The *San Antonio Texan* noted the visit of 30 or 40 emigrants who passed through the city en route to the gold fields of California, as well as Charles Wiggins' wagon train that left San Antonio in the spring of 1850 for El Paso and the Chihuahua trade. The editor also reported that several other merchants were loading their goods at Indianola and Lavaca in preparation for the trip to Chihuahua. An encouraging account of the route and conditions came from a traveler who made the journey from Fredericksburg. "I had as pleasant a trip as could be expected," he reported. Following such successful journeys, the editor of the *Western Texan* declared the search for a route to El Paso and Chihuahua over. "It is now reduced to a 'fixed fact' that the best, safest, and shortest route . . . is through Texas, by way of San Antonio."[22]

Conflict with the Indians

Although newspapermen boosted the route for the good it would do their cities, they all realized the primary difficulty with the western route–the Indians. Many Argonauts had made the trip through the Big Bend without a fight, but the Comanches and Apaches were becoming increasingly inhospitable. A "reliable gentleman" who traveled through northern Mexico in 1849 reported that there was "scarcely a ranch throughout all those states that has not been sacked by the Indians." Durand and Holliday, on their return trip from El Paso, found the road to be "much infested" by them. The "insolent and hostile disposition manifested by these savages" forced the pair to confine their traveling to night. A party of travelers arrived in La Grange from Presidio del Norte to report that the Apaches were "almost daily committing depredations . . . plundering the inhabitants and driving off their stock." The country was in "miserable condition" according to James T. Peacock, a member of the expedition. Indians constantly crossed the Rio Grande into Mexico, where they robbed and killed the inhabitants "with impunity," then returned to Texas. Another party was stopped by Mescalero Apaches, probably led by Chief Gomez, who demanded cattle but refused to specify how many, preferring to leave that to the discretion (or fear) of the owners. Considered the terror of Chihuahua and West Texas, Gomez and his warriors claimed the Davis Mountains and the Big Bend as their domain and challenged anyone who entered. Other parties were raided, travelers wounded, and cattle stolen.[23]

The Comanches and Apaches were protecting their last

stronghold: the *despoblado*. Applying to the newcomers what had been an enormously successful formula in Mexico, they had ruled supreme in the Trans-Pecos ever since the departure of the Spaniards, when Mexico won its independence in 1821. Weakened by internal difficulties, Mexico had never been able to establish any measure of control over the Big Bend, then lost the region entirely in 1836 when Texas won its independence. Nor could the Texans exert any influence beyond the Pecos River. For years the Big Bend was left to the Indians, who rode from their homes in present-day New Mexico, Oklahoma, and West Texas through the Big Bend into Mexico, where they killed and plundered the settlements along the northern border in what has become recognized as one of the most sustained devastations of the advancing frontier. Then they returned, leaving a path of destruction and prairie fires as they eluded their pursuers, much as their ancestors had done in the previous century. The struggle for supremacy began when the newcomers seeking trade with El Paso and Chihuahua, gold in California, or settlement in the Big Bend itself infringed on what the Indians had kept to themselves for decades.

Apaches and Comanches occupied the Big Bend more or less by default. Buffeted and forced from more fertile lands to the north, they had moved into the void known as the *despoblado* and adjusted their life styles. The meager existence they gleaned from the sparse plants and fleet animals of the Big Bend soon convinced them that they could live better by stealing from the frontier villages and frequent wagon trains that ventured through the region, a logical conclusion for a people that had been driven from their original homelands and continually pressured by the advancing Anglo-Americans, who took the land for their own sustenance.

The Indians were difficult to defeat, for they alone knew how to exist in the Big Bend. The Sol family of the Comanches, for example, lived for years in West Texas and Mexico, ravaging Mexicans to earn their living. Led by Arriba el Sol, the matriarch of the clan, they made their permanent home somewhere along the Colorado River of Texas, but roamed for much of the year in the Big Bend and northern Mexico. Arriba el Sol had two grandsons, Bajo el Sol and Mague, who were talented leaders and

A Lipan warrior encountered by the U.S. Boundary Survey. From a lithograph in Emory's *Report*.

excellent warriors. Because Comanche warriors were free to choose their own leaders, the Sols had a large following.[24]

The Great Comanche War Trail

The Sols entered Mexico over the Comanche War Trail, which crossed the Trans-Pecos from the northeast, then split into

Muchos Toros, a sub-chief in Bajo el Sol's band.

two forks when it reached the Big Bend. One fork crossed the Rio Grande near present-day Lajitas, then continued into Mexico via San Carlos and the Río Conchos valley. The main trail crossed the Rio Grande at the Chisos ford, between Santa Elena and Mariscal Canyons, then continued by the Laguna de Jaco into the eastern portion of the *despoblado*. So distinctive was this trail that explorers never failed to mention it if they saw it. A mile wide in places, it was littered with the skeletons of livestock driven from Mexico. Colonel Langberg reported that it was "wider than any 'royal road,' " and "so well beaten that it appears that suitable engineers had constructed it." The land was rutted and in some spots vegetation was burned off, graphically revealing the extent to which the Comanches had subdued the heretofore untamed Big Bend country.*

The Sols spent most of each summer camping in abandoned mining districts, around waterholes, and at times near springs known to the Mexicans. While their horses and animals grazed on

---

* Today the great trail is almost invisible, even to the trained eye. A research team from the University of Texas found that erosion and vegetation have changed the complexion of the thoroughfare and made it almost impossible to distinguish the trail from the surrounding desert.

The Chihuahua Trail

the best grass the *despoblado* could produce, the warriors participated in several camp games: horse racing and a form of ball playing probably similar to lacrosse. Because they were not disturbed in the *despoblado,* the Sols could establish fairly peaceful camps and disperse small raiding parties in all directions.

The warriors prepared for a raid by gathering at Bajo el Sol's tepee and dancing to rhythms beaten out with sticks. Then the warriors met in council with the elders to ensure a successful mission. The warriors spent the night at the edge of the camp, and the next day began their march, riding all of each day until they reached their destination. The raiding parties were sometimes quite large; often they were as small as half-a-dozen warriors. They raided any tempting target along the route. When they reached their destination, they spent the night nearby and attacked the following day. They took everything they could: livestock, blankets, church ornaments, harness gear, housewares, and captives.

They herded their booty back through the Big Bend via the Chisos ford to avoid coming too close to Presidio del Norte. Once again in Texas, they traded the livestock, sold the other goods, and ransomed the captives. In return they received rifles, bullets, swords, tobacco, whiskey, and other goods from the American traders, and iron for arrow tips and spear points from the Mexicans at San Carlos, which often made them better armed than the Mexican army. Col. Emilio Langberg, Inspector of the Military Colonies of Chihuahua, complained to Maj. Jefferson Van Horne that Ben Leaton had been supplying the Apaches and Comanches with lead, powder, arms, and "other articles of ammunition." Chihuahua Governor Ángel Trias charged Leaton with "a thousand abuses, and of so hurtful a nature, that he keeps an open treaty with the Apache Indians . . . ." [25]

The Sols managed by shrewd diplomacy to prevent the Mexicans from organizing a unified effort to exterminate them. When the Mexican government declared a "war of extermination" on the Indians of the north, the Sols responded by making treaties with the local governments, agreeing that they would not raid in that particular area and would help fight the Apaches. This not only left the Sols free to raid in other areas of Mexico, but it also gave them protection in the region where they concluded the treaty. Other Indians performed similar feats with the United States and Mexico, reaching an agreement with one country while continuing to raid in the other. Indian Agent Robert S. Neighbors feared that was the arrangement some Northern Comanches had with Chihuahua in 1854. The United States had difficulty making treaties with the

Indians of the Big Bend, on the other hand, because contact was sporadic. The Indians were not only hostile, they were also elusive. When Agent J. A. Rogers dispatched an interpreter to arrange contact with the Mescaleros, for example, he found only a few near Presidio del Norte, because a drought had driven them from the Big Bend.[26]

The Southwestern Scalp Hunters

The Mexican government tried several measures to stop the Sols and their allies. The military was seemingly useless because

James Kirker, also called "Santiago," whose name usually struck fear in the hearts of Mexicans and Indians alike.

William A. "Bigfoot" Wallace delivered the mail and fought Indians in the Big Bend.

the officers did not know either the ways of Indian warfare or the *despoblado*. Individual ranches, even the large ones, were virtually helpless against the hit and run raids of the Sols. For their own defense citizens constructed featureless houses of thick adobe. There were no windows or chimneys. "Many are built like forts, and may be considered as such," concluded George Evans, who viewed them in 1846. Ben Leaton copied the pattern for his ranchhouse near Presidio, which still stands, as did Milton Faver at his La Ciénega Ranch. In desperation, the local governments in Chihuahua and Durango offered bounties on scalps of unfriendly Indians, sometimes as much as $200 for each scalp, with additional money for the hair of a leader like Bajo el Sol. Dozens of Americans went south during the 1830s and after the Mexican War to take advantage of the opportunity. Some, who had intended to go to California and search for gold instead, soon found that scalp hunting was like "discovering a mine." Joel Glanton and James Kirker became near celebrities on the border because of their prowess in gathering scalps. Adventurers, ex-Texas Rangers, former U.S. soldiers, and villains joined them in the "vile industry." They were not always too careful about whose scalp they collected, because it was difficult to distinguish among Anglo, Mexican, or Indian once the lock had shriveled and dried, but the Mexican officials might have felt their cause had been served anyway. Samuel E. Chamberlain, famous for his paintings of the Mexican War and himself a scalp hunter for a short time, noted that Gen. José Urrea encouraged the bounty hunters, but held them in such low esteem that he "seemed equally pleased when Ranger or Indian went under."[27]

When merchants and explorers crossed the Big Bend, therefore, they entered the domain of the Apaches and Comanches. As the trade along the trail increased, incidents of harassment by Indians became more frequent. South of San Antonio the Indians seemed to have "entire possession" of the road. By 1852 every arrival of the mail train brought tales of new depredations: Apaches riding down on teamsters en route from Fort Fillmore, N. Mex., to Leona Station (Fort Inge), Texas; Indians attacking the mail train itself. William A. ("Bigfoot") Wallace was in charge of the mail train when his party was attacked on the afternoon of September 9, 1852. While they were camped near the Painted Caves of the Pecos River, more than 30 redmen charged into their midst. "We raised our rifles to fire on them," Bigfoot later recalled. "The Indians . . . fell back, circling around us [and] took possession of the top of Big Bluff, directly over our camp, and then the *fandango* began . . . ." The fight lasted but a short time, and there were only a few casualties. Rather than risk death in another frontal assault, the Indians waited until the whites broke camp. Bigfoot had anticipated their move, however, and retreated. "I could not by any means pass the Indians with the mail on mule back," he claimed after he had returned to San Antonio. But, still hoping to fulfill the mailman's creed, Wallace took on reinforcements – bringing his total force to nine – and headed for El Paso again. "If we cannot clear the road," he promised, "we shall fight it out with them." Any survivors would make their way to El Paso for the return mail.[28]

Each wagon train had to be prepared for an Indian attack. August Santleben, who freighted on the Chihuahua Trail for several years, recalled that the teamsters in his train realized that they were watched throughout the trip. They always left two men to guard the mules, even during meals. If possible, teamsters stood watch from a prominent peak, so they could view the entire area around the camp. At night, four men stood guard and were relieved every 2 hours. While in transit the freighters always stood ready to circle their wagons to provide a makeshift fort for protection against the expected attack. Unless the teamsters were overpowered by superior numbers, said Santleben, this tactic usually worked. There was no delay in resuming the trip after the Indians retreated, for all but two teams remained hitched during the engagement.[29]

Barren Country

Indian attacks were not the only hardship confronting travelers. The country was deserted; where there were once continuous orchards, gardens, haciendas, and "happy peons, shepherds and goatherds" between El Paso and Presidio, according to a correspondent who signed himself Melnotte, now there was only a "collection of squalid mud huts. All is desolation and ruins" because of the raids. Scarcity of water and grass often forced the teamsters to travel from waterhole to waterhole. This procedure frequently slowed Santleben's progress, for sometimes he made only 30 miles a day, when he could have pushed on perhaps twice that distance in better country. D. A. Tucker wrote that he and the 72 men in his party remained "on the hinges of starvation" during more than half their trip from East Texas to California. Colonel Langberg of the Mexican Boundary Survey team discovered discarded wagons and graves of American travelers between Santa Rosa and San Carlos.[30]

The same factors that had defeated the Spaniards withstood the American assault. Harsh terrain was rendered even more inhospitable by the severity of the Big Bend weather. In the fall water and grass became scarce. Capt. William Smith described the immense "suffering and loss" among the pioneers headed for El Paso in August 1854. The Fairchild and McClure expedition lost 200 head of cattle for lack of water. Dunlap's party lost 700 cattle while passing through the Big Bend. Smith reported that the path was "literally strewn with their carcases [*sic*]." Terrain caused a particular problem because the freight wagons were built for level ground. The wagon bed was 24 feet long, but only 4½ feet wide. High loads usually made the vehicle top-heavy. Santleben pointed out that this made the wagons sway from side to side, putting the weight first on one set of wheels and then the other. The load was easier to pull, but when the teamsters encountered the rougher roads in the Big Bend, the wagons frequently turned over. So the teamsters used ropes to hold them upright while they passed through the roughest parts of the country. Sometimes a dozen men were needed on the ropes to keep a load from spilling. Santleben recalled that the route between San Antonio and El Paso was a "constant drag." [31]

Nor was there any law enforcement in the towns along the route. Tucker reported that everyone had survived the "difficulties and privations" along the road, except for Walter Beard, who had been stabbed by B. B. Lee, another member of the expedition in El Paso. James Poole, who passed through El Paso, decried the "lynch law" that prevailed in the town. [32]

Diplomacy

At Presidio the traders had to go through Mexican customs, which could be an ordeal. Since there were no firm customs laws, according to George L. Macmanus, the American consul in Chihuahua, the traders had to negotiate with the customs officer when they arrived at Presidio. When James P. Hickman arrived in Chihuahua in 1858, he was presented with a bill for the same tax he had paid in Presidio. When he refused to pay, his wagons were confiscated and the matter was taken to court. There a stalemate occurred. The justice of the peace, realizing that Hickman was being cheated, refused to rule against Hickman because he was right. But the justice also refused to rule against the government for fear that he himself would be punished. "The govor. is winking at the whole transaction," concluded Macmanus, "thus Mr. Hickman is swindled out of his money." The matter was resolved, of course, by Hickman paying the tax, but Macmanus asked the American government to protest the decision, claiming that "we are in constant dread of some new imposition . . . ." [33]

Because of the Chihuahua Trail, the Big Bend was on the verge of becoming an important trade route. The Hays expedition had attracted publicity throughout Texas and Louisiana. The Ford-Neighbors party found what probably was a better route to El Paso, and Forty-Niners, traders, and settlers began their move into the Big Bend. Yet if this upstart trail were to rival the established Santa Fe Trail, several things had to be accomplished. It had to be made safe from Indians, and it had to be further surveyed and physically improved. In 1850 the power to accomplish these goals rested with the Army and the Topographical Engineers.

4/The Topographical Engineers

The great Chihuahua Desert, capped by the Chisos Mountains and penetrated only by the Rio Grande and its tributaries, must have played through Lt. Col. Joseph E. Johnston's mind as he prepared the official report on his reconnaissance of the Big Bend in 1850. While searching for a wagon road through the Big Bend, he had crossed tiny streams and creeks that bore the names of mighty rivers and often lived up to their names during the rainy season. After studying Indian trails in Wild Rose Pass and Persimmon Gap, he had learned from the Mexicans south of the Rio Grande that devastating raids were a common occurrence and had to be accepted as a fact of life.

Johnston's immediate tasks were to explore the river and the Big Bend for a site for an army post. He probably noted, as he drew one of the first accurate maps of the region, that there were almost no permanent settlements or place names in the Big Bend, and he might have suspected that the Topographical Engineers would play a great role in opening up the country to settlers. He clearly made the most of a difficult situation, for there were few benefits attached to the job of chief Topographical Engineer in Texas when he was appointed to the post in 1848.[1]

Johnston first arrived in the Big Bend about the time merchants became interested in West Texas. The United States had acquired the vast Southwest in the Mexican War of 1846-48. Many people believed that this area could not be absorbed into the Union because it was so large and removed from the settled portion of the country. Col. John J. Abert, commander of the Topographical Engineers, believed the situation was so desperate that first priority should be assigned to completing a road into the new territory. The "integrity of the Union" was at stake, he said. Part of the proposed route that would extend from San Antonio, Tex., to San Diego, Calif., had been charted by Lt. William H. Emory, who had explored from Santa Fe to the Gila River as a member of Col. Stephen W. Kearny's "Army of the West" in 1846, but the 500-mile stretch from San Antonio to El Paso del Norte was an un-

The Rio Grande between Presidio and the western boundary of the park.

known highway of horrors to most merchants.[2]

Secretary of War William L. Marcy had already directed the engineers to find a better road between San Antonio and Santa Fe, and by 1849 they were hard at work. With the knowledge gleaned by the Hays-Highsmith expedition, Lts. William H. C. Whiting and William F. Smith had set out for El Paso to find a route that would serve both military and commercial purposes. Contending with hostile Apaches and lack of water, Whiting and Smith did improve upon the Hays-Highsmith route to the extent that their trail was used for the first mail run between San Antonio and El Paso in 1850, but they did not fully satisfy the requirements of the army. "Unless some easy, cheap, and rapid means of communicating with these distant provinces be accomplished," said Abert, "there is danger, great danger, that they will not constitute parts of our Union." [3]

The experience of Hays, Ford, and Whiting showed that the job would be strenuous. Assuming that the Indians could eventually be suppressed, Lt. William F. Smith, who knew the Big Bend first-hand, predicted that the foremost obstacle in their path would be the inhospitable terrain. "When the nature of the country is seen by those who may hereafter pass over the road," he remarked, "it may excite surprise; but it will not be that so practicable a route has been found, but rather that any was found at all." [4]

But in 1849 the Indians had not been conquered. The Mexicans were never able to pacify the frontier, even as successfully as Spain had. The Mexican War brought people into the Big Bend, and a process of reclamation began. Johnston and his men were among the first Americans to deal with the Indians of the Big Bend.

Exploration of the Rio Grande

Johnston divided up the exploration of the Big Bend. He first assigned men to explore further the routes that had already been mapped: Hays-Highsmith, Ford-Neighbors, and Whiting-Smith. Lt. Francis T. Bryan was dispatched to explore the Ford-Neighbors route, while he and Lt. Smith took the southern route. The harsh country forced Johnston to look for other routes as well. Although he was unaware of the thwarted Spanish dreams of navigating the Rio Grande, he probably knew of Gen. Thomas J. Green's claim in

1844 that "a steamboat can leave Pittsburg, and go to within three hundred miles of the navigable waters of the Gulf of California," presumably via the Rio Grande and the Río Conchos. Johnston hoped that the Rio Grande might be navigable and strongly urged that the engineers devote their time to its exploration between Eagle Pass and the confluence of the Rio Grande and the Pecos. He pointed out that by using the river the army could shorten the distance that goods had to be hauled overland. He also wanted to open the river to steamboat traffic, a much more economical means of transportation than wagons. Secretary of War C. M. Conrad's hope also soared as he informed the President that navigation of the Rio Grande would save the army both time and money. [5]

Acting on instructions from Abert, the engineers momentarily directed their efforts toward a thorough exploration of the river. They were probably influenced by the enthusiasm of Maj. W. W. Chapman, who reported Capt. John Love's trip up the Rio Grande in 1850. Chapman claimed that Love had navigated upriver as far as Presidio, a distance of approximately 1,000 miles. The land trip to El Paso could have been shortened by several hundred miles if Chapman's report had been true, but it did not take the engineers long to disprove it. Johnston instructed Lts. Martin L. Smith and Nathaniel Michler to begin at Ringgold Barracks, on the lower Rio Grande in Starr County, and proceed upriver. Lts. William F. Smith and Francis T. Bryan journeyed to El Paso, where they put in the water and floated as far downriver as they could. Smith and Michler explored the river to a point some 80 miles above the confluence of the Rio Grande and the Pecos, where they ran out of provisions and had to turn back. Even at that, one of their men said he had been with Love and insisted that the Smith-Michler party had gone further upriver than Love had. And their observations differed sharply from Love's, raising serious doubts as to the accuracy of Chapman's report. Although Smith recommended that some improvements be made on the river and felt that it could be navigated as far as Isletas, or Kingsbury's Falls, he certainly was not as optimistic as Love or Chapman. [6]

Lieutenants Smith and Bryan, coming downriver from El Paso to Presidio, suffered problems from the beginning. Finding the Rio Grande up several feet from normal and running swiftly, they immediately lost two provision boats, and required almost 2 weeks to travel 20 miles. After numerous other difficulties, they reached Presidio, where they concluded that the survey could not be conducted any farther because of the canyons. They had not yet seen Santa Elena, Mariscal, or Boquillas. [7]

Joseph E. Johnston's 1850 map was one of the
first accurate studies of the Big Bend.

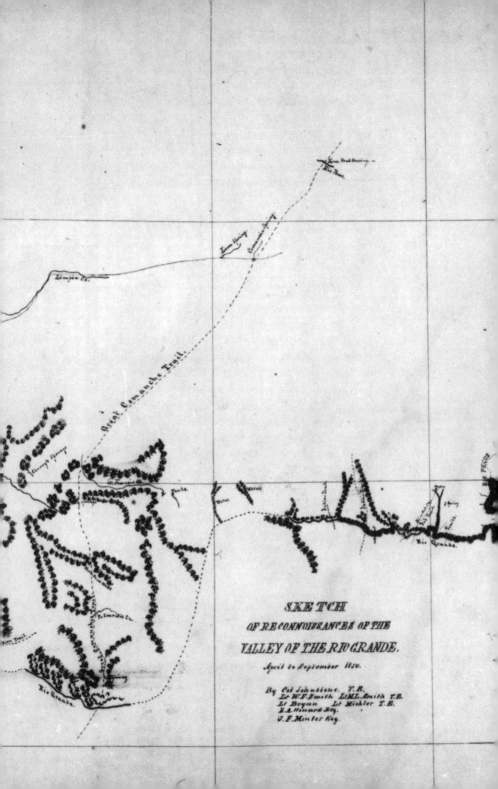

Great Comanche Trail.

SKETCH
OF RECONNOISSANCES OF THE
VALLEY OF THE RIO GRANDE.

April to September 1850.

By Col Johnston. T.E.
Lt W.F. Smith Lt M.L. Smith T.E.
Lt Bryan   Lt Michler T.E.
E.A. Howard Esq.
J.F. Minter Esq.

Johnston's men had tried. They had groped about the fringes of the Big Bend, but could not penetrate its heart. Johnston had ordered them to explore the Rio Grande, but saw them defeated by rapids, canyons, and a lack of supplies. "Strong armed parties" were forced to accompany the engineers throughout their trek because of the threat of Indian attack. As he drew the map that was to accompany his official report, Johnston had to admit that there was still much he did not know about the Big Bend. Confidently reporting that "the country in question is uninhabited, except the neighborhood of Presidio del Norte," he was forced to leave out important information: lengthy portions of the Rio Grande remained unmapped, key geographical and geological features were omitted, and only portions of the many Indian trails that crisscrossed the Big Bend were included. Just as in the Spanish era the fringes had been probed, but the Big Bend itself remained a mystery. Its exploration was left to yet another team.[8]

The Green-Chandler Expedition

The expedition that finally explored the Big Bend was a part of the joint boundary survey, required by Article V of the Treaty of Guadalupe Hidalgo. The treaty provided for two commissions, made up of representatives of both the United States and Mexico, to conduct a survey of the new border. John B. Weller was appointed the first U.S. Commissioner, while Gen. Pedro García Condé was named the Mexican commissioner. After establishing the westernmost boundary below San Diego, the commissioners moved to El Paso del Norte, where they met to locate the initial boundary point on the Rio Grande. On May 4, 1850, Whig President Zachery Taylor replaced Democrat Weller with a Whig, John Russell Bartlett, a prominent bibliophile and amateur ethnologist from Providence, R.I. Bartlett landed on the Texas coast and proceeded to El Paso where he began his work. The engineers worked westward first, then returned to El Paso. There Chief Surveyor William H. Emory discovered that Bartlett had not yet returned from the

William H. C. Whiting was the first man to use the term Big Bend in print.

John Russell Bartlett

William H. Emory

west and made plans immediately to complete the survey down the Rio Grande. By the summer of 1852, the survey had reached the Trans-Pecos.[9]

By then the surveyors were laboring under considerable hardship. Commissioner Bartlett's continued absence had fomented ill-will in the camp, leading one man to remark "that he came out here only to write a book." (Bartlett did, of course, write one of the classics of Western travel literature, his *Personal Narrative.*) "We as yet have not heard what part of the world he inhabits," continued the grumbler. Bartlett's spending added to the hardship, for the survey team was bankrupt. Some believed that he had already drawn on the next year's appropriation. Others, who were used to having their government drafts rejected by the merchants, were relieved when they arrived at Presidio del Norte, "a new field for credit – they have not found us out yet." The Indians further complicated the surveyors' job. They "are now becoming worse, they come now and take mules from under ones nose with no fear. I expect some night to hear the rascals in the house," commented G. Clinton Gardner, Clerk to the Chief Astronomer and Head of the Scientific Corps. If the engineers had known of Col. Emilio Langberg's troubles the previous year, they could have better prepared for their task. There was not even an open path, reported the colonel. They had "to pass the artillery by hand in various places because of the rugged terrain." To complicate their task, "the sun was beating down with all its force, and the camp gave few hopes for pasture for the horses, as two years of drought had nearly destroyed all the forage." [10]

81

Emory, nevertheless, decided that the river between Presidio and the mouth of the Pecos had to be surveyed. Short of able scientists and military men, he first selected his clerk, Gardner, for the task. Elated at the opportunity to receive the "credit of having carried a survey over an unknown country," Gardner hoped that the man most fitted for the task, Marine Tyler Wickham Chandler, would not arrive in camp in time. "My only hopes are that he will refuse it as rather a rough place for such a nice personage as himself," Gardner confided to a sister. The ambitious young man's chances faded, however, when Chandler returned to camp from a trip east and proved "desirous of taking charge." [11]

On August 8 Emory ordered Chandler to commence the survey at Presidio del Norte and proceed downriver to the mouth of the Pecos, or until he met another party coming upriver. Chandler was well qualified for the task. Born in 1819, he received his A.B. and M.A. degrees from the University of Pennsylvania. He worked as city engineer and surveyor for Philadelphia before joining the boundary commission, and gathered natural history collections for the Smithsonian Institution while in the Southwest. Aside from his personal enthusiasm, Chandler was also temperamentally qualified for his work. "You will find Mr. Chandler to be a bag of gass if you give him a chance to explode," Gardner wrote his father. "He can tell you more tales about the commission than I know you will believe, yet a great number of them I expect you will find to be so." [12]

Chandler was ordered to note islands or points where the boundary might be in doubt, because the treaty specified the border as the deepest channel of the river. Warning him that the "peculiar topographic features" of the Big Bend might force him to "deviate from the prescribed methods of operating," Emory gave Chandler a map made by Langberg. Though it was vague, the map indicated the forbidding landscape ahead and was far better than anything the Americans had. Because Chandler had the most difficult assignment of the survey, Emory gave him Lt. Duff C. Green and a 35-man escort for protection. [13]

The man who would make geological drawings and sketches for Chandler was Arthur C. V. Schott, a naturalist, engineer, and physician. A young man with little experience, he was hardly in the same class as the other artists on the survey: Seth Eastman, Henry C. Pratt, Harrison Eastman, and Bartlett, a good watercolorist in his own right. Since none of Schott's original drawings survived—we have only a few technical sketches—it's difficult to evaluate his work. He apparently served the scientific ends of the mission well enough, and must be judged as an artist by the engravings that appear in Emory's published report.

As the survey began, Lieutenant Green collected more men and supplies. "There is nothing to be had of any description of food between here and Fort Duncan," Emory had advised. Therefore Green traveled to El Paso, where he met Bartlett, who demanded that the lieutenant escort him to Eagle Pass. But Green refused and returned to Presidio, anxious to begin the survey before too much of the new food supply was gone. He expected the survey to take 100 days, even though Emory thought it could be done in 60 if the work was "prosecuted diligently."

Because Green was concerned that his refusal to escort Bartlett might endanger his career, he later pointed out in his report that his orders were to let nothing interfere with the survey. He felt justified in returning to Presidio and Chandler's party. He hoped that there were enough soldiers at Fort Fillmore to escort Bartlett, and he defended his decision by saying that the commissioner could have gathered an escort elsewhere if he had really tried. "Mr. Bartlett was very particular in his inquiries about the routes to Chihuahua, and it is my firm conviction that when I left him he made up his mind to go through Mexico, so he very readily seized the opportunity offered him by the Mexicans. . . ." Green neglected to say that Emory had promised him a promotion if he successfully completed the survey.[15]

The Bofecillos Mountains

Green and Chandler faced another problem as they started out: the rugged Bofecillos Mountains, which in Schott's sketches appear almost impenetrable. The valley around Fort Leaton, near Presidio, was most pleasant, said Chandler. But in the mountains the valley became only a small path, and rocks and tree branches impeded travel. Green had to take his escort to the Mexican side, leaving his wagons behind, to continue the march. When Green crossed, the river was three times its normal height. Before Chandler could follow him, the river had risen even higher, causing a 5-day delay in the march. In the first 3 miles on the Mexican side, most of Green's 80 mules became dispersed. Of the five left, only two still had their loads. Rounding up the others, he found that they

SURVEYS OF THE ENGINEERS

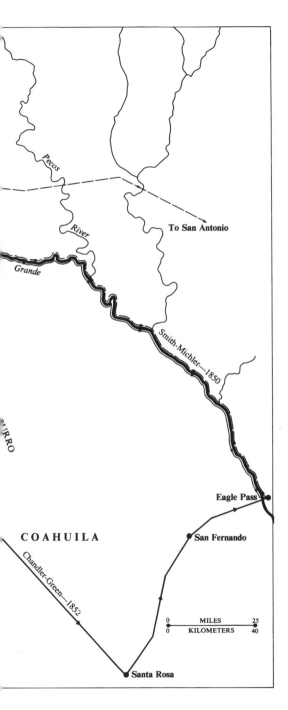

Pecos

River

Grande

To San Antonio

Smith-Michler—1850

Eagle Pass

COAHUILA

San Fernando

Chandler-Green—1852

0	MILES	25
0	KILOMETERS	40

Santa Rosa

ARRO

Lt. Duff C. Green, U.S. Army, commanded the military escort for the Chandler Expedition in what proved to be the first scientific exploration of the Rio Grande. Between September 12 and November 24, 1852, the party crossed the uncharted country between Presidio del Norte and Eagle Pass, traveling much of the time in Mexican territory. Green's report of the expedition is notable for its details on the field operations of the Boundary Survey. The young officer showed, too, the weakness of the Mexican frontier defenses and the impunity with which Texas Indians swept across the border to raid and plunder.

had lost all their coffee. "Knowing the necessity of contentment to perfect discipline," he commented, "I purchased some coffee for seventy five cents per pound." [16]

Although imposing, the Bofecillos Mountains were less treacherous than those farther downriver. It was "utterly impossible" for Green to take his mule train along the river bank, and because he was to survey the border as closely as possible, Chandler had to separate from Green and the escort party and float down the river in boats. Green, meanwhile, took the pack train and traveled as best he could along the Mexican side. Besides the rough terrain, he faced the "continual disengagement of mules from their loads." But Chandler was in worse condition on the river. He had lost his boats and supplies in one of the recurring "dangerous and long rapids" at the mouth of the canyon. Thereafter he found traveling on foot easier, and soon reached Comanche Crossing where he established his camp. Green located the camp, probably near the present village of Lajitas, as Chandler was "eating his last piece of pork . . . entirely destitute of kitchen furniture." Chandler decided to wait at Comanche Crossing until more supplies could be obtained from Presidio.[17]

Comanche Crossing, or Pass, as Chandler called it, had long been a famous ford where many of the Indians crossed the river with their booty from raids conducted in Mexico. Chandler observed "broad, well-beaten trails" leading to the Rio Grande from both sides. The country near the crossing was barren, but vegetation paralleled the river. "Sterile plains" stretched northwestward, with only the "rocky barriers" of the Solitario range in the north to break the monotony. While waiting for the supplies from Presidio, Chandler and Green met the famous Comanche Chief Mano, who was traveling with his band of Indians from the headwaters of Red River to Durango, Mexico. When the Comanches first approached, the Americans were, of course, cautious. Because he was in Mexico and anxious to avoid an international incident, Green sent a Mexican helper to confer with the chief and arrayed his troops across the river from the Indians. Mano claimed that he had been at peace with the Americans for more than a year and that he only wanted to cross into Mexico. He and Green entered into a "treaty," exchanged gifts – he gave Green a horse, Green gave him

This woodcut, reproduced from Emory's _Report_, shows the entrance to Bofecillos Canyon.

a beef that could not travel – and made as good a show of force as each dared. Mano then crossed the river headed toward the village of San Carlos. Only after he arrived at Fort Duncan did Green learn that Mano had attacked and killed four travelers on the San Antonio road and was headed to Mexico with his loot.

Santa Elena Canyon

Immediately downriver from the pass the Rio Grande winds through the San Carlos Mountains and into what Green called the Great Cañon San Carlos, probably Santa Elena Canyon. When the party came to the entrance to the canyon, Chandler stayed on the river. Schott paused to sketch the view for later publication, while Green was forced to try to find a more hospitable route for his mules. The following day they met at the entrance of the canyon and Chandler told Green the results of a reconnaissance by one of his assistants. On September 29 Thomas Thompson had gone into the canyon as far as he could. About 100 yards past the entrance Thompson discovered what are today called the "mirror-twins," a pair of canyons leading off both to the left and the right. They forced him to make a long detour and eventually prevented him from getting to the river. Before he returned, however, he observed a "perpendicular fall," probably a reference to the now famous rock slide that provides excitement for the float trips through Santa Elena. "One of the men with me is a boatman belonging to the survey," reported Thompson, "and he expressed the opinion that it would be impossible for the boat to pass this fall in safety." [19]

Using Thompson's information, Chandler decided to make as good a survey as possible without going through the canyon. Climbing onto the Mesa de Anguila, he saw the river hundreds of feet below him. "Dashing with a roaring sound over the rocks, the stream, when it reached the canyon, suddenly becomes noiseless, and is diminished to a sixth of its former width," he observed. "It enters the side of this vast mountain, which seems cut to its very base to afford a passage to the waters." Chandler saw numerous bends in the canyon, causing the swift current to crash against the vertical walls and rendering the river unfit for navigation. "The rapids and falls which occur in quick succession, make the descent in boats entirely impracticable," he concluded. Schott sketched the "falls of the Rio Bravo" from his vantage point atop the mesa. [20]

Chandler, too, saw the famous "rapids of the Rio Grande." "From the cañon wall the river may be seen far below," he wrote, "at a distance so great as to reduce it in appearance to a mere thread; and from this height the roar of the rapids and falls is scarcely perceptible." He estimated the fall in the river to be 12 feet during the course of the rapids, but he was so far away that it was little more than an educated guess. After viewing the mouth of

After viewing the "falls" from the top of the Mesa de Anguila (right), the Boundary Survey team decided not to try to float through Santa Elena Canyon.

Santa Elena Canyon, one of the most impressive sights in the Big Bend, Chandler reported that the river "is hemmed in" by the mesa for 10 miles, then "leaves it with the same abruptness that marks its entrance."[21]

Green soon discovered what he considered to be the best location for the fort that Johnston wanted to build. When Chandler had seen enough of the canyon, Green employed a Mexican, probably from nearby San Carlos, to guide them around Santa Elena on the Mexican side of the river. But they were forced to return to American soil to continue the survey because the river cuts through Terlingua Fault and emerges into flat land at the mouth of Santa Elena, leaving all the rough territory on the Mexican side. Two days' march from the mouth of the canyon, Green and the party camped at what he called "Vado de Fleche," or Ford of the Arrows, probably in the vicinity of present-day Castolon. Here "the country is more open, the valleys broader, and . . . susceptible of cultivation," wrote Chandler. "In the whole course of the Rio Grande," concluded Green, "I never saw a place so definitely marked for a miltary post as the valley near this ford." There were several reasons for his recommendation. The ford was the main Indian crossing, it was within two days' march of the only other ford of any consequence, Comanche Crossing, and a road could be constructed to join the San Antonio-El Paso road, more than 100 miles to the north. Cotton, timber, and good bottom land were immediately available.[22]

It was also at this point that the survey team had an excellent view of Mount Emory, or Emory Peak as it is called today. "Whenever the spectator was elevated sufficiently to see beyond the valley of the river," wrote Chandler,

> two prominent peaks were always presented to his view: one of these marks a summit in the range of the Mexican Sierra Carmel [sic]; and the other, from its peculiar shape and great height, was long and anxiously watched during the progress of our survey. From many places on the line it was taken as a point on which to direct the instruments; and, though the face of the country might change during our progress down the river, still, unmistakable and unchangeable, far above the surrounding mountains, this peak reared its well known head. The windings of the river, and the progess of our survey, led us gradually nearer to this point of interest, and it was found to be a part of a cluster, rather than range, of mountains on the American side, known as "Los Chisos." For this . . . we have proposed the name of Mount Emory.[23]

89

From that point Schott sketched several views of the Chisos, one trying to give an impression of the beauty and grandeur of the area, others to show the geologically diverse character of the mountains.

Mariscal Canyon

As the survey party reached Mariscal Canyon, where the river slices through Mariscal Mountain, the terrain grew rougher. Chandler stuck to the river and his surveying while Green took the remainder of Chandler's party and the pack train and headed for smoother ground. With the boaters, Chandler soon came on another "series of falls or sharp rapids far down in the abyss" where the "roaring of the waters announced a more than usual disturbance." They lost one of their boats. "It was impossible to carry the line nearer the bed of the river than the summits of the adjoining hills," Chandler determined. Two days were required to get out of the canyon, a trip which normally takes only 6 to 8 hours today. "Through these mountains the river forces its way, forming a cañon that equals the San Carlos in many places both in ruggedness and grandeur," he reported. Reaching San Vicente, the site of the abandoned presidio, Chandler left a survey flag and a note for the Mexican surveyor, Col. José Salazar Ylarregui, who had agreed to connect the point with his survey. A typical Spanish corral-type fortress, the presidio seemed ensconced in the last small clearing before the imposing Sierra del Carmen stops the eye. While at the presidio in 1851, Colonel Langberg noted that he could see the "half circle" of the river as it began its sweep northeastward to form the bend. He observed that the chapel was still standing, and that Comanches and Mescaleros had used the presidio patio after it had been deserted by the Mexican army. Standing on the American side of the river, Schott recorded Presidio San Vicente and the surrounding terrain. His is the only known view, although some ruins remain today.[21]

Boquillas Canyon and the Sierra del Carmen

Chandler had anticipated that the country beyond San Vicente would be smooth and less hazardous. That, unfortunately, was not the case. It proved to be just as "rough and broken" as that he had just covered. Green experienced "great trouble" in find-

The ruins of presidio San Vicente, on the Mexican
side of the Rio Grande, can be seen in the right
center of this woodcut from Emory's *Report*.

ing trails and water for his men and animals. As they progressed,
they found their route barred by deep arroyos that almost proved
insurmountable. They passed the Canyon of Sierra del Carmen,
probably what is called Boquillas Canyon today, another of those
"rocky dungeons" that imprisons the Rio Grande. Although the
traveling was rough, Chandler could still appreciate the virgin
beauty of the desert that he crossed. "No description can give an
idea of the grandeur of the scenery through these mountains,"
he reported. "There is no verdure to soften the bare and rugged
view; no overhanging trees or green bushes to vary the scene from
one of perfect desolation. Rocks are here piled one above another,
over which it was with the greatest labor that we would work
our way." [25]

The mules rapidly exhausted themselves on the long detours
necessary to move only a few miles downriver. Trying to find a
better route, Green crossed over to the Mexican side again, but
discovered that the "character of the country" there was just as de-
pressing. He located an arroyo which he hoped to be able to follow

92   **Capt. Arthur T. Lee was one of the few artists to paint the Rio Grande canyons during the 1850s. This view is probably near present-day Lajitas, the entrance to Santa Elena Canyon.**

to its source, where he then hoped he could find another farther east and follow it back to the river, thus avoiding the worst mountains along the banks of the river. But after marching miles from the river, he found no arroyo to lead him back. He sent out scouts with orders to find a way back to the river, but their search was in vain. Late on October 23 he saw a "fine new beaten trail" leading in exactly the opposite direction. Feeling anxious about Chandler and his party and knowing that they were without rations or bedding, Green ordered two men to follow the trail and if possible reach the river. They took bread and meat, in the event they found Chandler. The next day Green sent two more scouts out searching for Chandler, ordering them to stay close to the river. "Each hour my anxiety increased," he later reported, "for I saw most reasonable grounds to suppose that this party of gentlemen would be subjected to the awful pang of hunger and perhaps be so reduced in strength as when found to be unable to come into camp." [26]

Chandler surely was in trouble. Along with his boat he had lost all the extra clothing and provisions. His men had been reduced to existing on the barest rations and their "scanty wardrobes scarcely afforded enough covering for decency." "The sharp rocks of the mountains had cut the shoes from their feet, and blood, in many instances, marked their progress through the day's work." The same illusion that frustrates and defeats doomed men in the desert plagued Chandler's men. "Beyond the Sierra Carmel [*sic*], the river seemed to pass through an almost interminable succession of mountains," he said. "Cañon succeeded cañon; the valleys, which alone had afforded some slight chances for rest and refreshment had become so narrow and devoid of vegetation that it was quite a task to find grass sufficient for the mules." Finally, he crossed over to the Mexican side, hoping to find a passable route. Astonishingly, Chandler's party continued its survey work through all the rigorous march. With only this "slight interruption," he reported with much understatement, "the line of survey was carried on . . . ." [27]

Green, meanwhile, continued his march to the river, hoping to cross Chandler's path. About 11 p.m. on October 29 Chandler and his assistant, E. A. Phillips, found Green's trail and stumbled into his camp. They had marched in one day what had required two for the mules, reported Green. "Mr. Phillips and I walked . . . more than forty miles without water except once finding a little in a rock and for more than forty hours we were destitute for food," Chandler revealed. Two gentlemen had met in the desert. "After the usual salutation on such occasion," said Green, "I asked Mr. Chandler if he, from his knowledge of the position of his party, could think of anything I could do to relieve them." Chandler replied that there was nothing more to be done, that the men had been cared for as well as possible. The scientist in Chandler probably caused him to minimize the drama and danger of the situation, and this report is not so graphic as Green's because Chandler chose to omit "any but an incidental allusion to the difficulties of the survey." [28]

Maravillas Canyon

As the reunited party approached Maravillas Canyon, or Cupola Mountain in what is today the Black Gap Wildlife Management Area, they were in desperate condition, having lost boats, mules, and supplies. Again Schott's sketch gives some impression of the hopelessness that the explorers must have felt as they beheld the endless mountains before them. The river seemed to be so small as to be inconsequential, lost in the never-ending folds of earth that stretched as far as one could see. Temple and Reagan Canyons were monuments to the fact that the expedition would be unable to continue. The country was so rugged that Schott, unable to see all of it himself, had to depend upon the "primitive" sketches that Charles Abbott had made on his float trip through some of the canyons in order to map the region. Schott, in fact, left the party and returned to Fort Duncan by way of the San Pedro River and San Felipe Creek, rather than stay on the river. Green and Chandler sent out scouts to examine the routes back to the river. On November 3 Green informed Chandler that he felt they should discontinue the survey. The main problems were the character of the land they were approaching and the shortness of provisions. The following day Dr. C. C. Parry, a member of Chandler's party, referred to the "unexpected difficulty" of the country in also recommending that the survey cease. In addition to low rations and badly damaged boats, Parry mentioned the "destitute condition of the employees of the Commission . . . many of them are already nearly barefoot all poorly prepared for the prompt and efficient performance of their several duties over a country so rough and beset with thorns as this[.] I am therefore fully of your opinion that the work cannot be safely prosecuted further . . . ." Chandler himself admitted that some of his men had gone without food for 78 hours.[29]

Survey Suspended

With these reports in hand, Chandler then notified Emory that he had suspended the survey, having covered only 40 miles. "I have with great difficulty and exertion brought the line to the entrance of the cañon near this camp and after careful reconnoisances made both by myself and Lieutenant Green, I believe that the country in advance is impracticable to be surveyed with the means now at my disposal – my boats are unfit to transport the provisions necessary for the surveying party for more than one day . . . ." He would have had to depend upon the mule train for supplies, he said, and Green could find no accessible route to the river. After a brief conference, Green and Chandler started out for Fort Duncan via the safest route, through Santa Rosa, Coahuila, guided by a Mexican who knew the region. Not all the men stayed with the main party; some went by boat, preferring to risk "their lives in the remains of the best boat to walking with the train during the necessarily long marches that are before us, suffering as they are from want of shoes and other clothing," he wrote at the time. Chandler then, perhaps unwittingly, indicated the apprehension with which he undertook the march across northern Mexico: "I . . . expect (God willing) to report to you in person with my

Chandler and Green broke off surveying in Boquillas Canyon, almost out of supplies and with their boats wrecked, and headed across Mexico to Fort Duncan, near Eagle Pass, Texas.

notes in about eighteen days." [30] (Apparently the men in the boat arrived safely at Eagle Pass, presumably becoming the first men to float through the Hot Springs, Burro, and Upper and Lower Madison rapids of the lower canyons, because Chandler's letter reached Emory.)

Chandler and Green knew that the desperate party faced more than just desert country and a shortage of food. They also faced the very real threat of Indian attack. Writing from his camp on the San Felipe River, Schott, now surveying another part of the river, reported that about 25 armed and well-mounted Lipan Apache Indians had followed them for 3 days, and they were constantly afraid of being attacked. On his way to Chihuahua, meanwhile, Commissioner Bartlett, who had taken what he thought was a safer route, suffered the only full-scale attack in the area. One man was killed and several mules stolen. As they neared Santa Rosa, Chandler and Green were stopped by several Negroes, ex-slave members of the Seminole Chief Wild Cat's band who had fled to Mexico. Soon the party was confronted by Wild Cat himself, who threatened Green with a supposed 50 men concealed in the brush and who demanded to know why Americans had come into his country. After a short conference, in which Green claimed that he had three times as many men as Wild Cat, the chief withdrew and allowed the party to pass unharmed. The remainder of the march from Santa Rosa to Fort Duncan proved uneventful, and the party arrived on November 24. [31]

Michler Survey

The following spring Emory dispatched Lt. Nathaniel Michler to complete the survey from the point near Reagan Canyon to the mouth of the Pecos River, approximately the point at which Smith and Michler had stopped in 1850. Michler organized his party in San Antonio, including disassembled boats which he thought he might have to use, and rode west over the San Antonino-El Paso road. At Pecos Springs he turned south, hoping to strike the Rio Grande at the point where the survey was to begin. The road was rough, but Michler was equal to the task. The first 50 miles, from the Pecos to King's Springs, the course was nearly due west, enabling him to avoid the numberless "impassable arroyos" that cut abrupt swaths toward the river. His men scouted toward the Chisos Mountains, but found the country "cut up by immense chasms, closed in by steep cliffs, unseen until standing upon the very edge of their fearful depths." In the distance Michler saw the awesome Sierra del Carmen range, the primary obstacle that had blocked the progress of Chandler and Green's party. "The nearer we approached the river," he continued, "the more rough the country became; deep ravines and gullies constantly impeded the progress of the wagons, and the whole surface was covered with sharp angular stones and a growth of underbrush armed with thorns." [32]

About 10 miles from the river, the terrain became so difficult that the wagons had to be eased down the steep slopes by ropes. But Michler successfully located the initial point of the survey, the spot at which Chandler had suspended operations, and went to work. He found the same hostile conditions that had defeated Chandler, yet with fresh crewmen Michler pushed on. "It was impossible to approach the river from the first twenty miles of the survey," he reported, because it was "very tortuous." Michler thus bypassed Temple and Reagan Canyons, the names assigned to the canyons by Hill in 1899. Then he came to Irwin and Nichol Canyons, with their "banks . . . composed of high perpendicular masses of solid rock, resembling more the work of art than of nature." Rather than boat through the canyons, Michler first elected to work from horseback and wagons, but noted that they frequently had to make 25- or 30-mile detours to get around the arroyos that cut up the desert floor. South of present-day Dryden he located another fork of the Indian crossing and included a sketch of it with his report.

There the team was forced to use the boats. They unpacked them, only to find that the sun had warped the freshly cut, uncured lumber. After assembling the crooked planks and sending the wagons to Eagle Pass with the remainder of the party, Michler put the boats in the water. "Upon trial, we found the boats, which were our only resource, would float – the only thing that could be said in their favor," he dryly noted. With worried troops manning the oars, they set out in two skiffs and a flatboat. He probably was nearing Langtry Canyon.

He had entered the river at a "short break" in the canyon where the water rushed through "rocky banks" a dozen feet high. As the party drifted further into the canyon the wall grew higher, causing Michler to believe it "incredible that the bed of the stream could have been formed through ledges of solid rock." He described the narrow bed of the river that was "hemmed in by continuous and perfect walls of natural masonry" from 50 to 300 feet high. As the river narrowed, appearing "extremely contracted," the walls of the canyon appeared "stupendous" as they rose "perpendicularly" out of the water.

Immediately upon entering the most spectacular part of the canyon. Michler realized they were in danger. The boats were too small for the rough current and were viciously slammed against the walls. The first day out the crew floated through a canyon so narrow that the oarsmen could touch the walls with the tips of their oars. The river was only about 25 feet wide at that point. As they started through the pass they saw an "immense bowlder" dividing the main channel, leaving only a "narrow chute" for the boats. A rapids blocked the entire course of the river for several hundred feet, with the "whole mass of water" rushing through, "foaming and tumbling in a furious manner." Although the two skiffs made it safely through the narrow channel, the flatboat was not so lucky. "Totally unmanageable" said Michler, it ran "square against the rocky walls, splintering and tearing away her entire front." The crew was "knocked flat on their backs and the boat-hooks left firmly imbedded in the crevices of the rocks." As the boat started sinking, two Mexican crew members, both expert swimmers, jumped into the water, seized the lines, and pulled the boat to a sand bar, saving men and provisions. Michler and crew repaired the wreckage and continued their remarkable journey the following day.

As they passed canyon after canyon, they found the current so swift and the falls and bends so frequent that it was impossible to stop and take readings for the survey. Artist Schott sketched one of the canyons below Boquillas, perhaps Reagan or Nichol Canyon. The mountains there are not so imposing, but they still torture the river and imprison anyone who dares enter. "The only practicable way of making the survey through the cañon," reported Michler, "was by allowing the boats to drop down the channel, taking the direction of the courses and timing the passage from bend to bend; when opportunity offered, the speed of each boat was ascertained by distance accurately measured on land. . . ." The survey had covered approximately 125 miles when the team arrived at the mouth of the Pecos, which Michler described as being "a rolling mass of red mud, the water tasting like a mixture of every saline ingredient. . . ." (The water of the Rio Grande is also extremely high in mercury content because of the quicksilver deposits in the Big Bend.) They continued downriver to Fort Duncan, where they met the other members of the party. Michler and party had floated down one of the wildest rivers on the continent.

When Michler covered the distance from the Maravillas Canyon area to the mouth of the Pecos, the entire length of the Rio Grande that comprised the international boundary had been carefully surveyed by the Topographical Engineers. Smith and Michler reported on the portion from Ringgold Barracks to several miles past the mouth of the Pecos; Michler from the Pecos to below Boquillas Canyon; Chandler from Boquillas to Presidio del Norte; and Smith from Presidio del Norte to El Paso. Other excursions, such as that of Captain Love, had also covered parts of the river.

Even before all the reports were in, Colonel Abert knew that it was not likely that steamboats could navigate past the point they already served. He did ask M. L. Smith whether he had accurately calculated his estimate for improving the river as far as the Isletas, but finally concluded that there were too many disadvantages. The river itself, first of all, was simply too shallow and contained too many obstacles for a steamboat of any size. Improvements would have been costly if, indeed, they had been feasible. Then, should Abert have decided to improve the river, the question would have had to come before an international arbitration board with Mexico, for Article VII of the Treaty of Guadalupe Hidalgo stipulated that neither country should "construct work . . . not even for the purpose of favouring new methods of navigation" without the consent of the other Nation. Congressman D. L. Seymour of New York, a member of the House Committee on Commerce, asked the Corps of Engineers about possible improvements, but his efforts got no further than committee discussions. The hope that the Rio Grande might ultimately be found navigable died slowly, for it would have made travel through one of the most remote sections of the country less expensive and less dangerous.[33]

The chief means of transportation for years to come obviously would be the wagon road built by the Topographical Engineers. It had taken several explorations of optional routes and hard work once the path had been selected, but the engineers were confident that they had chosen the road that best took advantage of the existing waterholes and grasslands.

The first step to replace the old wagon road west were taken

100

when Andrew P. Gray surveyed West Texas for the Texas Western Railroad Company in 1854. A former member of the Topographical Engineers, Gray organized his party of 19 men in San Antonio and on January 1, 1854, set out for Fort Chadbourne. The trip across the Llano Estacado (the Staked Plains) and the northern part of the Trans-Pecos was accomplished with relative ease. The proposed railroad route, of course, did not enter the Big Bend region of the Trans-Pecos because it was too rugged.[34]

Fort Davis

To protect this western road the army established Fort Davis in 1854. Several sites were considered. All the engineers and surveyors who had trekked through the Big Bend had offered recommendations as to where the fort should be constructed. Green had opted for either of two points near the Comanche Trail: near present-day Lajitas or between Santa Elena and Mariscal Canyons. Bvt. Maj. Gen. George M. Brooke agreed with him. "There should be strong Garrisons in the Great Bend opposite San Carlos, which is the key to the country called on Disturnell's map 'Bolson de Mapimi.' Indians passing at this place go to Chihuahua, Monclova, Parras and Durango – laying the whole country to waste," concluded the general. Brooke also believed a post should be located

Arthur T. Lee's watercolors are probably the best record of Fort Davis's early years.

opposite Presidio del Norte. Another site under consideration, and the eventual location of the fort, was Painted Comanche Camp. The actual location of the fort was determined by Bvt. Maj. Gen. Persifor F. Smith, who visited the Trans-Pecos himself in September and October of 1854 to investigate the potential sites. Painted Comanche Camp offered more wood, water, and grass. It was strategically located, commanding the western road, yet was within

The Topographical Engineers

Not all the West Texas Indians were hostile. These Indians probably traded with the soldiers at Fort Davis, where Capt. Arthur T. Lee made this painting.

striking distance of the Comanche Trail. The post was named for Secretary of War Jefferson Davis.[35] Now preserved and partially reconstructed, the fort is a National Historic Site.

One of the officers stationed there in 1855 was Zenas R. Bliss, a youthful graduate of the U.S. Military Academy who had already tasted frontier service at Fort Duncan. After making the 17-day stage trip from San Antonio to Fort Davis, Bliss realized that Indians seemed to attack about half the stages. One of Bliss' friends was a good-humored captain named Arthur T. Lee, an artist with a good eye and considerable talent. Lee left a remarkable record of the fort during the mid-1850s, including several of the Indians who frequented it. After living at the post for several months, both Bliss and Lee realized that they were in danger of being attacked by Indians if they ventured so much as a couple of miles from the post. The army clearly had a difficult task ahead.[36]

The Camel Experiment

Because of its harsh terrain and climate, the Big Bend was the scene of an unusual experiment in desert transportation in 1859 and 1860. Secretary of War Jefferson Davis authorized the importation of camels for use on the western frontier in 1855. This was not the first time the army had contemplated using camels in the West. Twenty years before, Maj. George H. Crosman, who was then serving in Florida, had recommended their use. Maj. Henry C. Wayne took up Crosman's idea in 1848 and recommended that the War Department bring camels in from the Middle East. Wayne also contacted then-Senator Jefferson Davis of Mississippi, who became interested in the idea. In 1854, while serving as Secretary of War, Davis teamed up with Senator James Shields of Illinois to persuade Congress to vote money for the project. A bill providing $30,000 for the importation of camels passed Congress in 1855. The first load of 34 camels landed at Indianola on May 14, 1856. The second shipment of 44 arrived on February 10, 1857.

Major Wayne took the camels to San Antonio, where he set up camp at Val Verde, or Camp Verde, as it became known, a few miles outside the city. The first experiments with the camels were immediate successes. Many San Antonio citizens, thoroughly familiar with oxen and mules on the Chihuahua Trail, doubted the merit of camels in West Texas. Seeking to quiet their skepticism, Wayne gave a demonstration for an impromptu crowd gathered around the plaza. He ordered a camel to kneel, then had two bales of hay tied onto him. Realizing that each bale weighed over 300 pounds, the crowd feared the camel could not get up. Then, emphasizing his point, Wayne tied two more bales on the animal, a total of more than 1,200 pounds. The camel rose without difficulty and walked off, carrying the load. The Texans were so convinced that one of the "poets of Texas" composed some lines to commemorate the occasion, said Wayne.[37]

When President James Buchanan took office in 1857, John B. Floyd replaced Davis as Secretary of War, but the experiments with camels went on. Floyd ordered the wagon road from Fort Defiance, New Mexico, to the Colorado River surveyed with camels. Lt. Edward F. Beale, a veteran of the Mexican War and Superintendent of Indian Affairs in California and Nevada, was chosen to head the Camel Corps. He reached Fort Davis in the summer of 1857 and soon left with his camels for the assignment in the West.[38]

Camels in the Big Bend

Using camels Beale left behind, 2d Lt. William H. Echols of the Topographical Engineers and Lt. Edward L. Hartz conducted experiments in the Big Bend in 1859. In that year Maj. Gen. David M. Twiggs, commander of the Department of Texas, wanted a thorough reconnaissance of the country to locate supply routes for the far-flung posts in the Trans-Pecos. Twenty-four camels, loaded with between 300 and 500 pounds of equipment and supplies, were marched westward to the Pecos, then on to Fort Davis.[39]

Lieutenant Echols departed for the Big Bend on July 11. He varied the burdens of the animals, but they each carried an average of 400 pounds. The march continued uneventfully until they reached Nine Point Draw, or Dog Canyon. While trying to weave their way through the intricate passages, several camels fell down with their loads, and had it not been for the Indian trails Echols could hardly have gotten his party through the canyon. "A rougher, more rocky, more mountainous, and rugged country, can scarcely be imagined," wrote Hartz. After leaving the canyon, the soldiers probably followed Dog Canyon out onto the prairie, which was covered with luscious grass only recently watered by one of the cloudbursts typical of the Big Bend. Echols found water in several places, but correctly guessed that it was not permanent. He let the camels drink their fill, expressing surprise when their capacity proved to be nearer 15 or 20 gallons than the 20 or 30 pints the Secretary of War had led him to expect.

On July 16 Echols found the Comanche Trail and camped near a small spring, perhaps near present-day McKinney Springs. The Rio Grande was still 27 miles away, over a "most laborious and exhausting march." Echols bypassed Roy's Peak, Rice's Canyon, and the watershed of Tornillo Creek on the way to the river. He also discovered one of the characteristics of the Big Bend country: the infrequent but torrential rains which cause flash floods and erode the chalky, dry soil. "Our trail crossed, in the course of the day, no less than fifty-seven arroyos, some of them from fifty to seventy feet in depth, with plane banks inclining frequently as much as forty-five degrees," Hartz reported. At the Rio Grande, the soldiers had to abandon a horse and a mule that had become exhausted by the heat and distance.

On July 18 the train moved down the river, finding grass and water opposite the old Presidio San Vicente. As they headed farther downriver, however, the terrain grew rougher. On the 19th Echols decided that they had accomplished their mission and could return. The same hostile ground that had forced Chandler and Green to discontinue their survey now caused Echols to turn northward. Marching between the Comanche Trail and Tornillo Creek, Hartz described their relief at finding more grass and water, thus ending the mystery of how the Indians could so easily penetrate the *despoblado* while the Spaniards entered only cautiously. The Indians knew the country and the favors it offered. But even the Indians, used to seeing the pack trains of the army or Chihuahua traders silhouetted against the horizon, probably were now surprised by the awkward forms of the camels, seemingly "perched in mid-air" as they traversed the foothills of the Sierra del Carmen.

The party camped near Roy's Peak after a march of 21 miles. Another horse had to be abandoned since there was no water at the camp. The next day Echols found the trail he had followed en route to the Rio Grande. Hoping to return by another route, he headed eastward away from his trail, probably marching southeast of Dagger Mountain. This detour presented new problems. First, they encountered a dense growth of soapweed, whose slender, short blades tipped with tough thorns about an inch long could lame the camels. But the camels knew how to walk through them, putting their feet alongside the plant, then crushing them over to avoid the thorns. The growth was so dense, however, that progress was slow. Second, the terrain grew rougher as the party attempted to descend the cliffs of a small canyon. Several of the camels fell, narrowly escaping injury. After clearing the canyon, Echols turned northward, located his trail again, and followed it back to Camp Stockton.

After the force reached Camp Stockton, Hartz attempted to summarize the camels' performance. They had climbed hills and mountains of the "most difficult nature," crossed streams and prairies made almost impassable by deep arroyos, ravines, and maguey, gone nearly 5 days without water, and eaten much less

An unknown artist, probably a soldier, painted
this small watercolor of camels crossing a West
Texas stream on the way to Big Bend.

food than a horse or a mule. Covering between 20 and 34 miles
a day, they had marched through the "most difficult country in
northwestern Texas," reported Hartz, who had his directions
slightly askew. Nor did they appear to suffer physically. What
Hartz said about the camels also reveals the true nature of the Big
Bend. The army had sought a rough country in which to try the
camels, and they had found it in the Big Bend.

Echols had another opportunity to take the camels to the Big
Bend the following year. General Twiggs still hoped to build another fort in the region, and he also wanted a good road constructed between that post and Fort Davis. Leaving Fort Davis on
July 14, Echols marched down the Fort Davis-Presidio del Norte
road, searching for a favorable site near the San Carlos Crossing,
because it would have easy access to the road. He found the road
"magnificent," but might have guessed that the expedition would
have trouble when one of his men tested the water at nearby San
Esteban and found it undrinkable. The men were also hampered

by the "old song of 'the falling of packs,' " because the camel drivers had not yet learned how to secure the loads.[40]

As he pushed farther into the desert, Echols, by now a veteran Big Bend explorer, wryly observed that, "I cheerfully concur with all who regard this region as impassable." He found no suitable site for a fort at the San Carlos Crossing. He headed downriver, circling around the Mesa de Anguila, toward Comanche Crossing, which Green and Johnston regarded as the best possible location for a fort. Marching down the Lates Laguna, probably Terlingua Creek, he beheld a "wonderful curiosity," a "place where the stream runs through a mountain precipice, about 1,500 feet high." The guide had directed the party to Santa Elena Canyon, one of the first tourist attractions in the Big Bend, which Echols called "The Grand Puerta." A few miles farther downriver Echols located the crossing, which he, too, agreed was a good site for a fort.

On July 27 Echols headed back to Fort Davis by a different route. After striking Terlingua Creek, he turned due north, probably marching into the Terlingua area. He believed that a road could be built through that area easily enough until he encountered a mountain, perhaps Wildhorse Mountain. After climbing the

Camels made several trips across the Southwest, but the experiment was discontinued when the Civil War began.

mountain to survey the area, he concluded that much work would have to be done to make the road usable. As he started down the mountain, he saw a pool of water some 1,000 feet below. Because they could not reach it, he named it "Inaccessible Tank." The next morning Echols rode into the canyon, hoping to find a way through. He found that the canyon got deeper, but was able to lead his party safely through. As the terrain worsened, Echols realized that he would not be able to locate the road and headed back to the trail. He had found a fairly good road – but there was an obstacle, "the precipitous side of a mountain, rugged, rocky, and several hundred feet high" that could not be overcome. Because of injury to the camels and mules, the party could go no further. They had to discontinue the reconnaissance without finding a satisfactory route. After 3 days without water, they finally found some on August 1. Echols passed by what was rapidly becoming a well-known landmark to the Topographical Engineers – Camel's Hump, a small mountain in the prairie between Adobe Walls Mountain and Red Bluff. Today a curiosity, it is marveled at by travelers who have little idea that camels once roamed the Big Bend.

A combination of circumstances insured that camels would not be used on a large scale in West Texas. There was, of course, the cultural bias toward the "Missouri mule" that the camel could not overcome. But the Civil War ended the experimentation before pragmatic teamsters and surveyors could render their decision. When the Union army vacated Fort Davis, several camels were simply turned loose. Some of them ventured into Mexico, where they turned up in circuses years after the trial in the desert had been forgotten. A few fell into the hands of promoters, who tried unsuccessfully to wring a living from them. The experiment was not resumed after the Civil War, because the railroad became the dominant mode of overland transportation for the country.

Further exploration in the Big Bend, as well as the construction of the fort that General Twiggs had wanted, was also cut short by the Civil War. The Engineers had, however, made several important contributions in the Trans-Pecos. First, they had opened the country to travel both by the military and by merchants and travelers. Second, they had charted routes across West Texas that rendered defense of the region easier. Indian strongholds were penetrated; pursuit was surer. Third, the line of communication that Colonel Abert had wanted was established, although it would not prevent the disruption of the Union. Finally, the Engineers gave many enduring place names to the Big Bend, such as Emory Peak and Camel's Hump.

5/Settling the Big Bend

From the settled portions of Texas, the trails pointed westward toward the Big Bend country, and during the last half of the 19th century emigrants slowly made their way through the Trans-Pecos to California or some other El Dorado. Many travelers elected to settle in Fort Davis, Marfa, or Alpine, or on isolated ranches farther south after seeing the Big Bend only one time. Word of mouth advertising brought others to live there, to improve their health, to start over, or just to settle in a "new" country. It is a "fantastic country, like no other I've ever seen," said one traveler after his first glimpse of the Big Bend. Another was impressed with the "cool, bracing and invigorating" air after spending his first few nights in Marfa. But newcomers, more accustomed to the "human proportions" of the eastern or midwestern landscapes, were more taken with physical features of the land. "I was raised in a country where trees of a fair size were not uncommon, and where the prevailing and general hue was green or yellow in spring, summer and fall, and white in winter," recalled Judge O. W. Williams of Fort Stockton. "The everlasting neuter grays and browns of this arid country, not relieved by any trees, have for many years been monotonous to me. Yet, this dry, drab country charms one in its own way," he admitted. "The air is generally clear, the sunsets gorgeous, and the general scope of view large." [1]

The Chihuahua Trail

Many emigrants saw the Big Bend for the first time as they traveled along the Chihuahua Trail. Moving over paths blazed by Hays, Ford, and Johnston, the traders increased as the exchange grew more profitable after the Civil War. "The commerce is entirely inland and mostly in the hands of foreigners," reported Charles Moye, from his vantage point as U.S. Consul in Chihuahua, "particularly the wholesale establishments." Several families earned a livelihood from it, although few became wealthy. In San Antonio John Monier, a Frenchman, was the first merchant to send mule trains to Mexico via the Big Bend, followed quickly by John Gargin and August Santleben. Mexican companies like Rocke Garady and David and Daniel Sada of Monterrey, Nuevo León, and the González brothers of Saltillo, Coahuila, offered

The ruins of Mariscal Mine, near Terlingua.

goods for sale in Chihuahua. The goods moved in wagons drawn by mules or oxen across the "great deserts" between Chihuahua and the dispersal points – San Antonio and Independence, Mo. The trade across Texas had an advantage, because transportation cost only 10 cents silver per pound, reported Moye, while the cost on the Missouri route was 12 cents per pound.[2]

Fairly well-defined by the 1870's, the Chihuahua Trail began on the Gulf Coast in Powderhorn Bayou. Indianola was the principal port. The ponderous wagons reminded Thomas Ruckman, a resident of Helena, Texas, of a "great cloud of smoke" when he saw them "winding and worming" their way through the town northwestward. They passed along the Guadalupe River, through Victoria and Goliad. After Helena, the wagons jolted to a ford on Cibolo Creek, then to the San Antonio River, which they followed into the Alamo City. There the poet Sidney Lanier saw the "long train of enormous, blue-bodied covered wagons," which "lumbered" through the city, spending as little time as possible in San Antonio before setting out on the long road to Chihuahua.[3]

From San Antonio the route ran due west through Castroville and Uvalde to Fort Clark, 150 miles to the west, the real "jumping off place." Thirty-five miles farther west the trail hit the Rio Grande, turned northward and paralleled Devil's River almost to its source. There the wagons cut westward again, to Fort Lancaster. As they entered the Big Bend they gradually turned southwestward to Fort Stockton and Fort Davis and picked up the route to Presidio that John D. Burgess had charted when he supplied beef to the soldiers at Fort Davis. Passing by the present location of Marfa, the merchants could see Cathedral Rock looming several hundred feet in the air to the southeast. The Chinati Mountains and Elephant Rock broke the monotony of the desert en route to the small border village of Presidio. Many travelers purchased supplies from Ben Leaton, whose fortified adobe structure still overlooks fertile fields of cotton and corn along the Rio Grande.[4]

Forty miles south of the border the wagons entered the worst part of the Chihuahuan Desert. Terrain that had successfully defied the Spaniards and early Anglo-Americans only gradually yielded to the commercial thrusts of entrepreneurs. There were no wells between Rancho de la Mula and Chupadero, and it was 150 miles to

August Santleben's stageline, shown here in
1866 in San Antonio, made one trip a month
to either Monterrey or Chihuahua.

Julimes, the site of the old Spanish presidio on the Río Conchos.
The worst was over at Julimes. They then swung westward to
Bachimba, then northwestward to Chihuahua. The arduous trip
paid off handsomely for wary merchants who negotiated successfully with their Mexican counterparts.[5]

The Chihuahua trade with San Antonio and other Texas cities was well established by 1851 and continued, except during the
Civil War, until the Southern Pacific and the Texas & Pacific railroads completed their tracks across West Texas in 1882. The Chihuahua Trail was significant for several reasons. First, it diverted
some of the lucrative trade from Santa Fe and El Paso to San Antonio, giving merchants along the route a saving in transportation
costs and helping San Antonio become the chief distribution center
for goods throughout the Southwest. Second, it helped open the
Big Bend and led many persons to settle permanently in the region. The trail provided a livelihood for persons in the Big Bend
who would have had difficulty living there without the trade.[6]

The economic assets of the Big Bend – virgin grasslands,
minerals, fertile river valleys – remained untapped. Only after the
Topographical Engineers had opened the country to exploration
were they generally rumored, but for all practical purposes these
resources remained inaccessible until the U.S. Army tamed the
Indians and the railroad made transportation easier. Texans thus
longed for completion of the railroad across the Trans-Pecos.
They had been encouraged by Andrew Gray's Texas Western Railroad survey in 1854 and by the predictions of those who visited
the proposed route. One traveler who crossed the prairies in 1868
noted that it would not be difficult to find a route. A few years later
the editor of the *Austin Statesman* pointed out that the railroad

113

would soon open the State's last unknown region. He correctly forecast that it would stimulate ranching and mining and concluded that the Big Bend would then be one of the best sections of the State to settle in. He envisioned a "plain covered with farms and villages and cities" throughout West Texas, a land that at one time had been the home of the wild Comanches and Apaches.[7]

Conquest of the Indians

The Big Bend was still the home of Indians in 1867. Even Fort Davis had been left to the mercy of the Mescaleros. After the army withdrew from the fort in 1861, the Confederates lacked adequate forces to maintain it. When Union troops arrived from California a year later, they found it deserted, some of the buildings burned, others wrecked. Relations with the Trans-Pecos Indians were so bad in 1867 that Gov. J. W. Throckmorton of Texas asked the army to escort a trial judge to El Paso. "Unless the military authorities can furnish him an escort it will be impossible for him to make the journey in time," Throckmorton pointed out. Three children and one woman were reported captured by the Indians in January and February 1871.

It was not until 2 years after the Civil War that Federal troops reoccupied Fort Davis. After Capt. Edward S. Meyer reopened the old military road, the new commander, Lt. Col. Wesley Merritt, tackled his threefold job of reconstructing the fort, reclaiming most of the Big Bend from the Indians, and controlling his newly-assigned Negro troops.[8]

Merritt built the quarters from stone, as originally planned. Defeating the Indians proved more difficult. Although the all-Negro regiments of the 9th and 10th Cavalry and the 24th and 25th Infantry quickly proved their worth against the Apaches, solving his third problem, they often could not find the quarry. The area the "buffalo soldiers" had to patrol made their job difficult. "These posts are so distant from each other that marauding parties of Indians can easily pass between them without being discovered," claimed Maj. Gen. David M. Twiggs in 1857, "and, if discovered, it is very difficult to overtake them; indeed, there is not one case in fifty where a command can come up with them." A year later General Twiggs again called attention to the problem of space. "Fort

Davis is one hundred and eighty miles from Fort Lancaster . . . it is between these points [that] most of the depredations on this road are committed."

Knowledge of the land gave the Indians an advantage in the Big Bend. After robbing several sheep camps and killing two herders, a party of Comanches, including a captured white man named Clinton L. Smith, "pulled for the breaks of the Rio Grande, somewhere in the Big Bend country. . . . We sure had to ride to out-run our pursuers," Smith recalled, but they were safe after they reached the river.

The military pressure initially proved effective. In September 1871 the principal bands of the Mescalero Apaches came to Fort Stanton, New Mex., and agreed to a peace that lasted only 4 years. By 1876 depredations were increasing and civilian authorities again demanded action. While Apaches elsewhere in the Southwest had settled on their reservations, Chief Gomez kept his warriors in the Big Bend busy.[9]

The Indians did not attack wagon trains and ranches simply because they were warlike. They were desperate for food. With both white men and Indians hunting wild game, the supply thinned, leaving redmen without any adequate source of food. In the past they had been able to raid into Mexico almost at will, but the United States had agreed in the Treaty of Guadalupe Hidalgo to stop the international raids, denying them another source of supplies. Most of the Mescaleros were unsatisfied with the reservations on which they were placed. After studying the Indian situation in 1854, Capt. Randolph B. Marcy and Agent Neighbors concluded that "the Mescalero . . .will not willingly remove from their old planting grounds between the 'Presidio del Norte' and the 'Horsehead Crossing' of the Pecos where they have planted corn for several years." Marcy and Neighbors recommended that they be given the lands which they already lived on in the interest of a "speedy, peaceable, and permanent settlement." But the Apaches were not given lands in Texas because the State kept all its public lands when it joined the Union. Texas Indian policy was later characterized by the great photographer of Indians, Edward S. Curtis, as " 'Go elsewhere or be exterminated.' " Indians were a Federal problem as far as the State's officials were concerned, and they would have to be given Federal land. Many Indians were, therefore, placed on land in New Mexico that they considered inferior to what they had surrendered.[10]

Upset at this disregard for their rights, the Apaches grew discontented. The small groups scattered across the Big Bend raided

Men and officers of Troop D, 3d Cavalry, at Fort Davis about 1880.

Victorio led the last resistance of the Apaches to the U.S. Cavalry in the Big Bend.

isolated areas. In August 1878, Victorio, a chief who had ridden with the great Mangas Coloradas, led 80 of his people from their New Mexico reservation into the Sacramento Mountains and became a rallying symbol for all the discontented Indians in West Texas. Most white men thought that the Indian menace would eventually pass away, as surely as the whites would one day own all the land. But before this could occur, Texans had to deal with the reality of hostile Indians.[11]

While increasing numbers of travelers were becoming impressed with the beauty and uniqueness of the country, the Indian threat grew more serious. A correspondent for the *San Antonio Daily Express* wondered at the "scene of legends both of war and of love" that must have taken place within the "frowning heights and narrow passes . . . sylvan retreats and ferny grottos" of Wild Rose Pass, but facts jolted him back to the reality of 1877. "However this may be, there is nothing romantic in the unpleasant fact that the red man still lingers here, and avails himself of every chance to steal and murder. The canyon has always been dangerous ground, and up to this time the Apaches commit frequent depredations in the vicinity." Scattered raids were reported throughout the Big Bend by Victorio's warriors filtering southward from the San Carlos reservation. "The country is inhabited, and furnishes a favorite haunt for thieving and marauding bands of Indians." Another reporter noted that a party of 15 Indians had stolen more than 200 horses and mules from an area ranch in January 1879. "The country from . . . [Del Rio] to El Paso has not been a safe one by any means," another traveler concluded. The editors of the *Daily Express* feared their city might lose some of the Chihuahua trade because of the depredations. "What is the remedy?" pleaded the writer. "The present system of military protection is totally inefficient. With the utmost zeal on the part of the officers and men, who are stationed at such great distances apart, it is frequently impossible to catch the Indians, who plan their devilment with great cunning and elude pursuits by means of their superior knowledge of the country." There is good evidence, too, that many soldiers feared Victorio and did not want to catch him. Capt. George A. Purrington encountered Victorio on the Rio Grande in 1880, but left his commander powerless to "explain satisfactorily why he did not follow and attack." [12]

By June 1879, Victorio had proved to be an able, aggressive match for the cavalry. After leaving the reservation, he had headed for the Big Bend, where he was joined by Chief Caballero and another party of Mescaleros. Some have speculated that Caballero had volunteered to go out and try to convince Victorio to surrender. If this is true, he failed, for his warriors joined the rebel chief. Raiding on both sides of the Rio Grande, Victorio attracted the attention of the warriors who had remained on the reservation, and many slipped off to join him. From 80, his band soon had increased to between 200 and 300.[13]

Victorio would not be easily defeated. In contrast to past failures at cooperation, the United States and Mexico agreed to band together. Col. Joaquín Terrazas of Chihuahua coordinated his forces with those of the United States, permitting American forces to cross into his State in pursuit of the Apaches. The Americans, meanwhile, adopted a different approach. After years of futile effort, Brig. Gen. Edward O. C. Ord created the District of Pecos and appointed Col. Benjamin H. Grierson to pacify the Indians. Grierson established subposts to watch the principal waterholes and trails. His soldiers patrolled the entire Big Bend, gathering much information that aided them in their pursuit. Grierson himself toured the country and sent detailed reports to headquarters.[14]

Hearing that Victorio had emerged from the mountains of northern Mexico, Grierson took to the field with a small escort. He learned that the chief was headed in his direction. Grierson, another officer, six men, and Grierson's teenage son, Robert, fortified the Tinaja de las Palmas, near Quitman on the Rio Grande. Hearing that the Apaches were camped only 10 miles away, Grierson sent for reinforcements and got 14 additional men. The Apaches rode into the ambush on the morning of July 30, 1880. Trapped, they turned to flee, but were cut off by Lt. Leighton Finley and 10 cavalrymen. When Capt. Nicholas Nolan arrived from Quitman with reinforcements, Victorio retreated and scattered his warriors in Mexico.

Grierson knew that Victorio was not defeated. In early August the chief crossed into Texas en route to New Mexico and again encountered one of Grierson's patrols. Believing that the chief would have to visit Rattlesnake Springs, Grierson fortified that waterhole and waited. The Apaches attacked the troopers there, but found them too well dug in. Hoping to distract the soldiers, Victorio then turned on a passing supply train, but Grierson's men

Col. Benjamin H. Grierson chased
Victorio into Mexico.

Col. William H. Shafter followed Grierson as
commander and continued the Army's
"pacification" program.

attacked his rear as he closed in on the wagons. Victorio was again
forced to retreat into Mexico. Grierson had not captured the chief,
but he had prevented him from returning to the New Mexico reservation, which probably would have been a source for new
warriors.[15]

Peace finally came to West Texas when Victorio was killed in
a skirmish with Mexican troopers at Tres Castillos in northern
Chihuahua. Colonel Terrazas with a force of volunteers and Tara-
humari Indian scouts engaged the Apaches in October 1880.
When the battle was over, Terrazas, who had never seen the chief,
learned from two Mexican captives that Victorio was among the
dead. By the time Col. William Shafter arrived at Fort Davis for
his second tour of duty in March 1881, the Indians had been quieted. There were still occasional raiding parties of desperate Indians that swooped down from their hideouts in the mountains, stealing a few cattle or horses, but none of Victorio's band remained.
"There were some roving bands of the different tribes that found a
refuge in the mountain fastness of the Rio Grande where game and
fish were abundant and where a vast country two or three hundred
miles in length on either side of the river was totally uninhabited,"
wrote Capt. W. J. Maltby of the Texas Rangers, but as settlement

119

increased and game decreased, even they joined their countrymen on the reservation. Colonel Shafter had little problem driving the tired and hungry natives out of the Big Bend and forcing them onto reservations.[16]

Coming of the Railroad

The following year two railroads linked the Big Bend region with the rest of Texas. The task was difficult, for bridges had to be built over almost 200 rivers and arroyos, and water tanks had to be placed at 20-mile intervals. Over 300 construction workers and 100 trackmen were employed on the job by the Texas & Pacific Railroad by the fall of 1881. Seventeen cars of iron and 40 cars of ties were used each day. Crews strung telegraph wires along the track as it was completed, and a contractor followed the company with more than 180 beeves for food. When H. N. Dimick, from Uvalde, visited one of the construction camps in April 1882, he reported that the company had 3,000 Chinese at work on the tracks. They lived in a "town of tents covering an area as large as the town of Uvalde," he reported. Marveling at the cluster, he noted that a "regular store" on one of the railroad cars provided the workers with anything they wanted. A combination of the Southern Pacific and the Galveston, Harrisburg and San Antonio, a part of the Texas and Pacific, extended service to what became Alpine in 1882, with the Southern Pacific building from the west and the GH & SA working from the east. They drove the last stake just west of the Pecos River on January 12, 1882. "The huge Chihuahua wagon will be a thing of the past, traditional and somewhat doubtful," exulted the Fort Davis correspondent for the *San Antonio Daily Express,* but the future was less certain. "We are no longer the frontier, for we will have fallen into the embrace of the iron monster and will possibly perish beneath its wheels." [17]

The twin obstacles of Indians and poor transportation had now been removed. For the first time many prospective settlers realized that the Big Bend was more than inhospitable desert. Soon ranchers and miners, health seekers and opportunists, began combing the Big Bend in search of unclaimed grassland or undiscovered minerals. Enough were successful to encourage others to try.[18]

Ranching in the Big Bend

The ranchers were the first to come. The foundation for the cattle industry was laid early. Formal ranching did not begin until after the Mexican War, but cattle had roamed the Big Bend for centuries. The frequent Spanish expeditions to New Mexico brought cattle with them to supply food and milk for the travelers. The Indians brought back cattle after their raids in northern Mexico. One of the main cattle raising areas of Spanish Texas was the Rio Grande Valley, where cattle roamed free as far upriver as the Nueces.[19] Some probably wandered even farther, perhaps reaching the Big Bend. Herds also were brought to the Spanish presidios of San Vicente and San Carlos. Stray cattle undoubtedly became the nucleus of the wild bands that roamed the country. Thus cattle were in the Big Bend long before men moved in to organize one of the best ranching areas in the State.

There were several reasons why the industry itself did not develop more rapidly. Although the Spaniards ranched in both New Mexico and Texas, rugged country and the hostile Indians excluded them from the Big Bend. There were other difficulties. The Big Bend was a disputed land until the United States defeated Mexico in 1848. In addition, it was too far from centers of commerce to make ranching profitable. Most settlers came only after the railroad arrived in 1882.[20]

The Big Bend was ideally suited for ranching. This "natural cow country" is rich in grama grasses, shrubs, trees, and edible cacti for hungry cattle. The soil is good; the rainfall limited but timely. Water is scarce, but plentiful enough in the springs and creeks for ranching. James B. Gillett, a former Texas Ranger who became foreman of the G4 Ranch, found Terlingua Creek to be a "bold running stream, studded with cottonwood timber and . . . alive with beaver," even as late as 1885. Much of the land in the Big Bend is above 3,000 feet in elevation and is thus free from the 100 degrees plus temperatures of the desert in summer. The winters are rarely harsh.[21]

The First Ranchers

The first ranchers to settle in the Big Bend were fiercely self-reliant. Ben Leaton, John Spencer, and John Burgess felt that ranching would be profitable, but marauding Indians did not allow them to realize a profit. Cattle were brought into the area after Fort Davis was established in 1854. Spencer, probably the first important rancher in the area, and a handful of competitors were lured into supplying beef to the fort garrison. He had tried to raise horses on his ranch near Presidio, but there was no nearby market, and the Indians preyed on them. Knowing that the redmen wanted horses more than cattle, and that the soldiers needed the beef, he decided to change to cattle ranching in the mid-1850s. He negotiated a contract with Col. Washington Seawell, commander at the fort, and bought a herd of Mexican cattle to move to his ranch.[22]

The first large-scale cattleman in the Big Bend was Milton Faver, a former freighter on the Santa Fe Trail. Little is known about Faver, and much of that seems contradictory. An Englishman, or perhaps a Frenchman, he reportedly spoke Spanish, French, and German besides English. He was frequently referred to as baronial in appearance, and liked tailor-made suits, rare meat, good wine, and peach brandy. Faver told Zenas Bliss, who was stationed at Fort Davis, that he was a Virginian who had come west because of consumption. Others said that he left Missouri because he thought a man he had shot had died. He described to Bliss his trip across the plains to Santa Fe, his wanderings in Mexico, his eventual settling in the Big Bend. Although Faver lost much of his land late in life, he never seemed to lose his discipline and confidence.

In 1857 he operated a general merchandising store in Presidio, but soon turned to the livestock business. After he took up ranching, it was evident he had a talent for it. Moving away from the security of Fort Davis in 1856, he located his fortress-like headquarters on Cibolo Creek near the Chinati Mountains, 30 miles north of Presidio. To combat the hostility of the Indians and

Milton Faver was one of the first ranchers in the Big Bend.

of nature, Faver built his residence with thick adobe walls and heavy gates. Gunports were spaced evenly across the walls, and a small cannon, obtained from Fort Davis, guarded the area. The house is still occupied today, making it one of the oldest ranches in the Big Bend. Faver soon established several more ranches, including one stocked with sheep. He traded with the Indians, endured several of their attempts to wipe him out,* and prospered. Faver's herd eventually grew from the original 300 head to an estimated 10,000 to 20,000. When Bliss visited him in the 1880s, he was a wealthy man.[23]

Other Ranchers

While Spencer and Faver built the large herds, smaller ranchers located near Fort Davis to supply the needs of the soldiers. When Bliss arrived at the fort in 1855, Daniel Murphy, whose herd was located near the post, was the beef contractor. He later established a ranch in Toyah Valley in the Davis Mountains. Five miles down Limpia Canyon, Diedrick Dutchover raised sheep unsuccessfully because the Indians raided so often he could not make money. Bliss warned that no one was safe more than 2 miles from the post. In April 1877, two of Murphy's men were killed within a few hundred yards of another ranch as they gathered wood. Dutchover finally sold the remainder of his flock to the soldiers. E. P. Webster lived at the fort, preferring to take no unnecessary risks. He ran his cattle on the nearby range under army protection. Another early rancher who sought army contracts was Manuel Músquiz, a recent immigrant from Mexico who established his ranch south of the fort, in what is today Músquiz Canyon. Although he was frequently harassed by the Indians, he refused to leave the substantial home that he had built there for his family.[24]

After the Civil War, would-be ranchers moved rapidly into the Big Bend. Dutchover returned for another try, while Sam Miller, the civilian butcher at the fort, also decided to get a "beef contract" with the army. He soon had over 300 oxen and beef cattle pastured nearby. Colonel Grierson and Sgt. Charles Mulhern built herds while they were in the military at Fort Davis, then remained after their discharge. "Uncle John" Davis established his ranch not far from Faver's in 1870. Probably impressed by the fortress that Faver had constructed, Davis built a similar one on the

---

* Residents of the Big Bend still tell of an Indian who tried to sneak under the tin roof of the fortress during an attack. One of the defenders spotted the intruder and pinned him between the roof and the adobe wall with his saber.

One of Alpine's grocery stores about 1921.

Alpine grew quickly. This street scene indicates its affluence about 1900.

The courthouse and jail in Marfa in 1882.

By the turn of the century Marfa was a flourishing cattle town.

The depot in Alpine.

Although there were several settlements in the Big Bend before 1882, most of the larger towns grew up after the Southern Pacific Railroad crossed the Trans-Pecos. Marfa and Alpine both trace their beginning from the railroad. Today they are thriving centers for the Big Bend ranching country.

banks of Alamito Creek. He quickly developed a large herd of cattle and horses and was competing successfully with Faver and the others for the available market. Bliss commented in his reminiscences that fresh meat on the hoof was always available while he was at Fort Davis.[25]

George Crosson, a freighter who had traveled the Chihuahua Trail in the 1860s, became one of the better known ranchers in the area. Realizing that the railroad would soon come through the region, bringing with it a new form of prosperity, Crosson decided to establish a sheep ranch near Fort Davis. His operation was highly successful. A correspondent for the *San Antonio Daily Express* who visited the ranch in 1877 found Crosson's flocks in good condition, yielding a high quality wool. "His success has been satisfactory, notwithstanding attacks and depredations that would have discouraged a less energetic and determined man," the correspondent noted. Just before the traveler arrived, in fact, Crosson, his herders, and several soldiers fought off a party of Indians who were driving off his horses and mules. Crosson had 10,000 sheep in his pastures when H. N. Dimick, of Uvalde, visited his ranch in 1882. A later traveler pronounced him "one of the most successful sheepmen in the state . . . ."[26]

Another knowledgeable sheepman was Lawrence Haley, whose ranch Dimick also visited. After touring the land, the newcomer concluded that "Mr. Haley and Mr. Crosson have got the key to this country. They have the best range and the most water that I have found since I left home . . . ." Dimick was so impressed, in fact, that he leased an extensive parcel of land himself. Destined to become one of the largest landholders in the Big Bend, John A. Pool, Sr., arrived from Missouri in 1885. He bought Faver's Ciénega Ranch and eventually owned land from Marfa to the Rio Grande.[27]

One of the most beautiful spots in the Big Bend went to Lucas C. Brite, a young cowboy who reached Capote Mountain with his herd in October 1885. "Had one stood on the Capote Mountain and viewed the surroundings," Brite later recalled, "he would most likely have been impressed with the thought that the country was just as God had made it, not a trace of man was visible. Not a house in sight; no fences, no windmills, no water places, not even a road and no livestock of the domestic order." With his 140 cattle Brite built a large ranch and a fortune that allowed him to become a philanthropist in his old age.[28]

Another famous ranchman in the Big Bend was Richard M. Gano, former Civil War general and preacher. John, his son, moved to the Big Bend, where he served as deputy surveyor for Presidio County, which at that time included all of what would become Big Bend National Park. Gano was able to accumulate one of the largest ranches in the Big Bend. John, his brother, and a partner, E. L. Gage, even established a land office in Dallas. They organized the Estado Land and Cattle Company to handle their far-flung ranching activities in the Big Bend. The Ganos owned over 55,000 acres of land in the southern part of what is today Brewster County, in Block G4 of the survey. G4 became the name of the ranch.[29]

James B. Gillett, the ranch manager, recalled that the "Ganos had it all to themselves." In 1885 they shipped 2,000 head of cattle from Dallas and Denton counties in north Texas to their ranch. From Uvalde County they drove another 2,000 head overland to the Big Bend. Meanwhile, they had purchased another 2,000 and shipped them by rail to Marathon. By late summer they had 6,000 head of cattle grazing on their rich G4 pasture land. Initially the company prospered, increasing until the herd was estimated at almost 30,000 by 1891. But drought and other problems combined to decrease that number considerably. By the time the company was disbanded in 1895, only 15,000 head could be rounded up. Even at that the G4 did not suffer as much as the neighbors during the severe droughts of the mid-1880s. Most of the small cattlemen in the northern Big Bend lost heavily, but "not a head of G4 cattle died for the want of grass or water," claimed Gillett. Presumably, they died of natural causes, were rustled, lost or sold.[30]

Although the decline of such vast empires discouraged some smaller ranchers, others continued to settle in the Big Bend. Perhaps they were inspired by the example of W. L. "Uncle Billy" Kingston. Newly married, he set out for the West with 107 cattle, his wagon and team, and $4.70 in cash. At some point west of the Pecos River, he saw some cowboys dressing a calf that looked so good he inquired where it had been raised. Told that the calf had been nourished in the Big Bend, "Uncle Billy" forsook his plan of settling in Arizona and turned southward to the Big Bend. He soon agreed to buy 160 acres and leased another 2,500. Before he

**Stopping for supper during an 1895 trail drive.
These Big Bend cowhands are on their way to a
railhead in Kansas.**

died "Uncle Billy" had a 40,000–acre ranch. Others from all
parts of the State followed him. Some of the settlers were former
Texas Rangers who had guarded the railroad surveying team as it
inched westward, or who were stationed at Fort Davis as part of
the famous Frontier Battalion. There were novices like Capt. A. E.
Shepherd, who traded his interest in a fleet of Great Lakes freighters for the Iron Mountain Ranch, near Marathon. G. W. Evans
moved to the Big Bend because the country around Lampasas,
Tex., was getting too crowded. His brother-in-law, John Z. Means,
joined him in the move. "There were some cattle rustlers in the
country," said Mrs. Evans, "but things were fairly peaceful."[31]

The Big Bend was soon settled. John Beckwith brought 100
Herefords to his ranch on Maravillas Creek in 1878. H. L. Koker-
not and his uncle purchased extensive holdings in 1883. The fol-
lowing year Capt. Pat Dolan brought graded cattle to his range in
Limpia Canyon, and W. B. Hancock drove cattle from Uvalde to
Alpine. In 1885 W. T. Henderson settled at the mouth of the

These cowboys are doctoring a yearling infected
with the screw worm during a 1935 roundup.

creek, and Jim Wilson located some 30 miles upstream. Big Benders owned more than 60,000 head of cattle in 1886, the year of
the first big roundup.

Trail Drives

The ranchers faced many problems, some heightened because
of the isolation or harshness of the country. The first documented
trail drive in the Big Bend occurred in 1864, the result of the de-
bilitating effects of the Civil War. Conditions favored the growth
of the ranching industry in 1860; there was a steady influx of settlers, the mail route was frequently used, and Fort Davis remained
as a deterrent to Indians who threatened to steal the herds. But
when the war broke out, the troops were removed, several leading
citizens left to join forces with the Confederacy, and the passenger
and freight traffic along the Chihuahua Trail diminished considerably. Because the State's resources went toward the Confederate war
effort, residents of the area turned to Mexico for markets and supplies. Thousands of cattle were trailed through the Big Bend during the 1860s. W. A. Peril organized a herd and drove it from
Fort McKavett country, near the old San Sabá presidio and mission in present-day Menard County, over the Chihuahua Trail to

129

Starting the roundup, 1889.

Mexico, and in 1868 Capt. D. M. Poer took 1,200 head from Fort Concho to the Terrazas hacienda in Chihuahua. W. O. Burnam and several neighbors in Burnet County organized a herd to take to Mexico in 1868. They reported no trouble from Indians, but said that Mexican rustlers stole some of their longhorns.[32]

Will Tom Carpenter was an experienced cowhand by the time he reached the Big Bend in the early 1890s. A veteran of long trail drives through Fort Worth, he moved to a ranch south of Alpine and operated it for the Hereford Cattle Company. "It was an incorporated company, a bunch of Boston Guys," Carpenter later wrote, "it wasn't a big Ranch, only about 3,000 head of cattle." During Christmas week 1892, Carpenter began driving 1,760 head of cattle into the teeth of a norther. "It was trying to storm and do Everything Else but something nice," he recalled. "The fog would be so thick of nights that we couldn't see the cattle, and they would just walk off from 7 or 8 men on gard. We lost the herd 3 different nights before we got off with them . . . it was right in their Range and they wanted to get away and did," he explained. The situation improved slightly when it snowed and the sky cleared, leaving two and one-half inches of snow on the ground. When they reached the Pecos River, Carpenter had difficulty getting the cattle to enter the water, although they could walk across on firm river-bottom. "Those cattle had been raised in those mountains south of Alpine," said Carpenter, "the biggest water they had ever seen was a spring, only when a big rain happened along, which wasn't very often. So they was afraid of so much water." After coaxing them across the river, Carpenter and his crew herded the cattle on to their destination with little problem, but cold weather cost them several cattle.[33]

Rustlers

There were other hazards as well. Rustlers were common because of the many unbranded longhorns roaming the region. Even those with brands often had such simple marks that they could be easily altered. The Mexican border was close and enticing. Nobody was immune. Even the Texas Rangers themselves were once victimized by a daring gang of rustlers near Fort Davis in January 1882. While the Rangers were occupied elsewhere, Dave Rudabaugh, an escapee from the Las Vegas, N. Mex. jail, stole their horses. After securing other horses from the fort, the Rangers followed the bandits' trail, but by then it was cold, and they got away.[34]

A gang that specialized in stealing herds from settlers who had not yet located their land conducted several thefts near the Davis Mountains in 1885. They were captured by local cattlemen working with Texas Rangers, and more than 300 head of cattle were recovered.

The stereotype of the Big Bend bandit soon became the Mexican rustler who dashed across the river to gather in some longhorns, then retreated to safety across the Mexican border. But it did not always work. After losing 1,200 head of cattle from their ranches along Maravillas Creek in 1893, the cattlemen pursued the Mexicans across the river and recovered their cattle. The Big Bend ranchers were probably more troubled by Americans, or at least residents of Texas. Ranger Capt. Charles Nevill pursued Tom Blue and two Mexicans to Presidio del Norte in December 1881 because they were suspected of stealing several mules at Carrizo Springs. Still, rustling was one of the problems that caused Milton Faver to quit ranching.[35]

The Big Bend ranchers began to record their brands in 1875, indicating that the cattle industry had become so widespread that identification was necessary and that cattle rustling was a problem. Diedrick Dutchover and John Davis recorded their brands in 1877; George Crosson followed in 1878.[36]

Stampedes

Perhaps even more hazardous than rustlers were the occasional stampedes that took a heavy toll in stock and, sometimes, cowboys. According to the old-timers, most of the stampedes took place near the Pecos River, where the grass and water were so salty that the cattle became tense and irritable. In addition, the region was swamped with kangaroo rats that frequently set off stampedes by spooking or irritating the cattle. Probably the most famous Big Bend stampede took place at Robber's Roost in 1896. "I saw a sight I never expected to see again," recalled Arthur Mitchell. "Mountains of meat – gory from torn flesh. Grotesque shapes with broken necks, broken horns; here and there a slight movement indicating that somewhere below were a few not yet smothered." It happened during the annual roundup on the Mitchell ranch. The cowboys had corralled 1,500 head of cattle near the rim of Robber's Roost. Something, probably a coyote or panther, set off the herd. The cowboys realized instantly that they had a stampede on their hands. "Snatching whatever was handy – a slicker, a saddle blanket, or better still a flaming torch from the camp fire," remembered F. A. Mitchell, "they leaped into the corral brandishing their assorted weapons in the face of the maddened herd." But they were too late. Literally hundreds of cattle plunged over the cliff. The cowboys worked through the night to save those they could reach, but it was not until morning that they realized the hopelessness of their task. "It was an appalling sight," continued Mitchell. "By a miracle no human body had been added to this gruesome mound." [37]

Tom Granger, a trail hand with Norman and Morgan of Presidio County, recalled the most peculiar stampede of his life. As a 16-year-old boy, he was helping drive a herd to Amarillo in March 1890 in an electrical storm. "The cattle were milling and hard to hold," he remembered, "then electricity got to playing over their backs, and running along their horns like lights." Granger confessed that he was frightened as the thunder and lightning cracked and the cattle charged – but so were the more seasoned hands. A stampede was not to be taken lightly.[38]

Drought

The drought of 1885 left most Big Bend cattlemen desperate. The pastures suffered, waterholes dried up, and the pools and streams that still held water were badly overcrowded by thirsty cattle. Then a bad winter caused the stock to scatter. The drought of 1886 proved equally harsh. The cattle were moved from poor ranges to good pasture wherever possible. But still they died. Nineteen were left dead on one campsite. Uneasily noting that they needed to take action, the cattlemen began talking of a general roundup. Finally, they set aside 2 weeks in August for it. Two groups of cowboys swept through the Bend, saving most of the cattle.[39]

But some ranchers could not go on. One of the most notable failures was Frank Collinson, an Englishman who immigrated to Texas in 1872 at age 16. After learning the trade at the Circle Dot Ranch in Medina County, Collinson came to the Big Bend in 1882. "At the time it was a veritable 'no man's land,' " he recalled, "and few people had ventured into its deep, rugged, and almost impassable canyons." At first Collinson thought the Big Bend would have been poor ranch country, but he soon changed his mind. By 1888 he had convinced the Coggin brothers (Samuel and M. J.) and Henry Ford, a Brownwood banker, to invest in a ranch in the Glass Mountains, near Marathon. But the droughts continued, and the cattle market fell sharply. By 1891 the Big Bend had received no measurable rainfall for 3 years. Collinson drilled wells, but did not find sufficient water. "Over half the cattle from San Antonio to the Rio Grande are dead," he informed his partners in 1892. The following year was no better. "The Pecos is nearly dry and is so strong of alkali that it take[s] the skin of[f] the tongues of any animals that try to drink," he wrote Samuel Coggin. By June 1894, Collinson had been whipped. He had found by hard experience that the sod was poor and the water scarce. "I faced such problems half my life and concluded that the Big Bend is another Pharaoh's Dream," he later wrote; "a few good years are followed by more lean years, which eat up all that the good years have made, and then some." [40]

Barbed Wire Empire

The open-range days in the Big Bend were numbered. The roundups and other cattle industry procedures worked only so long

133

as the range was available to everyone. The coming of many small ranchers to the Big Bend led to widespread fencing. There might have been some fencing as early as 1885, but W. F. Mitchell did not close in his pastures near Robber's Roost until 1888. Pat Coleman and W. W. Bogel renewed the trend in 1893, when they enclosed their pasture. By 1895 Humphris and Company had fenced a 16-section range. The last stronghold of the open range was gone by 1900.

When fences closed the range, they changed the nature of the cattle business. Fences made possible the improvement of herds, thus numbering the days of the wild Texas longhorns, which could no longer compete successfully in the eastern markets with the better breeds from other ranges. By 1876 W. S. Ikard, a central Texas rancher, had already imported Herefords. The Northwestern Texas Cattleman's Association, meeting in Dallas in 1883, adopted resolutions urging the improvement of Texas cattle. John Beckwith, George W. Evans, Jim and Beau McCutcheon, Pat Dolan, and Jim Hilder had brought better stock into the Big Bend in the 1880s, but most ranchers had not yet fenced their lands and could not participate in the herd improvements. By the 1890s most of the area cattlemen were raising the quality of their herds with Shorthorns, Durhams, and Herefords. The *Marfa New Era* proudly boasted of a steer raised on the J. B. Irving ranch at Alpine in 1911. It was "said to be a many record breaker, weighing on the hoof 1740 pounds . . . ." [41]

Folklore in the Big Bend

One of the great legacies of the cattle industry is the folklore it has provided for the Big Bend. One of the most intriguing legends concerns the MURDER calf. The incident that inspired the story occurred during the general roundup of January 1891. Henry H. Powe, a rancher, disputed with Fine Gilliland, a cowboy working for one of the big ranches, the ownership of an unbranded calf. After a heated argument, both men drew their pistols and Gilliland shot Powe to death, then fled. He was later tracked down by the Texas Rangers in the Glass Mountains and shot. The cowboys who saw Gilliland kill Powe commemorated the occasion by branding the disputed calf with the word MURDER and turning him loose. There the legend takes over. Although there is evidence that the yearling was taken to Montana in the drive, some contend that it stayed in Texas, wandering through the Big Bend, shying away from other cattle, an outcast. Others insist that it turned prematurely gray, that the hair on the brand turned red, and even that the brand grew with the calf until the word MURDER practically covered his side. Thus marked, the steer supposedly wandered throughout the Big Bend looking for the man who made him a grim reminder of a violent event.[42]

Mining

The Big Bend was more than good ranching country; it was also rich in mineral resources. Spaniards and Americans alike searched the region for gold and silver. The Spaniards stationed at Presidio San Vicente reportedly had a mine in the Chisos Mountains that could not be worked because the expense of getting the metal out cost more than it produced. Other Spaniards were supposed to have buried treasure in the mountains, while legends tell of silver supposedly hidden at several sites. The tales of buried treasure and gold and silver mines later led many prospectors on futile searches, and still lure hundreds of treasure-hunters into the Big Bend each year with their hunches and electronic metal detec-

Ore wagons load up at the Shafter mine in the 1890s before heading for Marfa, 45 miles away.

A firewood train arriving in Terlingua, 1934.

tors. While the Big Bend has produced no lost Spanish treasures --
and it is not likely to – it has yielded some silver ore and great
quantities of quicksilver.[43]

Silver mining lasted only a short time. Ore was discovered in
the Chinati Mountains, near Milton Faver's ranch. John W. Spencer mined there on a small scale in the 1860s, taking what he could
to Mexico in burro carts to be smelted. Professor Wilhelm H. Stee-
ruwitz, a well-known geologist who visited the region in 1878, reported the presence of gold and silver, but it was not until 1882
that Spencer found evidence of enough silver to enlarge his operations. A vein in the Chinatis seemed to have a high ore content,
according to Fort Davis assayers. Gathering capital from California, where entrepreneurs were more willing to invest in mining,
Spencer formed the Presidio Mining Company, with W. S. Noyes
of San Francisco as president and Lt. John Bullis and Gen. William R. Shafter of Fort Davis holding interests.[44]

Because of the deserted nature of the country around the
Chinatis, everything had to be brought in by wagon. The machinery was transported to Paisano Pass on the Southern Pacific Railroad and hauled to the mine site by wagon. Humphris and Company of Marfa supplied 4,000 cords of wood annually, because
timber was scarce in the Chinatis. The company even cut lumber in northern Mexico, ignoring the international complications, in
order to get wood for the furnace. [45]

Marfa could have been the market for the silver miners. Four
years after Spencer began working his claim, the *Marfa New Era*

found the prospects "most encouraging" for both the miners and the city. "It will not be long before Marfa will be shipping more silver bullion than any point in the southwestern silver district," wrote the editor. He even predicted that when the riches of the Chinatis became well known, easterners would be anxious to invest in the venture. That would mean "prosperity and wealth for Marfa," he concluded. What wealth there was, however, went through the town of Shafter, which was established to accommodate the miners.[46]

If not large, the Chinati silver mines at least proved profitable. The Shafter mine changed hands in 1910, and the new owners announced their intention of introducing a new cyanide process. Oil replaced wood as fuel, keeping wagons busy hauling oil from Marfa. In 1913 the 50-ton mill was replaced with a 300-ton mill, and the refining process was improved by replacing quicksilver with cyanide, permitting 600 tons of ore to be treated in 24 hours. The miners encountered veins as rich as $500 per ton and others as poor as $8 per ton. Nevertheless, they made money. They tunneled through the Chinati Mountains, running shafts in every direction until they had more than 100 miles of tunnels that finally yielded over $20,000,000 in silver. At times the mines employed as many as 300 men and built Shafter, a company town between Marfa and Presidio consisting of a club house, a hospital, a boarding house, and family houses. The partially abandoned town stands today as a physical reminder of the strike. When the silver ran out, mining ceased as quickly as it had begun.[47]

There were hints of coal in the Big Bend. In 1886 a prospector named McKenzie found some coal seams northwest of Marfa, near Eagle Springs. Although he was not overwhelmed by the production, he found the yield "highly satisfactory" and still had capital to invest in cattle. O. W. Williams noticed a vein of poor quality coal in the Chisos Mountains while surveying in 1902. Coal was mined in the 1930s near Terlingua to provide fuel for the quicksilver furnaces after the companies began to run short of wood, but production was never impressive.[48]

In what might have been a unique discovery, W. A. Robbins and S. H. Eaton announced in 1909 that they had discovered the kind of lime rock in the Solitario Mountains that made good lithographic stones. The finest lithographic stones were imported from a Bavarian quarry discovered by the man who perfected the lithographic technique, Alois Senefelder. Robbins and Eaton felt that they had found a stone good enough to be commercially valuable, but little came of this discovery.[49]

Some of the more interesting artifacts in the Big Bend – remains of old wooden towers and pieces of cable and ore buckets – owe their existence to the Corte Madera Mine in Mexico near Boquillas. The editor of the *Alpine Avalanche* reported in February 1910 that 250 tons of lead and zinc ore were to be transported across the river on a 6-mile-long cable, then shipped to the Southern Pacific station at Marathon in cars pulled by traction engines. The cable tramway was an ingenious device to avoid hauling the ore over rough terrain and floating it across the river. The tramway's 90 ore buckets and 15 water buckets could carry 7½ tons of ore an hour. The mines, offices, and living quarters were in Mexico; the terminal was in Ernst Valley, on the American side. Today the ruins of the tramway can still be seen by hiking along the Ore Terminal Trail.[50]

Quicksilver

Although reports of quicksilver in the Big Bend had circulated for years, no one had ever taken them seriously. The Indians had used cinnabar for their war paint and for the red pigments in paintings that can still be seen in scattered shelters of the Big Bend. In 1847 Dr. Ferdinand Römer, a German scientist visting Texas, traded an Indian a leather lasso for a small quantity of quicksilver, or mercury. Both Texans and Mexicans heard reports before 1850 of the quicksilver, but no serious explorations were undertaken until 1884 when Juan Acosta reportedly showed a specimen to Ignatz Kleinman, who operated a general store in Presidio, Texas. Kleinman took up a claim near what became known as California Hill and went to work. He failed to find sufficient quantities to make the mine profitable, but did interest a California company in taking over the search. They abandoned the attempt after finding little ore, although they were on top of one of the richest fields in the country. The site of their operations became known as California Hill when one of the miners carved that inscription on a rock.[51]

Quicksilver mines quickly dotted the landscape around Terlingua. Mining began there in 1894 when George W. Manless and Charles Allen investigated the rumors of rich quicksilver deposits in the region. They found the deposits about 90 miles south of Alpine, at that time little more than a station on the Southern Pacific Railroad. The Marfa and Mariposa Mining Company, named after the town and Mariposa County, California, where a huge quicksilver mine was located, was the first to profitably extract quicksilver from the Big Bend. Organized in 1896, the company took up a claim near present-day Terlingua, where the California company had failed, and extracted over 9,000 flasks of mercury (3 quarts, or 76 pounds per flask) by 1903. The gross sale for the company in 1901 and 1902 was more than $350,000. After the "easy" ore had been mined, however, the company disbanded.

At its height the Marfa and Mariposa Company employed 1,000 to 1,500 persons. The four or five white families lived in stone houses belonging to the company, but the Mexicans lived in tents or crude stone huts. The laborers were paid with a punch-out check redeemable anytime at the company store or in cash at the end of the month. Although the store stocked only the barest necessities, it did a good business. Sugar, corn, beans, and flour were brought in by the carload. Work clothing, a few bolts of calico, blue denim, and shirting also were stocked. The store's revenue was usually $100,000 to $150,000 annually. A popular saying in Terlingua, reported C. A. Hawley, the company bookkeeper, was that the mine was a silver mine, but the store was a gold mine.

The ore proved to be rich but the mines were almost inaccessible. The wagon road from Marfa, about 100 miles to the northwest, was at best a difficult route. Six miles from the mine it became impossible for wagons. The supplies had to be loaded on pack mules for the trip across dry and badly eroded paths. Everything except fuel (the plentiful mesquite trees) had to be hauled in. Several Mexicans made a little money hauling goods to Terlingua and quicksilver to Marfa with their Studebaker wagons. Strong enough to carry 3 to 4 tons, the wagons required 10 days for a round trip to Marfa. There was little profit in the freighting, for the Mexicans charged only a half-cent a pound and the only thing they could carry out was quicksilver.[52]

The first miners employed only primitive methods and used shafts no deeper than 200 feet. After the ore was brought to the surface it was loaded into a small car and transported to an aerial tramway. The car was then hand-pushed back to the mine, while the ore was transported over the tramway to the ore crusher, half a mile away. From the crusher, walnut-sized chunks of ore were taken to the smelter.

Waldron Mine

Mexican miners loaded up to 80 pounds of ore on their backs before heading for the surface.

A tram car carried the cinnabar ore to the crusher, which reduced it to walnut-sized lumps.

The entrance to the main shaft.

Quicksilver mining in the Big Bend boomed in World War I, and slowly played out afterwards. One of the latecomers was the Waldron Mining Company, which began operation in 1916. Production ended before World War II. Few documents of the company have survived, and there is little record of its activities other than a remarkable series of photographs made during the mine's early years.

Condensers liquified the mercury, which was collected in reservoirs and bottled in standard 76-pound flasks.

Inside the extracting furnace, a hot fire vaporized the mercury in the crushed ore.

The brick furnace measured about 20 feet square and 40 feet high. Two or three weeks of continuous heating was required for the furnace to reach 360 degrees, the temperature at which quicksilver vaporizes from ore. The fumes went out the top of the furnace through a series of 8 or 10 slightly smaller condensers, connected by a pipe. A partition alternately extended from the ceiling of the condenser almost to the floor, then from the floor almost to the ceiling, forcing the smoke from the furnace to describe an upside-down arch in passing through each condenser. The quicksilver gathered in the condensers and ran into buckets. A smoke stack 30 to 40 feet high attached to the last condenser carried off the rest of the vapor and smoke.[53]

Work in the mines was difficult. The miners worked 10 hours a day, most of the labor underground and all of it manual. The ore was loosened by pick and hammer and gathered up by shovel. The work was also dangerous. In February 1908 a blast killed one man and seriously injured another at the Shafter mine. Even the candles used to light the shafts proved dangerous, for they often gave off too little light for the men to avoid open shafts and other hazards. "Miner's consumption," caused by the polluted air, killed several workers every year.

There was no hospital but the company employed a doctor who cared for all the employees. Although the treatment ostensibly was free, the Mexican laborers had one day's wages per month withheld for the medical fund, but white men only $1. The men worked 7 days a week for $1 to $1.50 per day. Sometimes an exceptional worker would be paid as much as $2 per day. Yet C. A. Hawley, the bookkeeper for Marfa and Mariposa Company, got $100 a month plus free rent and goods from the company store at cost.[54]

Several other companies competed with the Marfa and Mariposa Company. Howard E. Perry, a Chicago businessman, organized the Chisos Mining Company in 1902. By 1905 the Terlingua Mining Company, Colquitt-Tigner Mining Company, Texas Almaden Mining Company, Big Bend Cinnabar Mining Company, and Excelsior Mining Company were all in operation in and around Terlingua. When O. W. Williams saw Terlingua in early 1902 he

The water was free at the Chisos Mine, but
everyone had to come to the tank to get it.
The house commanding the view of Terlingua
belonged to Howard E. Perry, the mine owner.

noted that considerable improvement had been made in the last
2 years. The companies employed probably 300 men to haul wood,
water, and ore, and work the furnaces. The freight teams kept the
road dusty as they brought in supplies and hauled quicksilver to
the railhead at Marfa. Texas soon was the number two quicksilver-
producing State in the Nation.[55]

Perry's Chisos Mining Company lasted longer and produced
more than any other. Perry bought his land in the Big Bend in
1887 and turned down several offers to sell it at a slight profit before he decided to investigate. He found that his land contained
quicksilver and set out to mine it. After opening the mine in 1902,
he returned to Chicago to direct his affairs there, leaving the mine
in control of a succession of managers.

Perry made several changes in his operation. At first using the
crude methods of the Marfa and Mariposa Mining Company, he
improved his equipment, enabling his men to dig deeper and extract more ore. James Lafarelle reported in 1910 that the depth
had already reached 520 feet and that they were planning to go to
1,000 feet in the new shafts.[56]

The quicksilver industry received a good boost when James
Norman took some Terlingua ore to the Saint Louis World's Fair in
1904. The specimens were so good that several companies filed
claims in the region, but most were never more than small-time or
non-producing companies. Capitalized at $500,000 when it
opened, for example, the Terlingua Mining Company installed a
45-ton furnace, but fell on hard times and was worth only $35,025
when it closed in 1903.[57]

Perry's success drew other prospectors to the Big Bend. They quickly learned that the secret of his success was that his tract was the richest in the region. The quicksilver ore was limited to a relatively small area near Terlingua. Within an area about 14 miles long by 4 miles wide, 30 or more mines were dug, but most of the 150,000 or so flasks of mercury produced came from about 6 mines. The Chisos Company produced more than two-thirds of that total. The Marfa and Mariposa Company produced between 20,000 and 30,000 flasks, leaving all the other companies with a total of less than 30,000 flasks.[58]

Today Terlingua is one of the best known ghost towns in the Southwest and a monument to the lively industry that once flourished in the Big Bend. The site of the World Champion Chili Cookoff, a highly promoted and colorful celebration dedicated to boosterism and local chauvinism, it has also been designated a historic site by the State. The deserted general store, post office, movie house, jailhouse, and church suggest the activities that Terlinguans participated in each week during the heyday of the village. But the nearby cemetery is a reminder that life in the mines was hard, for most of the gravestones tell of those who died young. Dominating the entire perspective is Perry's abandoned house. Located on a hill overlooking the village, this sturdy, two-story building is symbolic of what has happened in Terlingua. From the front porch one can see the deserted mine shafts that brought hundreds of workers to the Big Bend early in the century, and in the distance Santa Elena Canyon and the Chisos Mountains, the impressive landscape which attracts visitors today.

Mariscal Mine

The discovery at Terlingua sent prospectors searching throughout the Big Bend for quicksilver ore. The site that became known as Mariscal Mine was discovered in 1900 by Martin Solís in Mariscal Mountain, just a few miles north of the river. It was not effectively mined until a store owner from Boquillas, D. E. Lindsey, filed a claim on Solís' site and began operation of what he called the Lindsey Mine. His profits were cut considerably because he transported ore via pack mules to the Chisos Mining Company for refining. He finally sold out to T. P. Barry and Isaac Singer, who, in turn, sold out to W. K. Ellis in 1916. Ellis installed his own refining plant and between July 1917 and May 1919 shipped 894 flasks of mercury. When the price of quicksilver dropped after World War I, Ellis sold his holdings to the Mariscal Mining Company, a New York corporation that worked the mines until 1927 when it finally declared bankruptcy. The mine was sold at a sheriff's auction in 1936. William D. Burcham, the company's president, tried to open it again during World War II, but produced only 97 flasks of mercury and soon closed it. Today the mine and old buildings are one of the more interesting remains in the southern part of the national park.[59]

Other Settlers

Settlers came to the Big Bend for various reasons. Max A. Ernst immigrated from Germany to Texas in 1873 at age 16. He lived in Alpine a few years before moving to La Noria, on Tornillo Creek. In 1898 he leased a section of land containing a waterhole called the Big Tinaja. He established a small store by the same name, and later became justice of the peace, coroner, law enforcer, marriage bureau, notary public, and postmaster of Boquillas, Tex. For a time Kit Williams of Louisiana acted as postmaster, because Ernst could not legally hold the jobs of mail carrier and postmaster simultaneously, though he would relinquish neither. Jesse Deemer, later a storekeeper in Boquillas, was a German mining operator working in northern Mexico when he first arrived in the Big Bend. Cipriano Hernández, a native of Camargo, Chihuahua, and an employee in the Shafter mines, moved to a plot of land near Santa Elena Canyon in 1903. He ran a small supply store in a community called Santa Helena, Tex., until 1914 when the name was changed to Castolon. Today the small village of Santa Elena, Chihuahua, is located across the river from Castolon.[60]

Several persons moved to the Big Bend for their health. Milton Faver might have been the first one, arriving in the early 1850s to alleviate a severe case of tuberculosis. After the railroad linked the Trans-Pecos with the rest of Texas, the word spread quickly. J. R. Landrum, who later managed Ernst's store and post office, suffered from chronic bad health and hoped that the dry climate of West Texas would help him. So did J. O. Langford, a malaria sufferer who took up a claim at Hot Springs on the Rio Grande in 1909. A skinny, wan man with thin lips, deep-set eyes, and a pleasing personality, Langford decided to make a health resort out of the hot springs. He received plenty of publicity from the Marfa and Alpine editors, who published accounts of those who had been cured as a result of the treatment and his plans for the

A candelilla wax maker and his family, in front of their home at Glenn Springs in 1917. They lived in this shack until they could build themselves an adobe home.

Burros at Bullis Gap, loaded with candelilla wax plants gathered in the mountains, 1913.

C. D. Wood's wax plant in full operation, 1917.

resort. There were even suggestions that a second resort be built at another set of hot springs near Castolon on the Mexican side of the river. T. J. Miller, who operated a small store at San Vicente, came to the Big Bend hoping that his wife's health would improve.

By the late 1890s there were enough people scattered throughout the Big Bend that two second-class roads were opened, one from Marathon to Boquillas, the other from Alpine to Terlingua. When a man named Pitts drove his 4-cylinder Acme over the hills from Marfa to Presidio in 1908, he received excited attention from the townspeople along the route and praise from the editor of the *New Era*. At Shafter the school children were dismissed from class and followed the car through the dusty streets. "Actual running time to Presidio, counting out stops, 70 miles in 3 hours 53 minutes," declared the editor. "Chauffeur Pitts states the roads out of Marfa are as good as any in the state...."[61]

Guayule

As the new age of chemistry dawned, scientists found uses for Big Bend plants. "Guayule, the rubber plant, formerly despised and useless, has produced a few hundred million dollars worth of rubber in Mexico and Texas," reported the editor of the *Alpine Avalanche* in 1911. "It has brought riches to those who took advantage of the opportunity when they were asked to invest in the guayule rubber enterprises." Several factories were established along the railroad, but the industry did not last long. The guayule was soon exhausted, and Big Benders turned to other ways of earning a living.[62]

Wax Making

The candelilla plant provided the raw material; unemployed Mexicans supplied the muscle; white men usually provided the capital. In 1911 Oscar Pacius, a director of the Continental Wax Company of Little Rock, Ark., visited Marfa and Alpine and announced his intention of establishing 10 wax factories in the Big Bend. The company already had four producing factories in Mexico, he explained. Pacius declared that his company expected to be able to make about $600 per ton of wax. By the time he reached Alpine in the fall of 1911 the name of his company had been changed to the Rio Grande Wax Company, but the enthusiasm had not diminished. Another important producer was C. D. Wood, who established factories at McKinney Springs and Glenn Springs in 1911.[63]

Wax making is still a major industry in the Big Bend on both sides of the border. In Mexico the government monopolizes production, assigning quotas to producers and guaranteeing them a certain income each year. In the United States a small number of firms buy most of the independently produced wax. Because the Mexican wax makers have no market for their product after they fill the government quota, some observers claim that smuggling wax into the United States is common. Although candelilla wax has been in demand since 1911, the process by which the pure wax is secured has changed little. The plant, which grows wild in the Big Bend, is heated in a mixture of water and sulfuric acid. When the wax loosens from the plant, it floats to the top of the vat, and is scooped off and put into barrels to harden. It is used in candles, phonograph records, insulation of electrical wires, leather and wood polishes, as an agent in the manufacture of celluloid, and as a waterproofing. Early in the century it was an important sealing wax. Today most of the wax goes to the chewing gum industry. Ruins of old wax-rendering operations can be found throughout the park, and wax factories still operate outside the park.

Fur Traders

A common frontier livelihood that might not be expected in the Big Bend was fur-trapping along the Rio Grande. T. M. Meler floated down the river trapping beavers at the turn of the century. Perhaps the best known trapper in the Big Bend was James Mc-Mahon, who escorted Hill through the canyons in 1899. He lived well into this century, trading furs for goods at Johnson's Trading Post, in the southern part of what is now the national park.

Elmo Johnson buying furs at his trading post in the Big Bend, 1929. He enjoyed a good reputation among trappers for his fair prices.

The trappers brought the furs of fox, coyote, wildcat, and skunk into the border trading posts. Often they skinned goats to supplement their income. Many pelts were captured in the mountains along fur trails that stretched sometimes 100 miles through the wilderness. As barter, Elmo Johnson offered wood, other kinds of fur, chino grass, ropes, and various finished items or food. Regular fur traders, in fact, made up his best customers.[64]

The Unwritten Code

By the turn of the century the Big Bend was fairly well settled. Small villages had grown up near waterholes – Tornillo Creek, La Noria, Glenn Springs, and Robber's Roost – and along the Rio Grande. A number of farms flourished in the Lajitas-Castolon area. Ranching, mining, wax making, merchandising, law enforcement, and the military provided a living for the early settlers. Society began to organize into various groups. Livestock associations, promoting pure-bred cattle, exerted strong influences. Rev. William B. Bloys, the "Cowboy Preacher," held annual camp meetings in Skillman's Grove. Soon Bloys Camp Meeting was an event that not many Big Benders missed. Disciples of Christ, Baptists, Methodists, and Presbyterians attended the affair.[65]

The early settlers gradually evolved a code of unwritten laws that governed their community. Probably the most obvious one was the frontier's raw, aggressive brand of equality. A white man was accepted at face value. No questions were asked about the years before he came to the Big Bend; no information was usually volunteered. Texas had much the same reputation during its youthful years when "GTT" meant "Gone to Texas," usually for a bad reason. In the Big Bend it was accepted that a man might be using an assumed name. Thus there are several stories about Milton Faver's background, including the possibility that he was a murderer and that he had been jilted by his Mexican girlfriend. C. A. Hawley was hardly surprised when a neighbor calling himself Tom White came into the post office at Terlingua and claimed a pension check addressed to John M. Southard. He cashed the check with no questions asked when White explained that he was Southard and had changed his name when he moved to the Big Bend. Perhaps the point is better made by the cowboy who, when conversation around the campfire lagged, challenged his companions to create a little excitement by telling their real names.[66]

The fact that white men were accepted as they were emphasizes a second unwritten law of the Big Bend: dark-skinned men were not accepted at all. Racial prejudice in various forms was evident to the newcomer. Hawley, a mid-westerner unaccus-

This family, living near Polvo in 1916, built their
adobe house between boulders.

tomed to the racial segregation of the South and Southwest, was
surprised to discover that the Mexican stage driver rode with the
whites but did not eat with them. Working for the Terlingua mining companies, he also learned that Mexicans were employed for
menial jobs and manual labor, but not for the management positions. "In this state," a Brewster County lawyer explained, "we
have one set of laws for white people and one for Mexicans, all in
the same words and in the same book." Prejudice tainted every relationship between white and brown, even to the point that Hawley, as manager of the company store, intimidated a poverty-
stricken Mexican woman into buying her groceries at more
infrequent intervals and in larger quantities because he had grown
tired of selling her a small amount each day. Only later did he
learn that she bought meagerly because she usually did not have
enough money to buy in larger measures. When a ranch or store
was robbed, the authorities immediately assumed that Mexicans
were to blame. Pilares, Chihuahua, was attacked without warning
in both 1917 and 1918 by Americans seeking revenge for raids on
Texas ranches. Several residents were killed, including the mayor of
nearby Candelaria. The amazing explanation, accepted without
qualm by the Anglo-Americans, was that "anyone living in that
particular area, and those who were familiar with it, were aware
that no innocent Mexicans lived in Candelaria and Pilares, Mex-

Nick Merfelder at his Fort Davis home, 1896.
He was the post's musician, barber, photographer,
and justice of the peace.

ico." An army lieutenant searching for bandits in northern Mexico revealed a similar attitude. Flying over the Río Conchos, he saw four mounted horsemen. "I shot a few rounds at them from about 1,000 feet altitude (too high to hit them), to see if they would return the fire. Since they dashed into the high brush without responding, I concluded they were not bandits, but Mexican cowboys. The only way to tell a bandit from a cowboy was to use such a test."[67]

The prejudice extended to Negroes, but had less opportunity for expression because there were few blacks in the Big Bend. The editor of the *Alpine Avalanche* opposed further Negro immigration into Alpine in 1909. Under the headline, "Not Wanted in Alpine," he editorialized that they would disrupt the community. He also suggested a few months later that those already in the city would have to behave in an exemplary manner or be run off. At that, Alpine was hardly different from any other Texas city of the day.[68]

A third unwritten code, which lasted well into the 20th century, required everyone to arm and defend himself. A peaceful

151

Frontier Life

A Shafter family, photographed in the 1890s, in their two-seater carriage.

A wedding in 1898 at Boquillas, Mexico.

This baptism took place a few miles from Marathon, during the early 1900s.

This Marathon saloon, shown in 1910, kept a pet bear so customers would buy it a beer.

Mexicans gambling in Polvo, Texas.

Although life on the Big Bend frontier was more strenuous than in settled parts of the West, residents found time to be social, often by taking a Sunday ride in the surry, attending a friend's wedding, or visiting the local saloon.

man who disdained liquor and "gun-totin," Hawley abhorred such practices. But he had little influence. As justice of the peace, he frequently asked men charged with violation of the law why they carried weapons. Their invariable response was that no one would respect them if they went unarmed. They apparently feared the social pressure more than the consequences.

The result of disputes involving a deliberate or insulting wrong usually was a gunfight. Hawley remembered hearing the calm pronouncement of final judgment several times: "Well, somebody has got to be killed." This unwritten rule was responsible for the death of Roselle Pulliam, a Big Bend rancher who crossed paths with Jim Gillespie, a well-known cowboy. After purchasing hundreds of cattle in Mexico, Gillespie brought them into Texas, probably without paying all the duty required by law. He cut the fences as he crossed Pulliam's ranch, and Pulliam sought revenge by reporting the approximate number of cattle Gillespie had brought in to the Customs officers. The officials impounded the herd, waiting for the question to be settled. Gillespie's consequent grudge against Pulliam could be settled only by a gunfight. Pulliam moved to New Mexico to avoid the confrontation, but the episode ended tragically when he returned to Alpine to visit his father and Gillespie killed him. It would have been virtually impossible to have secured a conviction, said Hawley, because the murderer had followed the unwritten laws of the country. In this instance, the jury never had the chance because Gillespie himself was killed before his case came to trial.[69]

Law Enforcement

The arrival of the railroad spurred the growth of several towns in the Big Bend: Marfa, Alpine, Marathon. As the unruly element moved in with progress, so did the few individuals who became lawmen. The Texas Rangers patrolled the region throughout the last quarter of the 19th century. Their famous Frontier Battalion did everything from chasing Indians and bandits to accompanying surveyors down the Rio Grande. After retiring from the Rangers, Capt. Charles L. Nevill remained in the Big Bend, first as sheriff of Presidio County, then as a rancher. An even better known lawman who settled in the Big Bend was James Gillett, who retired from the Rangers to become marshall in El Paso. After Nevill and Gillett bought a small ranch in the Big Bend together, it was not difficult for Nevill to convince Gillett that he had been a lawman long enough. He left his marshall's post to become foreman of the G4 Ranch, which was owned by the Ganos and was near enough to his own ranch that he could also care for it. Another popular Ranger who spent a few years in the Big Bend with Nevill was Jeff Milton, who left the service in 1883 and went on to serve with distinction in the U. S. Customs Service.

D. E. Lindsey, the man who filed the claim on Mariscal Mine, first came to the Big Bend as a mounted inspector for the U.S. Customs Service. But the man who perhaps best symbolizes law enforcement in the Big Bend is Thomas Creed Taylor, who was stationed at Pena Colorado, near Marathon, shortly after the turn of the century. He quit the Rangers in 1904 and ranched until 1918, when he joined the Customs Service. In 1942 he was elected sheriff of Presidio County, and held that office for 4 years.[70]

The man who later became known as the "father of the Big Bend National Park" also initially came as a law enforcement officer. Born in Colorado County, Tex., in 1871, Everett Ewing Townsend joined the Texas Rangers at age 19, but resigned after only 18 months with the Frontier Battalion. Moving to Presidio, he joined the U. S. Customs Service and became familiar with the Big Bend while fulfilling his job of scouting along the borders for smugglers. The enthusiasm he gained for the Big Bend while employed by Customs was the foundation of the Big Bend National Park.[71]

Americans came to the Big Bend in three phases. First, the traders and explorers passed through, finding the region neither hospitable nor available, for the Indians controlled it. Then, the U.S. Army and its associates moved into the Fort Davis area. Only vital occupations such as beef contracting could flourish. Not until the Big Bend had been pacified did the third phase – miners, farmers, ranchers, merchants, health seekers, and settlers – begin. Another barrier was isolation. As the Big Bend was drawn into Texas commerce through the Chihuahua traders and later through the railroad, more people settled there – and with them an unsavory element of frontier society.

6 / Bandits Along the Border

The same conditions that rendered the Big Bend difficult to explore and even harder to homestead attracted dozens of bandits during the two decades both before and after the turn of the century. The region's sparse settlement, isolation, and rugged terrain seemed at times to constitute an environment more favorable to the lawbreaker than to the settler, and the arroyos, canyons, caves, and mountains that had first found use as campsites for Indians and explorers now served as hideouts for what historian J. Evetts Haley described as "the backwash from the frontiers." But the natural features of the Big Bend proved to be more than just hideouts as Indians and bandits alike transformed them into fortresses. After a firsthand look in 1899, just a few years after the last conflicts with hostile Apaches, geologist Robert T. Hill concluded that, "Few Americans realize the impregnability and isolation of this frontier." [1]

The litany of criminal acts that came with the end of New Mexico's Lincoln County War, which drove desperados such as Jesse Evans and John Selman south, and the hooligans and tricksters accompanying the construction of the railroad across West Texas seemed to bear out his observation. There were, of course, the routine, racially tinged incidents that law enforcement officers had to contend with throughout the post-Civil War South. Texas Ranger Sgt. J. T. Gillespie of the Frontier Battalion reported on January 10, 1882, that an Indian woman had been "brutally murdered" only 2 days before at Fort Davis, and that he suspected a black soldier of the deed. When the post baker, John Schueller, was killed in February 1882, as usual, the authorities suspected a Mexican of the murder. [2]

The 1881 arrival of more than 2,600 Chinese railroad workers in West Texas to complete the nation's second transcontinental railroad, the Southern Pacific, complicated the situation further. The Chinese seemingly suffered racial hostility wherever they went in the West, and Texas was no exception. On December 31, 1881, a band of Apache Indians attacked a Chinese surveying party

A rocky perch on the south rim of the Chisos.

near Eagle Pass, killing them all. Later, several Mexican section hands beat up some Chinese laborers outside of El Paso, and the murder of another by an Irish worker led to Judge Roy Bean's infamous finding that there was no law in Texas that prohibited "killing a Chinaman." The region "is a favorable resort of the murderers and desperadoes driven from other sections of the state," claimed a Pecos County delegation as they requested more Rangers for their area. Such conditions required the Texas Rangers to establish Company E under Lt. Charles L. Nevill in July 1880 with headquarters in Fort Davis.[3]

With the completion of the track through the Trans-Pecos, trains established more or less regular schedules, and some of the more daring bandits added the short-lived but tempting job of robbing trains to their repertory. In October 1891, as the Texas Rangers closed in on five members of the gang that had held up a train in the vicinity of Samuels station near Langtry, the gang leader was wounded in the ensuing shoot-out. Ranger Capt. Frank Jones reported that, rather than be captured, he "took out a book and pencil, wrote his will, bequeathing all his property to his brother, took out his pistol and blew his brains out." The other bandits were taken to El Paso for trial, and the Southern Pacific soon had guards riding all its trains.[4]

Only the military was authorized to cross the Rio Grande in pursuit of raiders, and then only in special cases, but the laws were often violated. After trailing adversaries deep into the Big Bend or Mexico, U.S. authorities, Texas Rangers, and vigilante bands alike sometimes forgot about due process of the law and the rights of their victims. Thus Rancher Jim P. Wilson explained the result of a search for a band that reportedly had murdered a family and stolen some horses in the evasive but highly esteemed manner of the frontier: "When we overtook them, it just naturally scared them to death, so we rounded up our horses and come on back." [5]

Robert T. Hill obviously had heard many of these stories as he planned his 1899 float trip through the canyons of the Big Bend. Old-timers counseled that the Big Bend was infested with thieves and murderers who disliked any intruders and felled their prey by

Camp King in the 1890's. Nevill's Texas Ranger battalion patrolled the frontier from this outpost 12 miles north of Alpine.

shooting into sleeping camps at night, and Hill reported that the storekeeper at Polvo, just upriver from Bofecillos Canyon, showed his party the "splotches of blood" on the floor where the previous merchant had been robbed and murdered the year before. "Sheer fright" prevented two members of Hill's party from going any further, and the others proceeded only with caution, keeping their rifles handy and hiding their camp in bushes wherever possible. E. E. Townsend, former sheriff of Brewster County, believed that Hill had exaggerated the danger, but others took his concern literally: "Away from the railway," concluded Hill, "the Big Bend – sometimes called the Bloody Bend – is known as a 'hard country,' . . . in which . . . civilization finds it difficult to gain a foothold."[6]

The Mexican Revolution and the Big Bend

The most serious violence developed after the turn of the century as a direct result of the Mexican Revolution, which exploded in 1911 and suddenly ended the more than three decades dictatorship of President Porfirio Díaz. The uprising was the product of decades of economic poverty and political suppression. When a Coahuila *hacendado,* Francisco I. Madero, revolted against Díaz, several of the initial conflicts occurred along the U.S.-Mexico border largely because the insurrectionists either had sought exile in the U.S. or had come to recruit Mexicans living in the United States, and rebels from every segment of society joined him. Francisco (Pancho) Villa and Pascual Orozco, Jr., presented Madero

159

with his first big victory in Chihuahua, when they took the city of Ciudad Juárez in May 1911.

That victory, however, was only the beginning of the devastating conflict, rather than the end. The country entered a chaotic period when Madero himself was murdered in February 1913, leading to a series of conflicts in every section of the country and starving guerrilla bands roaming throughout northern Mexico, striking fear in the hearts of settlers all along the international boundary. There were at least 20 large ranches and several mines in a 250-square-mile area of the Big Bend that were patrolled by only a few cavalrymen, Texas Rangers, and mounted customs officers. These officers worked together closely, and, according to C. A. Hawley of the Chisos Mining Company, they felt relatively safe. "The revolution in no way affected the usual course of life at the mines in Terlingua," he later recalled. But the task of patrolling such a huge area would have been impossible even for twice the force, for the territory was extensive, the hiding places numerous, and access too easy. Gen. Frederick Funston reported in 1916 that the Big Bend Military District alone was 500 miles long and that "practically all" the combat-ready army in the United States, almost 50,000 troops, was stationed along the international boundary. Still, it was impossible to patrol the entire area.[7]

Pancho Villa's 1911 attack on Ojinaga sent refugees fleeing into the United States and led one New York newspaper to report

After the Mexican revolutionaries attacked Ojinaga in 1911, refugees fled to Marfa and settled into camps

erroneously in 1911 that Terlingua had been devastated by Mexican desperadoes and many people slain.[8] Another reporter wrote of his adventures along the combustible border. As the revolutionaries regrouped in the Big Bend, Associated Press reporter E. S. O'Riley ventured down the river to El Polvo, where he encountered two Mexicans who offered to take him to meet José La Cruz Sánchez, a prominent guerilla leader and a well-known ranchman in Chihuahua. O'Riley accepted their offer and accompanied them to a nearby vacant house, where he waited for Sánchez to appear. Overhearing that his hosts were *Rurales* and that they did not intend for him to write any stories about the insurrectionists, however, O'Riley announced he was leaving. The men jerked out their pistols and ordered O'Riley to go with them to Ojinaga. Thinking fast and recklessly, the correspondent hit the man nearest him and drew his own weapon. "The first shot dropped an assailant before he could fire. Each of the others got in a shot at close range, but by a miracle, went wild, and before a second round could be fired, O'Riley's deadly aim had done its work. One he was compelled to shoot the second time." The reporter then rode back to the American side of the river and filed his remarkable story.[9]

Just a few months later, in June 1911, Inez Salazar and a band of 30 revolutionists surrounded the ranch house of Lamar Davis, an American, at nearby San Antonio, Chihuahua, and demanded provisions, guns and ammunition, horses and saddles. Francisco and Dario Sánchez, the ranch managers, were able to contact the government commander at Presidio, who sent a party to chase the raiders away, but not before they had gathered up a large number of guns and supplies. Again, refugees poured into Texas, and the commander of the Southern Department at Fort Sam Houston used the raid as the excuse to keep a few troops in the Big Bend there, rather than withdraw them, as some military men had pressured him to do.[10]

Similar incidents up and down the river made crossings even at established border checkpoints difficult. The Mexican commander at Ojinaga likewise limited entry, provoking a complaint from Congressman William R. Smith, whose district included Presidio.[11] When a government officer scattered a band of 25 bandits just across the river from Candelaria the following year, he left a dozen troops at San Antonio to help the Americans under Capt. Frank A. Barton pacify the area.[12] J. O. Langford, who operated a bath concession at Hot Springs, realized that danger was near when he heard that residents had vacated San Vicente, Coahuila, the village that had grown up near the old presidio, and he advised his guests to gather at his house, which could be transformed into a fort if necessary. When he heard that the bandits had plundered Boquillas and San Vicente, he concluded that he was in imminent danger. Langford and Jesse Deemer of Boquillas rode to Marathon and requested that troops be stationed near the river. Lt. Everett Collins and 25 men were dispatched to La Noria, where they took up their patrol along the river.[13]

Troops Leave the Big Bend

Early in 1913, however, the troops were withdrawn. Lt. Collins advised Langford of their departure and recommended that he move his family to a safer location. "That word shook me up," recalled the resort owner. "I realized that Collins would not have risked court martial for revealing army secrets if he had not felt that our danger here was immediate and great." [14]

Perhaps the most feared raiders were the Cano brothers, José, Manuel, and Chico. They were suspected of ambushing U.S. Customs Inspectors Joe Sitters and J. S. Howard and cattle association inspector J. W. Harwick in January 1913, killing Howard and wounding Sitters. "They were not Carranzistas, they were not Villistas, they were not anything," claimed E. W. Nevill of the Canos. "Whoever is in charge on the border . . . they are with." Some thought that they might have been responsible for the ensuing raids of the Lee Hancock ranch, 14 miles northeast of Alpine, and the Lawrence Haley ranch. "The lower part of Brewster County is a desolate and broken mountain country," reported the *Alpine Avalanche*, "and . . . it would be a hard matter to locate anyone familiar with that section who was trying to avoid detection. As the Mexicans are known to be bad men and are armed to the teeth, there has been much uneasiness felt about those who are pursuing them. . . ." [15]

Such incidents provoked citizen demands that soldiers be returned to the Big Bend. J. R. Landrum, postmaster at Boquillas, appealed to Texas Senator Morris Sheppard, pointing out that Boquillas was 100 miles from the railroad, was "scarcely settled," and provided an inviting target for raiders. The *Alpine Avalanche* joined in the campaign, and Texas Governor Oscar B. Colquitt authorized Sheriff J. Allen Walton to deputize as many men as he felt necessary to "properly safe-guard the interests of the citizens" and wired President William H. Taft to send help. Still, the commander of the Southern Department, worried about the need for troops in other areas, concluded that he had no troops to spare.[16]

Texas Governor James E. Ferguson saw a May 1915 murder as characteristic of the violence occurring all along the state's southern border. In response to the discovery of the *Plan de San Diego*, a revolutionary document that called for Hispanics on both sides of the border to rally in a combined revolution and race war, Ferguson had sent virtually the entire Texas Ranger force to the Rio Grande Valley. Just as in South Texas, Mexican raiders had crossed the border into Texas: Capt. G. C. Barnhart of the 15th Cavalry reported that some supposed Villa men had shot and beaten Pablo Jiménez. "I have a piece of his skull," he claimed.[17] And, just as in South Texas, it now seemed that cultural upheaval cultivated the unrest in the Big Bend. While the percentage of Mexicans living there increased by more than fifty percent between 1910 and 1920, that figure alone conceals the population shift that occurred. Many of those who had been living in proximity to the border for years vacated in the face of increasing violence, to be replaced by newly-arrived refugees fleeing the bloodshed in Mexico.

Secretary of War Lindley M. Garrison initially agreed with Ferguson that additional troops should be sent to the Big Bend, but after consulting General Funston, commander of the Southern Department, he declined to recommend action. Believing that many of the bandits were citizens of Texas, Funston insisted that the Texas Rangers or the local sheriffs should handle the matters. "The distance from Brownsville to El Paso . . . is over twelve hundred miles, following the windings of the river," Garrison wrote, "and part of it is about as inaccessible and difficult a country as can be imagined, so that it will not in any circumstances be possible to station troops throughout that entire stretch. . . ." [18]

The chaos in Mexico continued to breed unrest and periodic border raids in the Big Bend. Four bandits attempted to wreck a train east of Alpine in March 1916, but alert soldiers prevented any damage. Most people felt that the raiders were members of Villa's band, which was a significant force in the Mexican Revolution until he was defeated at the battle of Celaya and driven into the desert of northern Chihuahua. Then, Villa turned to guerrilla warfare and survived on aid from the United States, rendered in many cases by several Big Bend businessmen, merchants, and even Howard Perry, owner of the Chisos Mining Company in Terlingua, who increased their profit margins by smuggling guns and ammunition to Villa in return for stolen cattle.

When President Wilson discontinued all aid to Villa in 1916, hoping thereby to end the revolution and enable President Venustiano Carranza to restore order, Villa retaliated. On March 9 he attacked Columbus, N. Mex. In addition to obtaining food and supplies for his ragged troops, he hoped to force the United States to react, thereby embarrassing President Carranza. Many felt that the attack on Columbus was also a signal to army deserters and local gangs that they could now raid the isolated U.S. settlements along the border with impunity.[19] The President, of course, did send Gen. John J. Pershing into Mexico in an attempt to chastise Villa for the raid at Columbus, but the Big Bend itself remained unprotected.[20]

Raids on Glenn Springs and Boquillas

On the evening of May 5, raiders hit both Glenn Springs and Boquillas, thrusting the Big Bend into the international spotlight and creating what would have been a major diplomatic incident had it not been for Villa's raid on Columbus, N. Mex. A party of perhaps 80 bandits crossed the Rio Grande near San Vicente and attacked the candellia wax plant at Glenn Springs, while a smaller group headed toward Jesse Deemer's store at Boquillas. Located on a rise in the foothills of the Chisos Mountains, Glenn Springs was the home of C. D. Wood and W. K. Ellis, partners in a wax factory employing about 50 Mexicans. The bandits overwhelmed the small army detachment from the 14th Cavalry stationed there and fell on the small general store that Wood and Ellis had established to serve the needs of the workers and their families.[21]

Asleep in his home 2 miles from the village, Wood, a veteran of the Philippine campaign, was awakened by the sound of shots, but he was unable to offer any aid to the hapless victims. He first thought what he heard were the celebrative sounds of *Cinco de Mayo,* the holiday recalling Mexico's defeat of the French at Puebla in 1862. When he realized that what he heard were actual shots, he quickly dressed and aroused his neighbor, Oscar de Montel, another army veteran. Carrying rifles, they hurried through the night toward the flames and sound of shooting. "We stumbled through whipping brush and annoying cactus," said Wood. By the

Capt. C. D. Wood

After the raid on Glenn Springs, two troops of
the 6th Cavalry arrived and set up camp.

time they got there two hours later, the firing had stopped and the
flames had died, but the bandits were busily ransacking the store.

"Quién vive?" (literally, "who lives?") shouted the bandits'
picket as the pair approached. The response, common during the
Mexican Revolution, should have been "Viva Villa" ("Villa lives"),
but Montel replied, "Quién es?" ("Who is it"), and bullets soon
whistled by the pair as the sentinel began firing in the direction of
the voice. They hid in the hills until the bandits left at daybreak
with their wounded, the loot, and nine cavalry horses. Wood found
the body of only one bandit. Ellis escaped harm and drove to Marathon the next day to report the incident.[22]

The second group of raiders hit Boquillas, an even smaller
community. Situated directly across the river from the Mexican
village by the same name, it was the terminal for the aerial tramway that brought silver ore from the nearby mines in Mexico.
Realizing that they were outnumbered, Deemer and his black clerk,
Monroe Payne, offered no resistance. They gave the bandits all
their money, allowed them to select the merchandise they wanted
from the shelves, and helped them pack it. In no hurry because
they knew they were safe in such an isolated place, the robbers
worked methodically until 10 a.m. when the group that had laid

165

Several soldiers fought the bandits from this adobe cook house at Glenn Springs.

waste to Glenn Springs arrived. Taking Deemer and Payne captive, the bandits crossed the river. Deemer probably would have been killed immediately had not several of the party argued that he be spared because of the many kindnesses he had rendered to Mexican families around Boquillas, suggesting that some of the raiders might have been local residents.[23]

As the raiders passed through Boquillas, Coahuila, they split up. One group paused at the American-managed silver mine to rob the company store and take the mine payroll, along with six more prisoners, including Dr. Homer Powers, the mine physician, and the superintendent. Because they were so loaded with booty that they could hardly carry it, the bandits confiscated a mining company truck. Lt. Col. Natividad Álvarez piled the loot onto the truck and ordered Dr. Powers and the three mine officials to get in. The other group rode ahead with Deemer and Payne.

The truck driver took advantage of the raiders' ignorance, driving as slowly as possible and allowing the mounted horsemen to get several miles ahead. Then he stalled the motor, complaining that it had overheated. They waited for the motor to "cool off," then pretended that the truck was stuck and tried to push it. Feigning that they could not free it, they suggested that if the guards would push, they could get it started. When the horsemen complied, the driver slipped the gears into reverse and released the clutch, knocking them to the ground. The Americans quickly gathered up the weapons, captured the bandits, and delivered them to the Brewster County sheriff.[24]

Coming so soon after Villa's Columbus raid, and while Pershing was in Mexico searching for Villa, the Boquillas and Glenn Springs attacks became an international incident. The bandits actually had conducted their raids while Generals Hugh Scott, Army Chief of Staff, and Funston of the United States and Alvaro Obregón of Mexico were meeting in El Paso to negotiate Pershing's withdrawal. Now facing the possibility of another American invasion, Mexicans demanded that President Carranza take action, and both governments hardened their negotiating positions. Carranza denounced the raids, claiming that they were the work of lawless elements residing on the American side of the border, and demanded the withdrawal of American forces from Mexico before concluding agreements on any other pressing matters. Scott and Funston, meanwhile, concluded that the Big Bend was practically defenseless and predicted that such raids would continue. But they also believed that the Mexicans were powerless to stop such incursions, so they did not walk out of the meetings.[25]

The Little Punitive Expedition

Scott saw no alternative to sending more troops into Mexico if the bandits were going to be punished and Deemer and Payne rescued, and he assigned the task to Troops A and B of the 8th Cavalry under Maj. George T. Langhorne. A handsome, "dapper" officer, well-liked by his men, Langhorne was a decisive, courageous leader. A good horseman, the major led his men in drills as well as in combat. On the way from Fort Bliss at El Paso to Marathon, he and his men paused at Boquillas, Tex., to secure information, then on May 11 headed into the mountains, complete with reporters, photographers, and a motion picture crew in tow. The

Jesse Deemer   **Monroe Payne**

167

journalists rode in two Ford sedans, Langhorne in his chauffeur-driven Cadillac touring car, both loaded with grain for the horses. "The country isn't bad," one of the accompanying cameramen said. "It's just worse. Worse the moment you set foot from the train, and then, after that, just worser and worser." [26]

The bandits, meanwhile, had a 3-day head start in familiar country. They had split up, one group crossing the river at San Vicente and riding to El Pino and Sierra Mojada, the other fording the river near Deemer's store. Deemer got word to Langhorne that he and Payne were well cared for and being held at El Pino, and that the bandits wanted to trade them for Colonel Álvarez and the other prisoners who had been captured by the truck driver and his companions. Believing that the bandits did not know that he was within 15 miles of them, Langhorne dashed ahead in the cars with two dozen of his best marksmen. The cavalry was to follow as quickly as possible, but Langhorne made only 9 miles in 2 hours, so he decided to halt and wait for the cavalry. They made camp, slept fitfully, and spent the next day at a well called Aguaita, awaiting nightfall to begin the forced march.[27]

A few hours later Langhorne and his men surrounded El Pino. They advanced cautiously to within 400 yards of the village, but the bandits had been warned and were gone. They had left Deemer and Payne in the custody of the village *jefe*.[28] According to one reporter, Deemer revealed a proper perspective on the events, immediately asking one of the troopers, "How is the Verdun battle doing?" suggesting that he realized that far more turned upon that European battle than upon his capture. Deemer again drew the reporter's admiration when he turned down Major Langhorne's invitation to dine because of a previous engagement – dinner with some Mexican friends in one of El Pino's tumbled-down *jacales*.[29]

The troops had hardly settled in their temporary quarters when word came that some of the bandits had been spotted in the nearby village of Rosita, about 15 miles down the road. Langhorne now faced a difficult decision: he was already more than 100 miles into Mexico. Should he continue, knowing that Carranza's forces might soon be gathering to meet him? The captives were safe, so the only reason to continue was to punish the raiders and possibly

Natividad Álvarez, one of the raiders.

recover the loot. Feeling that the raiders should be punished, he yielded to the enthusiasm of his men: "I dropped my coffee, borrowed a rifle and two bandoleers of ammunition from the soldier nearest me [and] we started after them." [30]

As a dozen troops in the Cadillac and Fords approached the village of Rosita, four or five bandits dashed from a house into the brush in their view. The soldiers pursued them on foot, for the cars could not penetrate the thicket. Another bandit mounted a horse and rode off down the road. Returning to the Cadillac, several troops set out after him, their weapons blazing. "The last we saw of them" recalled Lt. Stuart W. Cramer, "the big car was bounding over the ditches and bushes like a steeplechaser, to the tune of a merry cannonading." When the other soldiers finally arrived at Rosita, they learned that the bandits had escaped again. [31]

While he waited for the rest of his force, Major Langhorne established a temporary camp at El Pino and sent out scouting parties. Lieutenant Cramer was given command of eight men and told to return to El Pino by a circuitous route that would allow him to search for a band of raiders who were reportedly staying at Castillón Ranch. When Cramer protested that the country did not offer anything in the way of food or water – a problem that hundreds before him had faced – and requested permission to pack rations, Langhorne refused, saying that it would be a "valuable experience" for Cramer, allowing him to "exercise . . . great ingenuity." [32]

Giving his sergeant time to secretly purchase what food he could from the soldiers and residents of Rosita, Cramer set out for Castillón. Approaching cautiously, he managed to surprise about

169

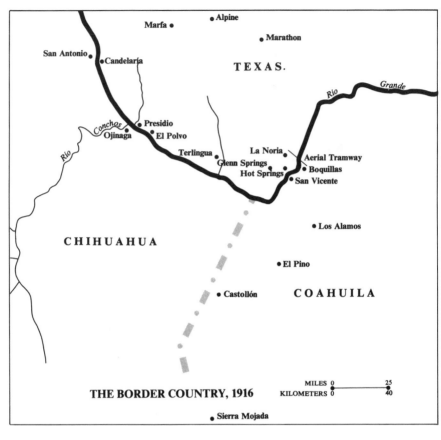

TEXAS.

Rio Grande

CHIHUAHUA

COAHUILA

THE BORDER COUNTRY, 1916

MILES	0	25
KILOMETERS	0	40

Alpine
Marfa
Marathon
San Antonio
Candelaria
Presidio
Conchos
Ojinaga
El Polvo
Rio
Terlingua
La Noria
Glenn Springs
Aerial Tramway
Hot Springs
Boquillas
San Vicente
Los Alamos
El Pino
Castollón
Sierra Mojada

The journalists who accompanied Langhorne
and their Mexican guards.

Col. George T. Langhorne was more successful but received less publicity than Gen. John Pershing in leading an American force into Mexico in pursuit of bandits in 1916.

a dozen armed men at the Santa Anita well. He correctly guessed that they were part of the bandit gang, although his logic – "the *pacífico* always wears a big straw sombrero" – was a bit flawed. Deploying his men along a crest overlooking the well, Cramer ordered them to attack about an hour after sunset. One bandit fell, and the soldiers rushed over the hill and down toward the windmill. Two other bandits now fell wounded. At the foot of the hill an old man held up his hands and pleaded that he was a *pacífico* who had been captured a few days before and forced to accompany the bandits. His hand had been shattered from a bullet wound. Cramer left him under guard and pursued the others. The bandits were soon lost in the darkness.[33]

Cramer returned to the windmill to survey the victory. In their fright the Mexicans had escaped with nothing more than their handguns and the clothes they wore, abandoning a wagon, 17 horses and mules, nine rifles, two swords, and several saddles, bridles, and packs. But not everything had gone well. For safekeeping the guards had put the old man in the well, which made an ideal prison, but his wound bled so profusely that it spoiled the water. As badly as they wanted rest, the weary troops had to continue their march in hope of finding drinkable water.

Before reaching camp, they had quite a scare. U.S. intelligence had picked up several rumors to the effect that an elite force of Yaqui Indians from the Mexican Secretary of War's personal guard had been sent to deal with the intruders. As Cramer and his men rode slowly toward Cerro Blanco with the captured goods, one of the troopers spotted a cloud of dust behind them. "My heart sank," remembered the lieutenant, "as I was not in any shape to fight, with my men nearly dead with fatigue, and all the plunder to hamper us. I saw visions of being attacked by a bunch of bandits

171

or by Carranza troops, and the spoiling of my success, and the losing of my loot, just as I was about to get into camp with it." Cramer ordered his men to set up an ambush, but there was no time. They simply laid down in the road and prepared to fight the column advancing toward them.[34]

Just before they opened fire, one of Cramer's men saw in the dim light of dawn that all the horses were black and of similar size and that the men were uniformed. He shouted that the approaching troops were Americans. The party turned out to be a detachment from Troop A that had seen Cramer's scraggly men and their plunder and had concluded that they were the bandits.[35]

The "little punitive expedition" into Mexico had proved to be a success. Deemer and Payne had been freed, most of the supplies taken from both Glenn Springs and Boquillas recaptured, and several bandits killed and wounded, five captured, and the others dispersed. Langhorne's report convinced Col. Frederick W. Sibley that the mission had been completed, and General Funston recalled the force. Langhorne's men had been in Mexico 16 days, had traveled more than 550 miles, and had suffered no casualties. Although the Carranza government was upset at the incursion, it was in many ways more successful than Pershing's more widely publicized pursuit of Villa.[36]

Occupation of the Big Bend

After the Glenn Springs and Boquillas raids, Generals Scott and Funston sent a joint telegram to President Wilson asking that the National Guard be called out to protect the Trans-Pecos. Acting according to a long-range plan intended to intimidate Mexico by placing guardsmen at strategic points along the border, on May 9 the President called up the Texas, New Mexico, and Arizona National Guards. By midnight, July 4, troops from 14 States had taken up positions along the Mexican border. By the end of the month over 100,000 men had been sent to four major assembly areas, three in Texas and one in Arizona.[37]

General Scott then continued his discussions with Obregón from a strengthened hand. Pershing's army was still in Chihuahua, and the National Guard lined the border, bored and anxious for action. "I told him that if he wanted to lose his country, the surest way to do it would be to attack Pershing," Scott later wrote. Under these circumstances, Scott and Obregón concluded their talks, penning a lengthy agreement that stipulated that Pershing would pull back but be allowed to remain in Mexico. Although President Carranza repudiated the agreement, Scott concluded that it "made little difference . . . since everything went on as if agreed upon by all."

One of the companies sent to the Big Bend was Company I, 4th Texas Infantry. After several months in Marathon, it transferred south to Stillwell's Crossing and La Noria, both on the Rio Grande. Their specific duty was to guard the region against further incursions by Mexican raiders. One member of the company, Lt. William P. Cameron of Mineral Wells, Texas, reported that the area was quiet while they were there and his many snapshots of the company prove it: troops on guard, troops at mess, troops cleaning up, troops at leisure. But no troops in battle. They spent most of their time stringing telephone wire through the Sierra del Carmen and Boquillas Canyon to Boquillas, Texas, to improve the area's communications.[38]

Another national guardsman who left a personal view of this police duty was Jodie P. Harris, also from Mineral Wells. A caricaturist, Harris drew cartoons on postcards and mailed them home to Mineral Wells, where his friends displayed them in the local drug store. He also lettered a four-page weekly newspaper called *The Big Bend, a Paper with a Muzzle: Without a Mission,* which was picked up by the *Fort Worth Star-Telegram* and included in its Sunday editions. Several of his cartoons pictured unhappy privates engaged in makeshift jobs, officers dreaming up busywork for them, and awe-struck soldiers taking in the spectacular scenery.

Although the soldiers felt that they were wasting their time – even though they knew of the Glenn Springs and Boquillas raids – that did not stop them from appreciating the beauty and uniqueness of the land. Some of Harris's cartoon cards called attention to well known landmarks, and he joined what had already become a popular movement by depicting two soldiers admiring the scenery and agreeing that the region should be made a park. Another humorously made its point by showing soldiers trying to move a wagon mired in sand up to its axle. In a refrain frequently heard about areas that became national parks, the soldiers suggested, tongue in cheek, that the Big Bend was good for nothing but a park. Harris also promoted the park idea in his newspaper, and when the bill to create Big Bend finally reached Congress years later, guardsmen from several States who had served there in 1916 supported it.[39]

In late 1916 Company I was recalled from the Big Bend and sent to Europe the following year. Although they were replaced with other guardsmen, the country was not patrolled as closely as before, and by 1917 the raiders were back.

Brite Ranch Raid

Many Texans were shocked on Christmas Day 1917 to learn that raiders had crossed the border and attacked the L. C. Brite Ranch. About sunup that day approximately 45 bandits rode into the ranch, located between Marfa and the Rio Grande about fifteen miles east of the river. The likely target was the ranch's general merchandise store, which served dozens of ranch employees and residents. Because of the ruthlessness – and because it happened on Christmas Day – news of the attack was carried in newspapers across the country.[40]

The bandits had probably chosen Christmas Day for the raid because they expected that few people would be at the ranch. Indeed, the Brites were at their home in Marfa that day, and only Van Neill, the ranch foreman, and his family were there. But others were expected for lunch, and the bandits soon faced what must have seemed like a continual parade of new arrivals.

Van Neill's father, Sam, was up early that morning sipping his coffee in the early dawn when he saw the bandits ride into the ranch complex and disperse. He ran into his son's room, grabbed a rifle, and quickly shot the man who appeared to be the leader. The bandits then returned the fire. Neill and his son held the bandits off from the house, but were unable to get any help. The raiders had cut the ranch's telephone lines.

The raiders took two ranch hands prisoner and sent one in to tell Neill and his father that the other would be killed if they did not surrender. Mrs. Neill begged Van and his father to stop fighting and to give the bandits the key to the store, hoping that they would then go away. Meanwhile, unknown to the Neills, the bandits had captured Mickey Welch, the postman, and two passengers in the mail stage who had ridden unknowingly into the ranch, and killed them, perhaps because one of them might have recognized some of the

Troop B, 1st Cavalry of the Texas National Guard on their way to Ruidosa in 1916.

gang. As the bandits looted the store and rounded up the best horses, guests began arriving for Christmas dinner with the Neills. The first was Rev. H. M. Bandy, the preacher for the First Christian Church in Marfa, and his family. Just as the bandits were about to open fire on them, Neill sent a Mexican boy out to tell them that Bandy was a *padre* (priest), and Bandy and his passengers were allowed to enter the house. Bandy knelt and led everyone in prayer, then asked for a rifle to help defend the house. Other dinner guests escaped when the store manager warned them and asked them to go for help.

Meanwhile, James L. Cobb, a neighbor, had heard the shots and had driven to the ranch to investigate. From a distance, he saw the Mexicans looting the ranch and drove to the nearest telephone and called the sheriff. Soon a large posse assembled and, traveling in automobiles, almost caught the raiders, who were considerably slowed by all their loot, but they got away by crossing the Candelaria Rim only 8 miles away, where the cars could not follow. The next day a larger party, including Troops M and G of the 8th Cavalry, gathered to pursue the raiders. Crossing the river at Los Fresnos, they engaged a number of the raiders near the Rio Grande and a running fight ensued, ending up near the Mexican village of Pilares. Several of the raiders were killed – no one knows how many – much of the loot recovered, and the troops returned to the American side of the river.

These soldiers replaced their hot tents with cooler mud houses that provided protection from the wind and helped settle the choking dust.

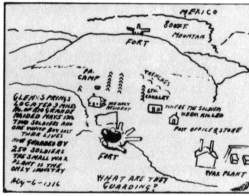

According to this Jodie Harris cartoon, the troops found little to protect at Glenn Springs.

One of Harris' characters declared that the Big Bend was good for nothing but a national park.

The Porvenir Massacre

The Brite Ranch raid shocked Big Bend residents, and, despite the army's success, citizens called for an official response. They formed a vigilance committee with the intent of registering and disarming all the Mexican population in Brewster, Presidio, Jeff Davis, Culberson, and Hudspeth counties. Racial tensions increased as the committee declared that suspicious individuals would be watched. With most of the army still in Europe, or miles from the border, the primary responsibility for the defense of the Big Bend fell on the Texas Rangers, who faced a difficult enough task, even without the circumstances under which they worked. C. A. Hawley recalled that their wages were low and the work hard. As a result, he said, the Rangers did "not attract very capable men. Those I met at Terlingua were a pretty cheap sort – men who loved to show their authority and swagger around with a gun on the hip, ready to shoot somebody."

Local ranchers intent upon vengeance for the raid convinced Ranger Capt. J. M. Fox that the Mexican population of Porvenir, across the river from the Mexican village of Pilares, were "spies and informers" for bandits living on the Mexican side of the river. The Captain authorized a group of Rangers accompanied by a number of locals to investigate and question the residents of Porvenir. At midnight on January 24, 1918, the party, some wearing masks, rode into Porvenir. They roused the sleeping Mexicans and held them at gunpoint while searching their *jacales* for weapons and loot. Finding two rifles, a shotgun, and a pistol, they confiscated the weapons and questioned three villagers who were wearing shoes of a type similar to those taken from the Brite store, then released them.

But this was not the end of the matter. On January 27, a group of Rangers arrived at Camp Evetts, an 8th Cavalry border outpost near Porvenir, and presented a letter from Col. Langhorne ordering the local commander to assist the Rangers in another inspection of Porvenir. The Rangers and army surrounded the village at about midnight, again rousting out the residents and searching their homes. This time they found only one old gun and several knives that had been overlooked in the previous search. They asked the troops to withdraw while they questioned their prisoners, then they separated the men from the women and marched fifteen men off to a rock bluff about a mile from the village and shot them. Quickly mounting their horses, the Rangers rode off into the night, leaving the stunned troopers to deal with the devastation. The survivors of the massacre abandoned the village and returned to Mexico before daylight. Some had lived in Porvenir for years, although most were newcomers, refugees from the violence in Mexico.

In his report of the incident, Captain Fox, who apparently was not involved in the affair, claimed that his men had come under fire while conducting their investigation and had returned the fire, killing the 15 victims. Fox also charged that his men had found property in the village that had been taken from the Brite ranch. Even the army participated in the coverup, later claiming not to know who had committed the murders and saying that they had found the bodies of the victims when they had arrived at the village at dawn.

One who refused to accept that explanation was Harry Warren, the schoolteacher in Porvenir, whose father-in-law was one of those murdered. Because of his continued efforts, the Mexican government finally took up the case, protesting the murders to the American government. That resulted in Texas Ranger Captain W. M. Hanson's visit to Marfa, supposedly to investigate the Mexican government charges, but, in fact, he was much more concerned about gathering support for his new boss, Texas Governor

Mickey Welch's mail stage.

Rev. H. M. Bandy.

After the 1917 raid, L. C. Brite built this adobe fort, but it was never needed.

178

William P. Hobby, who as Lieutenant Governor had replaced the impeached Ferguson and now faced election on his own. Despite the continuing coverup, Warren and others also forced the Army to reopen the incident, resulting in the charge that the Rangers were guilty of murdering the Porvenir residents. The Texas Adjutant General concluded that although the Rangers had handled the problem in an unorthodox manner, justice had been served, but Governor Hobby disagreed and dismissed Capt. J. M. Fox and his entire company of Texas Rangers, although no criminal charges were filed. Fox later claimed that his dismissal was politically inspired, but the Porvenir case was included as one of the most damaging bits of evidence in state representative J. T. Canales's investigation of the Rangers in 1919. The Senate ran out of time before it could be presented, and no criminal charges were ever filed, but the Rangers were completely reorganized as a result of the many charges brought against them.[41]

Nevill Ranch Raid

The Pilares and Porvenir attacks, although intended to impress upon the Mexicans that they would be punished for their misdeeds, only inspired additional vengeful acts. The raid on the Nevill Ranch 3 months later, the last large-scale raid in the Big Bend, was a direct payback for the Porvenir murders.

Capt. Jerry Gray's company of Texas Rangers at Marfa, 1918. They replaced the company dismissed after the Pilares raid.

On March 25, 1918, the army captain at Van Horn received a report from one of his informers across the border that some bandits were planning a raid on the nearby Bell Ranch. A patrol dispatched to the area found no bandits, but Ed Nevill, in Van Horn on his monthly supply trip, heard the rumors and returned to home. He and John Wyatt had leased a ranch about 6 miles up the Rio Grande from Porvenir. The nearest neighbor was about 12 miles away, and the ranch had no telephone. He arrived after an 8-hour ride to find a peaceful scene.

Relieved, he and his son were sitting in the front room discussing the next day's chores when some horsemen rode up. Believing that they were troopers returning from a nearby ranch, Ed was not alarmed, but as soon as the riders saw him, they opened fire. He grabbed his rifle and ran for a ditch about 250 yards from the house, because the bullets were easily penetrating the thin walls of the house. He made it, but his son was fatally wounded in the head just a few steps out of the house. The bandits also murdered the wife of one of the Mexican ranch hands and made off with the horses, ranch supplies, clothes, and bedding. Nevill wandered through the night until the raiders left at about 3:30 a.m. He recognized one of them as a resident of nearby San Antonio, Chihuahua, and credited Chico Cano and his gang with the raid.

Probably about the time the raiders were crossing back into Mexico, Maj. Henry H. Anderson of the 8th Cavalry arrived with some troopers. Langhorne, who had been promoted and named commander of the Big Bend district, had received word of the attack at midnight and immediately ordered Troop G to proceed from at a nearby ranch to Nevill's. Troop A was sent by rail to Valentine, where they disembarked, rode to the Rio Grande, and joined Troop G. They followed the bandits, who had crossed near Pilares. They rode into an ambush, and a vicious battle followed. Some reports claimed that 32 bandits and one American were killed. The soldiers continued the fighting in Pilares, destroying several houses. Again they found some of the stolen loot, adding to the village's reputation as an outlaw hangout. The Nevill ranch raid appears to have been carried out in revenge for the Porvenir massacres. Robbery could hardly have been the motive, for Ed

Chico Cano (center), the tough Mexican bandit,
and his pursuer, Capt. Leonard F. Matlack (right).

Nevill had little to steal. The proximity of his ranch simply made
him the most convenient target.[42]

There were several smaller raids, but surveillance in Texas
increased and the situation in Mexico began to stabilize. After the
National Guard was recalled from the Big Bend, Langhorne's 8th
Cavalry squadron was stationed at Marfa and given instructions to
patrol the Rio Grande country. Believing that the temporary posts
should be bolstered, the government leased land from Howard E.
Perry and Wayne R. Cartledge in 1919 to build Camp Santa Helena near what is today Castolon. The post was never constructed
as originally planned, for a large force was no longer necessary.
The final plans called for one officers' quarters, two barracks, one
kitchen mess, one lavatory, two quarters for non-coms, two stables,
one blacksmith shop-guardhouse combination, one hay shed, and
a grain barn, but only one barracks, a lavatory, a barn, a corral and
stables, and one building each for officers and noncommissioned
officers was built. The camp was ready for occupation in early
1920.[43]

The River Pilots

When Pancho Villa's men attacked Ciudad Juárez for the
third time in June 1919, the American government ordered the

**Several planes were lost in the Big Bend while
searching for bandits.**

Army Air Service to begin regular patrols along the river. Surveillance in the Big Bend was the responsibility of two military districts: the Big Bend District, which stretched from Comstock to Sanderson to Boquillas, and the El Paso District, which included Boquillas to Presidio to Marfa. The "Big Chickens," as the horse soldiers called the flimsy DeHavillands, were supposed to find out where Villa had gone. They were also to spot any bands and move in close to determine what they were doing and which direction they were headed. Any bandit movements were to be reported to the troops on the ground. Although the pilots were not supposed to cross the Rio Grande, they often did, particularly if they were looking for something or someone. As the raids in the Big Bend decreased, the ranchers grew appreciative of the "River Pilots." [44]

This esteem was proven in August 1919, when two flyers, Lt. H. G. Peterson and P. H. Davis, went down near Boyame, Chihuahua, while on a routine patrol. Flying upriver from Lajitas, Peterson and Davis mistook the Río Conchos for the Rio Grande and turned into Mexico. Four connecting-rod bearings burned out, forcing them to land in rough terrain. Still thinking they were over the United States, the airmen made certain that they landed on the northern side of the river, coming down in pasture covered with mesquites, paloverde, and greasewood. They broke the landing gear and wrecked the plane in the landing. (The DeHavillands, often called a "flaming coffin" by the pilots, had an unretractable axle connecting the two front landing wheels, rough terrain or brush would break the axle and sometimes flip the plane over.) Still believing they were in Texas, the lieutenants headed downriver, expecting to find Candelaria and the army post there.[45]

Peterson and Davis were captured by Chico Cano's gang, led by Jesus Rentería, variously called "Corklet," "Gancho" (or hook, because he had an artificial arm and steel hook), or "Mocho" (maimed). Rentería was well known in the Big Bend as one of Cano's horse thieves and robbers. During the raid on the Brite ranch he reportedly had sat on Mickey Welch's body while an accomplice held Welch's hair and slit the man's throat with a penknife. "Slim" Olívas and Delores Navarrette reportedly assisted Rentería in the capture.

The lieutenants were allowed to send out messages saying that they were being held for ransom, but that they were well treated and in good health. A messenger delivered Rentería's demand for a $15,000 ransom to Dawkins Kilpatrick, a storekeeper and a rancher at Candelaria on August 17: Send $15,000 in cash by midnight, August 18, or the flyers would be killed, he wrote. When word of the airmen's capture reached a group of Big Bend ranchers attending Bloys Camp Meeting, near Marfa, the money was raised in just a few minutes. Grateful for the aid they had received from the "River Pilots," the ranchers authorized the Marfa

The ransom money for the captured lieutenants leaves the Marfa National Bank.

National Bank to deliver the money to Capt. Leonard F. Matlack at Candelaria.

Negotiating with Rentería by notes delivered by Tomás Sánchez, Matlack arranged for ransoming the prisoners one at a time. Peterson was brought safely to the American side. When Matlack returned for Davis, he overheard the bandits planning to kill them after the money was delivered. Acting quickly, he drew his pistol on the bandits and ordered Davis to get on the horse behind him. Matlack returned to the Rio Grande by a different route, thereby avoiding the suspected ambush. Captain Matlack had brought the airmen safely back to the American side and saved $6,500 of the rancher's money ($1,000 was given to Sánchez for his assistance). Colonel Langhorne declared that the officer deserved a decoration.

As soon as the flyers were safe, Colonel Langhorne ordered troops into Mexico to chase Rentería and his men in what became the last of the punitive expeditions into Mexico. The "River Pilots" served as their "eyes," flying low over the harsh terrain, searching for any suspects. Messages were then dropped to the cavalry, indicating the direction the suspects were headed. The results were immediate. Sergeant William H. Nealing's patrol encountered three Mexicans who immediately surrendered. Although they were not members of Rentería's band, U.S. authorities wanted them on other charges. They were turned over to the civilian scouts, who took them off into a canyon and shot them. (An officer was later court martialed for the action.) Lts. F. S. Estill and R. H. Cooper spotted Rentería's gang on the afternoon of the first day. Flying low over the canyons and mountains, they suddenly realized that three horsemen below were firing at them with rifles. Turning the craft toward the trio (the Marlin machine guns were aimed by pointing the plane at the target), pilot Estill began firing. As they flew by, Cooper fired more rounds with the Lewis machine gun mounted on the rear cockpit. They reported that both Rentería and his white horse were killed. (Of course, stories still circulate in the Big Bend that Rentería survived the attack and lived along the border until he died of old age in the 1970s.)

The pilots communicated with troops on the ground by dropping messages.

Langhorne recalled the troops and proclaimed success. Rentería was reported killed, and the civilian scouts had killed four other bandits. The raiders, who at one time had seemed to reign supreme in the Big Bend, proved to be no match for the DeHavillands. The Big Bend was on the verge of peace after a decade of turmoil.

The Big Bend figured in another pilot search in 1921. Lt. Alexander Pearson, a crack pilot in the 12th Aero Border Patrol Squadron, attempted to fly from the Pacific to the Atlantic across the southern United States with only two service stops. The crankshaft broke, forcing him down near Columbus, N. Mex. After repairs, he flew into Fort Bliss at El Paso on February 8, 1921. He left Fort Bliss the next day, intending to land in San Antonio or Houston. But he encountered a fierce norther in the Big Bend and was blown far off course. Somewhere over the mountains the bearings of his crankshaft froze up, forcing him to land in rough terrain. Like Peterson and Davis, he thought he was in the United States when he was really in Mexico. He walked along the Rio Grande, hoping to find a ranch or a village. Two Mexican horsemen aided him, and he met J. E. Murrah, foreman of the Rutledge ranch, who loaned him a horse for the ride into Sanderson. "A good meal and bed was all I wanted that night, as I was pretty well exhausted," he told reporters. "The worst thing about this is that I lose my chance to try the transcontinental record." Pearson's plane was finally repaired and flown out of the valley where he had landed – "Las Vegas de los Ladrones" (the Lowlands of the Thieves) – on the Mexican side of the river east of Boquillas.[46]

**The 1st Cavalry Division, from Fort Bliss, Texas,
arrives in Marfa in 1929 for maneuvers.**

By 1921 the Big Bend had quieted down to a point where the army could discontinue aerial patrols. The circumstances that spawned the raids were unique. Mexico had undergone tremendous revolution and social upheaval. Settlement in the Big Bend was so sparse that defense was practically impossible. Several wealthy ranches, two large mines, and numerous wax factories were within easy striking distance of the Rio Grande. J. O. Langford operated his resort at Hot Springs. Jesse Deemer his store at Boquillas, and Brite his ranch in the Capote Mountains. Most of them evacuated their homes at one time or another during the chaotic years. One who stayed was Dawkins Kilpatrick, who mounted a machine gun on the roof of his store in Candelaria. Army occupation, increased settlement, and stability in Mexico combined to bring peace. Soon fur trappers hunted their prey in the Rio Grande and Río Conchos canyons, farmers moved into the Castolon area to raise cotton, and ranchers returned to their herds.

Geologist Robert T. Hill had written some of the most fanciful stories about the bloodthirsty thieves and bandits of the Big Bend after his seemingly uneventful trip down the Rio Grande in 1899, and the region's reputation for violence died hard. By the turn of the century, however, civilization had overtaken the region. With the end of the Mexican revolutionary era, a peace that had existed with a few sensational interruptions was reestablished. Outlaws, cattle rustlers, and smugglers did not disappear, and their feats became less colorful if no less publicized, but former Texas Ranger E. E. Townsend admitted 30 years after the fact that Hill had exaggerated the lawlessness of the Big Bend, and the dream of the early-day National Guardsmen – that the region be made a national park – grew into a reality.

7/The National Park

Quiet spoken and somewhat timid, Everett Ewing Townsend was nevertheless a man of deeds. Coming to the Big Bend young, he had seen firsthand its spellbinding mountains and canyons. He had ridden through the cacti and riverbottom on horseback as a customs inspector for the United States government and searched its valleys and deserts as a Texas Ranger. As sheriff of Brewster County the Big Bend was his paradise; as a member of the Texas legislature it became a personal cause. Throughout the struggle to establish a national park in West Texas, Townsend made contacts, wrote letters, and lobbied with the influential. He was a cowboy who had spent most of his life in the nearest thing to the frontier in West Texas, rather than a forceful man or a diplomat. He wanted to preserve what was left of the Texas wilderness for others, and by the time he was through, the Big Bend was a national park, and he was its "father." [1]

When Texas deeded 707,894 acres of the Big Bend country to the Federal Government in 1944, it was the fruit of many years of dreaming and working by scores of people. Townsend was, perhaps, the first to think of the region as a park. But the soldiers who came in 1916 helped spread the notion. Col. Frederick W. Sibley and Col. George T. Langhorne, who had spent several years riding through the rough country, recounted the splendor of the region. The early visitors were impressed with grandeur that local residents took for granted, and returned home carrying news of the Chisos, Santa Elena Canyon, and the great variety of bird life. So when the proposal for a Big Bend National Park surfaced in 1935, there was ready made national support for the idea.

One of Jodie Harris' illustrated postcards to the "folks back home" pictured a conversation between Major Coulter of the 10th Pennsylvania and Capt. E. A. Davis of Company I, 4th Texas. "The Big Bend is a wonderful country – moulded by nature for a park" says Coulter. "Sure!" answers Davis. "It's Great! When we get back home let's start a move to make it a *National Park*." Shown on a cliff overlooking the camp, the two men seem to be sharing what Harris terms a "new Big Bend." Picked up by the

"The Window" (sometimes called "The Pour Off")
in the Chisos Basin.

Fort Worth Star-Telegram, the picture was spread across the State.[2]

The Big Bend found new friends in the 1920s. Victor Schoffelmayer, agricultural editor for the *Dallas Morning News* and president of the Texas Geographic Society, first visited the proposed park with Dr. W. D. Hunter's entomological expedition in 1920. His writing popularized the region as, in Robert Hill's phrase, the "Garden of Gods." In 1923 Max Bentley, a freelance journalist, sat talking with a friend beside the placid waters of the Rio Grande. "Some day this will become a great national park," the acquaintance ventured. Bentley listened with curiosity as the man recounted the wonders of the Big Bend: the scenic attractions, the interesting geological and biological examples, the Chisos Mountains, the Rio Grande itself. Impressed, he returned to Alpine and wrote the first news article promoting the idea for a Big Bend National Park.[3]

Texas Canyons State Park

Still nothing was done to transform the idea into reality until 1931 when a newly-elected state legislator, R. M. Wagstaff from Abilene, became interested in the Big Bend. Wagstaff had seen the December 1930 issue of *Nature Magazine,* in which J. Frank Dobie, a folklorist and writer on the faculty at the University of Texas, had summarized the "distinctive charms" of Texas and lamented the fact that none of the millions of acres of Texas' public land had been set aside for a park. The scenery and international character of the Big Bend particularly intrigued him. During the second session of the 42nd legislature, Wagstaff began to investigate whether the State owned any land in the Big Bend that might be set aside for a park. As a lawyer, he was familiar with the laws regarding the State's public lands, so he called upon Land Commissioner J. H. Walker, feeling that there was real potential for a park in West Texas. Wagstaff and Walker discovered that the State did own thousands of acres in the Big Bend, and they also found out that several other tracts had been sold but had been forfeited within the last few months because of non-payment of interest. Walker could have proceeded with forfeiture of the land at that moment, but the policy of the General Land Office required that the owners be notified that the interest was overdue and that

Although the soldiers were glad to leave the Big Bend, they recognized the uniqueness of the country and suggested it should be a national park.

Everett E. Townsend, "father" of Big Bend National Park.

they be given an opportunity to pay. He suggested that Wagstaff defer filing his bill for a State park until the next session of the legislature, when the owners' options would have expired and they would know precisely how much land the State owned.

Wagstaff was ready for action when the next session of the legislature convened in January 1933. Checking with the land office, he found that none of the owners had paid the interest and that many more acres were now legally in the hands of the State. Since he was from Taylor County, a long way from the Big Bend, Wagstaff contacted Townsend, then the representative from the 87th District including Brewster County, and B. Frank Haag of Midland, the 88th District, for support for the bill. By then Wagstaff had found Hill's 1901 article on the canyons of the Rio Grande and had been transported by the scientist's descriptions and pictures. Thrusting the story before Townsend, he asked, "Is this article true? Do you have all of this wonderful scenery out in your district?" Although Townsend felt that much of Hill's writing about the bandits of the Big Bend was exaggerated, he readily confirmed that Big Bend contained all the scenes Wagstaff referred to, and more. "But 99 percent of the people of our own state don't know of its existence," he lamented.[4]

Wagstaff pursued the idea. "Don't you have a lot of unsold public school land along the canyons?" "Doubtless there is," answered Townsend. "It's not worth a damn for any commercial purpose, so why should people bother to own it?" Townsend was correct, but most of the river bottom, mountain, and scenic land was privately owned.

Wagstaff spurred Townsend into action. Not wanting to begin without consulting his constituents, Townsend first wrote to several, then returned to Alpine to talk with them. Assured of their cooperation, he came to Austin with a portfolio of excellent pictures of Santa Elena, Mariscal, and Boquillas canyons, the Chisos Mountains, and other scenic points in the Big Bend. Many of the pictures used to publicize the region were either taken by or gathered by a photographer who had first come to the Big Bend as a mule teamster in 1916, W. D. Smithers of Alpine.

Supported by Townsend and Haag, Wagstaff introduced a bill setting aside fifteen sections of land for a park. Given its first reading on Texas Independence Day, March 2, 1933, the bill called for an appropriation of $5,000 to be paid the public school fund for the land. The bill was referred to the appropriations committee, where Townsend, with his encyclopedic knowledge of the Big Bend, a no-nonsense attitude, and a portfolio of pictures, proved to be an excellent lobbyist. J. Frank Dobie, who had first caught Wagstaff's attention with his article, also testified effectively on behalf of the measure. The committee reported favorably on the bill, giving the three West Texas legislators what they considered a major victory during the economy-minded 1930s. Although the bill was introduced late in the session, they maneuvered to get it before the legislature before adjournment. On May 19, Speaker Coke Stevenson laid the bill before the House. It was amended to reserve all the minerals for the public school fund, to correct some descriptions of the land, and to lower the appropriation from $5,000 to $1,250. Still feeling that they had a good bill, the sponsors accepted the amendments, and Wagstaff moved that the law requiring the bill to be read a third time on another day be suspended. His motion carried, and the bill was passed 90 to 27.[5]

The measure was then sent to the Senate where Ken Regan of

Pecos was its sponsor. Although time was short, Senator Regan maneuvered the bill through without delay. The appropriation was further lowered to $1,000, but the Senate approved it 26 to 3 on May 24. The following day it went back to the House for concurrence. The House concurred by a large majority, 109 to 3. Enrolled, signed by the Speaker, and sent to the Secretary of State, the bill was signed by Gov. Miriam A. ("Ma") Ferguson on May 27. Since the law contained a clause making it effective immediately, Texas Canyons State Park was established upon the governor's signature.[6]

But the lawmakers were not through. When the legislature met in special session in September 1933, Governor Ferguson allowed two bills increasing the size of the park to be introduced. Townsend sponsored a measure transferring all lands that had been forfeited because of non-payment of taxes south of latitude 29° 25′ in Brewster and Presidio counties to the State for the park. Wagstaff introduced a bill to change the name of the park to Big Bend State Park and withdraw from sale all public school lands in Brewster County south of 29° 25′. Both bills were referred to the Committee on Public Lands and Buildings, where they were reported favorably. Townsend's bill came up first, so Wagstaff attached his as an amendment, and both bills passed as a single measure on October 4. The Senate added minor amendments, and 8 days later, on the last day of the session, the House concurred. Governor Ferguson signed the bill on October 27. An estimated 150,000 acres were added to the park.[7]

Big Bend National Park

Townsend was still not satisfied. He immediately began urging Congressman R. Ewing Thomason to introduce legislation creating a national park in the Big Bend. When Thomason was in Alpine, Townsend invited him to visit the park site. When the congressman refused, saying he did not have time, Townsend began to apply pressure. "Well, Ewing," Townsend reportedly said, "you're going to [visit the park] if I have to threaten you with your constituency or a six-shooter." The phone calls, telegrams, and letters of park supporters made Thomason aware of the significance of the project. "Tell that Ewing Townsend I'll come see the park if he'll call off his dogs." pleaded the congressman. Thomason visited the Big Bend in November 1933 and was so impressed with what he saw that he immediately began to work on a bill to establish a national park. Townsend continued to support the park concept every chance he got. "I am so full of it that I have got to unload on someone, and just at present you

Amon Carter Peak, the "Window," and Vernon Bailey Peak were first photographed by Hill in 1899 and named by Park Service officials decades later.

are the only available victim and will have to suffer the consequences," he wrote Col. Robert H. Lewis of Fort Sam Houston. Judge R. B. Slight had similarly talked with Senator Tom Connally during one of the senator's brief visits to Alpine.[8]

Before the legislation could be passed, much work had to be done. It fell primarily to Townsend to prepare for the distinguished visitors who must visit the Big Bend before any action could be taken on a national park. The park promoters hoped for a Civilian Conservation Corps camp for the Big Bend to do the necessary development work, but several applications had proved unsuccessful because there was no adequate water supply. One good source at Government Spring was unavailable because the owners wanted more than the Alpine Chamber of Commerce could afford to pay. On three occasions the chamber failed to get other sites approved.

Townsend's suggestion enabled the organization to succeed on the fourth try. Some of the best land in the hoped-for park was in the Chisos Mountains basin, where Townsend's nephew, Ira Hec-

The Civilian Conservation Corps built roads and blazed trails for the first visitors to the planned national park.

tor, owned a large plot of land. Thinking that water was available there, Townsend convinced Hector to deed the land to the county. Residents from Alpine and Marathon contributed money for the well. Townsend took the digging crew into the basin, while James Casner, president of the Chamber of Commerce, requested that the county commissioners build a road into the basin. By the time the crew began digging at a site suggested by Dr. C. L. Baker, head of the geology department of Texas A. & M. College, time was running out on the fourth CCC camp application.

The men were at work by 9 a.m. April 16, 1934. Mrs. Townsend cooked lunch and her husband carried it to the men so no time would be lost. By 2:45 p.m. they drew out the first bucket of water. The following day they rigged a gasoline pump to keep the water out of the well so they could dig deeper. Because water had to be found immediately, Townsend called the well *Agua Pronto*. A road grader soon cut a path into the basin, and the government approved the location for the CCC camp.[9]

Teams of specialists quickly visited the region. The National Park Service filed a report on the Big Bend in January 1935, pointing out the advantage of the area as a national park. Members of the CCC camp constructed barracks in the basin as headquarters for the operations and built roads and cleared trails in preparation for opening the park.[10]

Texas Senators Connally and Morris Sheppard and Representative Thomason introduced identical bills in Congress on March 1, 1935, calling for the establishment of the Big Bend National Park when Texas deeded adequate land to the Federal Government. The bill passed, and President Franklin D. Roosevelt signed it into law. Allowing for private donation of as much as 1,500,000 acres, the legislation was only an enabling act with no appropriation or enforcement provision. The actual acquisition of the land was left to the State of Texas. Newspapers across the state carried the news. "Sweeping vistas . . . will greet visitors to Texas' first national park in the Big Bend," a reporter for the *Fort Worth Star-Telegram* noted.[11]

Dream of an International Park

National Park Service officials, meanwhile, were at work on a more ambitious project. When Senator Sheppard presented the idea of a Big Bend park to President Roosevelt in February 1935, he suggested that it should really become an international park. The President liked the idea, and Secretary of the Interior Harold Ickes set about to make it a reality. Assistant Director Conrad L. Wirth of the National Park Service and several colleagues met with a Mexican commission in Alpine in August 1935 to discuss the prospects. The group made a pack trip into the mountains, climbed to the South Rim, and viewed the magnificent Sierra del Carmen on the Mexican side of the river, Elephant Tusk Mountain to the south, and Santa Elena Canyon 20 miles to the west. Following Wirth's report – which predicted that the international park would "be one of the greatest recreational and educational ventures ever undertaken by the National Park Service" – meetings were held in El Paso in October and November. As a result, a temporary joint park commission was established.[12]

The idea won new friends in 1936. Secretary of State Cordell Hull set up a formal commission to meet with the Mexican commission to plan the park, forest reserves, and wildlife refuge, not only for a Big Bend but for other prospective international parks. In February, the joint commission again met in Alpine to inspect the proposed Mexican park area. Entering through the small village of Boquillas, the commission spent several days in the

The Sierra del Carmen is even wilder and more impressive on the Mexican side of the border.

Sierra del Carmen, the Fronteriza range, and in nearby villages. They returned through San Carlos, visiting Castolon, Tex., as they emerged from Mexico. (This conference was marked by tragedy, when Roger W. Toll, the superintendent of Yellowstone National Park, and George Wright of the Park Service's wildlife research division, were killed in a car wreck. Toll Mountain, adjacent to Casa Grande, and George Wright Peak, both in the Chisos, are named for the officials.) Another meeting was held in El Paso in November, and boundaries for the proposed park were agreed upon: the western point was downriver from Lajitas, the eastern point just above Stillwell Crossing. Markers were set at these points.[13]

Creating a National Park

Meanwhile, the Park Service had sent a group of scientists into the Big Bend to explore its features and locate possible wild-life refuges. One of them was a young geologist who had recently received his Ph.D. from Northwestern University. Dr. Ross A. Maxwell had never been west of San Antonio, but the job in the Big Bend was a good one during the Depression. "I did not know what I was getting into," Maxwell later recalled. "When I

197

went out to Big Bend and took a look at it I was ready to throw in the sponge. I stayed at the CCC camp because there was nowhere else to stay." Former Texas Governor Pat Neff, chairman of the State Parks Board, visited the Big Bend in June 1936. "The Big Bend is the last Texas frontier," he wired the *Waco Tribune Herald*. Working diligently at their tasks, the boys of the CCC camp, said Neff, possessed the "atmosphere of an academy of science . . . ." The preliminary work was done, and the national park moved closer to reality.[14]

Enthusiasm for the Big Bend park climaxed in 1937. With so much publicity directed toward an international park, the State legislature moved to fulfull the terms of the Federal act. The lawmakers authorized an expenditure of $750,000 to purchase privately held land for the national park. As news of the action was carried in newspapers throughout the State, Walter Prescott Webb, well-known historian and member of the faculty of the University of Texas, embarked upon a trip through Santa Elena Canyon, hoping to call attention to the splendors of the Big Bend. As author of the famous *Texas Rangers,* Webb was familiar with the trouble Capt. Charles L. Nevill had in attempting the same trip in 1881. He was also advised by Hill, who had made the trip in 1899 and who now, in 1937, was a special writer for the *Dallas Morning News.* The party took several precautions. Guided by experienced river men, the expedition would be tracked by Coast Guard planes. They also had special, flat-bottom boats made of steel, instead of the clumsy wooden crafts that Hill was forced to use. "Four men in two steel rowboats required 30 hours to travel the 15 miles of treacherous rapids in the boulder-choked Rio Grande," announced the *Houston Chronicle* upon completion of the trip. In the tradition of other river men, Webb carved his name and the date of his float on a prominent rock in the canyon.[15]

Webb's trip also had another purpose. He had been commissioned by the Park Service to prepare a historical handbook that would serve as a visitor's introduction to the Big Bend. He rapidly acquainted himself with the existing historical material, and then he contacted several old friends in the region to begin preparation for the trip. In addition to the publicity expected as a result of the float, Webb wanted to get to know the Big Bend personally so he could write more knowledgeably. He also contacted several large newspapers across the state and made arrangements to sell them feature stories on his trip.[16]

Webb, along with thousands of other Texans, undoubtedly was shocked when Gov. James V. Allred vetoed the measure on grounds that no money had been appropriated for the land and that the general fund could not stand the strain. Both West Texans and the Park Service were upset. "Was very sorry indeed to read that Governor Allred vetoed the Big Bend Park Bill," wrote Thomas V. Skaggs, who guided Webb through the canyon. "To me our young governor is a funny edition. If and when he visits west of the Pecos again I think the residents out there may greet him with the welcome the Comanches greeted the buffalo, in season." On December 15, 1937, the Park Service abandoned the CCC camp, and Maxwell left; there was no place else to stay. "The whole Big Bend park idea seemed dead," he recalled. The citizens of Brewster County had taken the project about as far as they could.[17]

Texas Big Bend Park Association

But the Big Bend was too good an idea to die. When the *Fort Worth Star-Telegram* carried a vigorous editorial favoring the national park, the resourceful supporters of the idea saw another opportunity. The newspaper had suggested that instead of the State

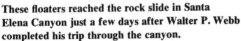

These floaters reached the rock slide in Santa Elena Canyon just a few days after Walter P. Webb completed his trip through the canyon.

A get-together at the Mariposa Mine Store, 1917.

Mexicans cross the Rio Grande near Lajitas with a load of stove wood and chinograss, 1916.

A Marfa school exercise on Liberty Loan Day, during World War I.

Early sightseers at Jordan's Gap, near Marfa.

A Baptist encampment at Paisano, 1921.

Shortly after the turn of the century, Big Bend residents found life a bit kinder. Mining brought in many new families, and the automobiles and the railroad ended the oppressive isolation. Social functions that were impossible earlier now became commonplace.

appropriating the money for the land acquisition, a million people should contribute $1 each. Herbert Maier, the Park Service's regional director, endorsed the proposal in a letter to managing editor James R. Record of the *Star-Telegram*. Maier's plea was supported by James E. Casner of Alpine and Dr. H. W. Morelock, president of Sul Ross State College, who met with Record. The result was the establishment of the Texas Big Bend Park Association, an organization of influential citizens across the State, with the goal of raising money to buy the land.[18]

The Executive Committee of the association met in May 1938 in Austin to discuss ways of raising the money. Amon G. Carter, publisher of the *Star-Telegram*, was elected chairman, and, in a politically wise move, Governor Allred was named honorary president. The committee viewed movies of the Big Bend and adopted guidelines for raising funds and putting out information. The members of the committee themselves pledged $12,500 and expected to raise another $12,500 in other cities. They hoped to raise money from popular subscription, wealthy persons and foundations, and legislative appropriation. The Depression, international difficulties, and finally World War II seriously impaired these plans, however, and the committee soon directed its efforts primarily toward securing an adequate legislative appropriation.[19]

Although the main thrust of the committee was to secure State funds, other possibilities were not overlooked. A. F. Robinson, an Alpine resident, donated 320 acres for the park. The public was invited to join the association. Chairman Carter hoped for 30,000 memberships at $1 each, and before the campaign was launched 53 persons had paid the token dues. The *Star-Telegram* successfully urged its readers to contribute to a general fund that would be turned over to the association for purchase of the needed land. In September 1942, when the newspaper closed out its effort, $8,346.88 had been raised from 659 persons, with donations ranging from 5 cents to $100.[20]

By mid-1941 the committee's efforts were bearing fruit. An executive headquarters had been established in Fort Worth. The State Parks Board had determined that the land necessary for the establishment of the park would cost almost $1,400,000, so the committee set its goal as a $1,500,000 appropriation from the legislature. Newspapers across the State announced support of the measure. Dr. Morelock had been given permission by his Board of Regents to spend as much time as necessary on the development of the park. He traveled more than 25,000 miles across the State in its support. H. R. Smith and J. E. Mowinkle, Texas oilmen, covered the expenses of a color movie about the Big Bend for service clubs, school groups, and anyone else who was interested. Carter himself took a great interest in the park and spent both time and money in its support. He issued statements to the press, gave interviews on radio station WBAP of Fort Worth, and continued to chair the meetings of the executive committee. Gov. W. Lee O'Daniel signed the bill appropriating $1,500,000 for the purchase of the land in July 1941.[21]

Land Acquisition

Then the first real difficulty with the Big Bend project arose. Under authority of the State act, the State Parks Board established the Big Bend Land Department to appraise and purchase the land. Eugene Thompson was named administrator of the department and chief appraiser and Townsend associate administrator. More than 3,000 persons owned land in the Big Bend, but only 55 of them lived there. The department's task was complicated by having to locate other owners throughout the world and because not everyone wanted to sell. It was eased somewhat by the fact that over half the land needed was owned by only 20 people.[22]

Some delay resulted when Rep. A. H. King of Throckmorton, Tex., filed an injunction to prohibit the State from spending the $1,500,000, but the State Supreme Court rejected the suit. Another possible conflict concerned mineral rights. When the legislature passed the original appropriations bill in 1937, it reserved mineral rights for the permanent school fund because the representatives feared the loss of a large amount of revenue. The 1941 appropriation also had the reserve attached, but Townsend fought hard to get it removed, for he knew that such a clause would be unacceptable to the National Park Service. [23]

When Gov. Coke Stevenson ceremonially presented the park to M. R. Tillotson, regional director of the Park Service on September 5, 1943, he again called attention to the proposal for an international park, which had lain dormant during the war years and the frenzy of land acquistion. The only thing that had happened since the boundary had been marked in 1937 was that both the United States and Mexican commissions had been reconstituted. As chairman of the U.S. commission, Tillotson visited Mexico City

A sheepherder's place, below North Peak in the
Chisos. Hill photographed this scene in 1899.

in June 1942 to discuss the matter with the new members of the Mexican board. Little more was achieved than an expression of interest and a promise to study the matter.[24]

In February 1944 Governor Stevenson delivered the deed to Amon G. Carter, president of the Texas Big Bend Park Association, for formal presentation to President Roosevelt. Carter formally gave the document to the President in a ceremony on July 6, 1944. Six days later the National Park Service announced that the Big Bend Park was officially open. Secretary of the Interior Ickes had already approved Ross A. Maxwell's appointment as superintendent, a logical choice since the soft-spoken geologist had conducted one of the initial park service studies of the area. In taking charge of the park, Maxwell noted that it included "scientific phenomena and scenic beauty mingled with historic incidents along the Texas-Mexico frontier that give it a charm and color that is not known in any other park." Interpretation in the park has tended to emphasize the uniqueness of its biological characteristics. It contains desert, shrubland, woodland, and grassland. Scientists soon realized that it also contained a remarkable number of bird species, making it a paradise for bird watchers.[25]

The New Park

Maxwell faced several problems. The most significant one was the presence of ranchers whom the Park Service had given permission to remain on the land until January 15, 1945. There were about 50 active ranchers in the park, running about 25,000 head of cattle, 20,000 to 30,000 head of sheep and goats, and 1,000 to 2,000 head of horses. The land was badly overgrazed. Nor could the people and stock be moved easily. Since 1944 was a very dry year, thousands of cattle would have died if the ranchers had been forced to move their livestock by that winter. Strays roamed through the park for more than 5 years.

Whatever maintenance and construction Maxwell did in the park was accomplished under wartime conditions. There was no food service, no grocery store, and tires and gas were rationed. Maxwell had a dump truck, a pickup, and a passenger car to conduct the business of the park. There were only five employees on the staff, including the superintendent, so "everybody was a ditch digger or a truckdriver."

Maxwell saw few visitors during the first years of operation, but he prepared basic facilities in case someone got stranded. He put some surplus army cots in the old CCC cottages for emergencies. The first visitors to the park usually fell into two categories: those in love with the area, and those who had not known what to expect and did not want to spend time there once they found out. Maxwell encountered a couple from Austin who had come to enjoy the solitude of the Big Bend. They had been warned to bring along food, but had not brought enough. They had a couple of cans of soup, some sausage, and other bland items. After 2 days Maxwell decided he had better check on them. He found them completely out of food but unwilling to leave. Since they had eaten nothing for 24 hours, he took them to his cottage and fed them beans and coffee. Another couple stayed a shorter time. When they drove into the basin, Maxwell started walking toward the car to see if he could be of assistance. "The man had gotten out of the car and taken two or three deep breaths of that sweet air, and was looking around just sort of awed by Casa Grande," Maxwell recalled. "The wife did not even get out of the car. She just shouted his name and told him to get back in the car and 'get me out of this place.' " [26]

When the time came for dedicating the national park, officials again brought up the idea of an international park. The dedication had been postponed by both World War II and the Korean War. In May 1954, Dr. Bryan Wildenthal, Morelock's successor as president of Sul Ross State College, wrote Carter about plans for the dedication. Meantime, Park Service officials and local Big Bend residents had been active, hoping to arouse interest in the international park in the neighboring Mexican states of Coahuila and Chihuahua. M. L. Tillotson had spoken over a Chihuahua City radio station. Former President Morelock of Sul Ross had contacted many individuals. Wildenthal thought that the occasion of the dedication would be the ideal time to renew discussion of the international project.

But the idea had not suffered from lack of attention over the years. President Franklin Roosevelt had written Mexican President Manuel Avila Camacho in October 1944 that he hoped that the project could be reviewed after the war. Avila Camacho responded in kind and ordered the Mexican park department to conduct studies in the region. After Roosevelt's death, President Harry S. Truman pursued the idea. In 1947 an International Park Commission was established. Apparently the main Mexican objection to the

Big Bend residents built their homes of whatever they could find. This is the home of a *curandero-avisador* and his family. As a *curandero*, this Mexican shaman "healed" the sick, using herbs from "nature's pharmacy." As an *avisador*, he gave warnings and advice to his patients.

park was that they did not have as much government-owned land as Texas did. Most of the land on the river was owned by miners, ranchers, and lumbermen who were loath to sell. The Mexican Federal Government did not want to act without the cooperation, or at least the consent, of the local States. Thus action on what the Mexican had planned to call *Parque Nacional de la Gran Comba* was postponed indefinitely.[27]

The Big Bend National Park was dedicated on November 21, 1955. Secretary of the Interior Douglas McKay delivered the main address. Gov. Allan Shivers of Texas and Gov. Jesús Lozoya of Chihuahua were present. Two men who contributed so much to the drive for a national park had died before the dedication took place: Everett E. Townsend and Amon G. Carter.[28]

The Secretary spent much of his time talking about Mission 66, a ten-year program to develop roads, bridges, trails, and other facilities that would make the national parks more accessible to the

207

The Chisos Mountains, wild, vast, and trackless,
are a fitting symbol of the Big Bend.

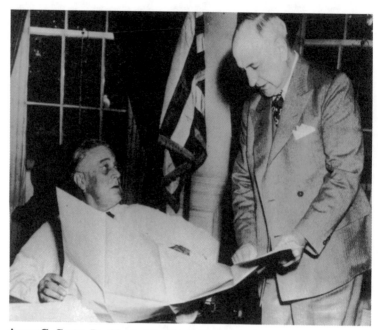

Amon G. Carter, President of the Texas Big Bend Park Association, presents the deed to Big Bend National Park to President Franklin D. Roosevelt.

public. Practically all the development in the Big Bend – the Panther Junction park headquarters, the tourist facilities in the Chisos Basin, the store and camping grounds at Rio Grande Village – took place during those 10 years.

This phase ended when Mrs. Lyndon B. Johnson visited the park in April 1966. Traveling with Secretary of the Interior Stewart Udall and Mrs. Udall, National Park Service Director George Hartzog, Jr., 70 members of the White House staff, the Washington press corps, and dozens of other reporters, photographers, and film crews, the First Lady brought in one of the largest entourages ever seen in the Big Bend.[29]

The numerous travel writers realized the uniqueness of the land. It was a wonderland for biologists and geologists; they called attention to the international aspects of its history, and they noted its overwhelming vastness. At least twice, for the U.S. Army's experiment with camels during 1859 and 1860 and for astronaut training in 1964, the Big Bend has been used for its harsh terrain and unforgiving climate.

The Big Bend, of course, has easily survived the successive waves of human occupation. The timeless face of the land emphasizes that fact. The Big Bend protected the Indians against the encroachment of the Spaniards and the Anglo-Americans. It gradually yielded to exploration, but the hostile environment helped insure the survival of one of the country's most fascinating regions. Relics of the historical drama are preserved at Fort Davis National Historic Site, Guadalupe Mountains National Park, Chamizal National Memorial at El Paso, and Fort Leaton State Park near Presidio, as well as Big Bend National Park.

The Big Bend is now a source of inspiration for artists, writers, photographers, scientists, and vacationers. The Chisos Mountains continue to shelter an isolated alpine environment; the desert nourishes hundreds of different species of cacti; and the Rio Grande erodes away a few more inches of limestone canyon every year. Today the sights that only a few 19th-century travelers saw after heroic efforts are available to nearly everyone. Hiking and horse trails lead up into the Chisos along the South Rim or Lost Mine trails. Most visitors drive across the desert in air-conditioned comfort to see the fossil bone exhibit, Dagger Flat, Mariscal Mine, or Wilson's Ranch. And float trips through Santa Elena, Mariscal, and Boquillas Canyons are almost a daily occurrence. E. E. Townsend's lament that most people in the State were unaware of the Big Bend is no longer true. It finally is recognized as one of the great wonders of the Southwest.

Following page: Homer Wilson was a late-comer to ranching in the Big Bend. He built this home in Oak Canyon, just below "The Window" in the Chisos, and a line camp in Blue Creek canyon. The line camp is well preserved and can be visited today by trail.

Historic Sites
of the Big Bend

Although some Big Bend place names recall the days of the Spaniards and Indians, most are of more recent origin, reflecting the Anglo-American society that settled the region as well as the pragmatic and common character of the settlers. The hopes and dreams of people, as well as their philosophy and vision, can often be seen in the names they apply to their surroundings. The dominant human thread running through the history of the Big Bend is that survival requires hard work. Practicality and directness are virtues in such circumstances, as the many obvious names signify.

In such country little was done if it did not have to be. Thus many landmarks went without names until 1903 when surveyor Arthur A. Stiles conducted a study of the region. He consulted the local citizens before applying the place names to his map. M. A. Ernst, storekeeper and justice of the peace in Boquillas, convened a jury for the purpose of considering and approving place names. Each member had a topographical feature named for him, but as Stiles reported, "there were barely enough people living in the country to furnish names for all the places." So they resorted to friends and relatives. Many of the more exotic sounding Spanish and Indian names were consequently forgotten. (In fairness to Ernst's jury, it must be pointed out that frequently the previously awarded names were unknown to them and have only been turned up by recent research.[1])

Most geographical features have obvious names. Mule Ears Peak is perhaps the best example. Located in the southwestern reaches of the Chisos, near Trap Mountain, these durable peaks were probably named by teamsters who were coaxing their mule teams through the Big Bend. Cow Heaven Mountain has a more obscure origin. Located northwest of Mariscal Mountain, this formation reportedly got its name when a local rancher observed that the land was so barren that a cow "would have to go to Heaven" if stranded on it, because there was no grass. Casa Grande, Santa Elena, Terlingua Creek, Burro Mesa, Mariscal, Boquillas, and numerous other points illustrate the Spanish-Mexican influence. Other names, such as Maverick Mountain, Cow Heaven, and Dogie

Mountain, testify to the importance of the ranching industry.[2]

It took little imagination to apply the names of common reptiles and animals, plants or legends to prominent landmarks—Panther Peak and Spring, Rattlesnake Mountain, Alamo, Willow, and Cottonwood Creeks, Ash and Oak Springs, Chisos Mountains. The presence of the National Park Service is evident in such names as Vernon Bailey Peak, Roger Toll Peak, George Wright Peak, and Carter Peak. Early pioneers are honored by such names as Nevill Springs, Stillwell Mountain, and Roy's Peak.

The land is still being named. During a recent study of the park, the Geological Survey searched for historic names for prominent landmarks, but applied their own creations when no historic names could be found. Such minute naming of features is only possible, or necessary, after the development of exact mapping techniques and aerial photography, and large numbers of visitors want to know what each hill or border is called and why.

The following guide lists only the most important extant historical sites. Most of them can be reached by car, but some require travel over primitive roads or strenuous hikes. Additional interpretative material is available at park headquarters on the better known sites. Sites marked with an asterisk * are located on primitive roads, where conditions change with the weather. A park ranger should be consulted before traveling in the back country.

Big Bend National Park

Barker Lodge Once a NPS ranger station, today a research station associated with the "Man and the Biosphere" project. Located northwest of Boquillas Canyon on a spur road.

The Basin of the Chisos Mountains Site of the Civilian Conservation Corps camp in 1934 that prepared the way for the national park. Now lodging facilities and a restaurant are located there.

Comanche Trail Marker A historical marker at Persimmon Gap commemorates the hectic past of the great Comanche War Trail. Beyond the gap the trail divided into several paths. One path crosses the Rio Grande near Lajitas, today a small community with a general store and a post office. Often a mile wide and lined with the bones of horses and cattle in the 19th century, the trail was the route Comanches took to and from Mexico during the raids of the "Comanche Moon," which one historian called the most sustained and devastating assault by one civilization on another.

La Coyota An abandoned Mexican farm village of some 10 adobe and stone ruins clustered on the west bank of Alamo Creek as it flows onto the Rio Grande floodplain. Across the creek, on an eminence overlooking the village, is a Mexican cemetery. Located along the paved road from Castolon to Santa Elena Canyon.

Emory Peak One of the highest peaks in Texas and the highest point in the Chisos Mountains at 7,835 feet. Named after Maj. William H. Emory, head of the Boundary Survey team that explored the Rio Grande in 1852. Although the engineers never climbed the peak, they used it as a point of reference throughout their survey. A hiking trail leads from the Basin to the top.

G-4 Ranch In 1880 the G-4 Ranch covered 55,000 acres of open range in Southern Brewster County (Survey Block G-4). This ranching operation consisted of 6,000 head of cattle, controlled by 10 cowboys and a foreman. The cowboys worked out of three camps; one at Aqua Frio, 18 miles north of Terlingua Creek near

Santa Elena Canyon, and a main camp west of Chisos at Oak Spring.

*Glenn Springs Located 9 miles down the unimproved Glenn Springs Road from the junction on the Panther Junction—Rio Grande Village paved road. The site of one of the earliest wax camps in the Park, Glenn Springs was also an army station and a small settlement. It is best known for the bandit raid that occurred in 1916. The rifle pits can still be seen lining the crest of the low ridge that overlooks the settlement site, along with the remains of a water system that brought water into the settlement and wax works. A large ranch house was located here; the holding pen, corral, and dipping chute are still visible.

*Johnson Ranch Located about 16 miles east of Castolon on the unimproved river road. Johnson's Ranch was a successful ranch, a border trading post, a wayside stop for travelers, and a landing area for flyers during the border troubles in 1919. After Elmo Johnson purchased the ranch in 1928, the landing field was developed and officially opened by the U.S. Army on July 6, 1929. Its purpose was to train young aviators and to serve as a lookout station and check point on the International Boundary. Johnson occupied the ranch until the Park Service purchased the land.

*La Noria Located a few miles up the unimproved Old Ore Road from the junction on the Panther Junction-Rio Grande Village road. The name is Spanish for "The Well." When the region was farmed, La Noria became a small village known for the post office which operated there and as a stopover point for travelers. It was formally called Old Boquillas when the first map of the area was published; changed its name to La Noria when the village moved to its present site on the Rio Grande. There are few visible remains today.

*Luna Jacal About midway on the unimproved road between Maverick and Santa Elena Canyon. One of the most photographic ruins in the park, the *jacal* of Gilberto Luna illustrates the struggle of man versus the elements in the Big Bend. Luna himself lived to the age of 109.

*Mariscal Mine   Located south of Glenn Springs on the unimproved river road, the main processing plant, building, paymaster's office, superintendent's house, employee's residences, company store, barracks and brick kiln still remain. Although the view from the mine is magnificent, the area is dotted with open mine shafts and extreme caution must be used in viewing the site.

Old Sam Nail Ranch   The remains of the adobe house built by Sam Nail in 1916 stand south of Santa Elena Junction, on the road to Castolon. His windmill and water tank continue to be a watering place for birds and other wildlife. Recommended as a pleasant picnicking and bird-watching area.

Persimmon Gap   The point at which the Great Comanche Trail penetrated the Santiago Mountains. Now the north entrance to the Park. A Historical Site Marker on Tex. 385 from Marathon points out the spot where the trail crossed the mountains.

Wilson Ranch   Located on the Ross Maxwell Scenic Drive (or Castolon Road), about 7 miles south of Santa Elena Junction. Homer Wilson, a relative latecomer to the Big Bend, built a line camp for his profitable ranch. The remains of the living quarters and outbuildings are probably the best preserved in the park. Here can be seen all the functions of a successful ranch's line camp: the bunkhouse, cistern, corral and stubbing post, dipping chute, and chicken coop and pens. A trail leads from the overlook to the ranch.

Castolon—Santa Elena Canyon Area

Castolon   Named after a settler called Castulo, the village was first a subpost of the border patrol (1910-14), then the site of an army post during the border troubles with Mexico. The mountain identified with Castolon is Cerro Castellan—from the Spanish word meaning castle. Located just above the river on the Castolon road, the village is a popular visitor stop. Farming, commerce, border troubles, and local dwellings—the four major historical themes of the Big Bend National Park—are all represented here.

Dorgan Farm House   Of exceptional architectural interest, this house stands just above the river road between Castolon and Santa Elena Canyon. It commands an outstanding view of the

217

Glenn Springs in 1917.

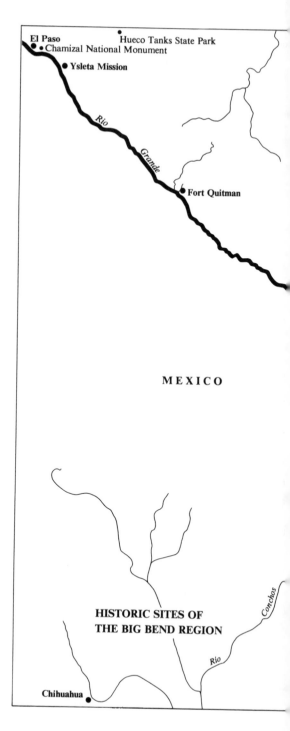

El Paso •   • Hueco Tanks State Park
• Chamizal National Monument

• Ysleta Mission

Rio

Grande

• Fort Quitman

MEXICO

HISTORIC SITES OF
THE BIG BEND REGION

Conchos

Rio

Chihuahua •

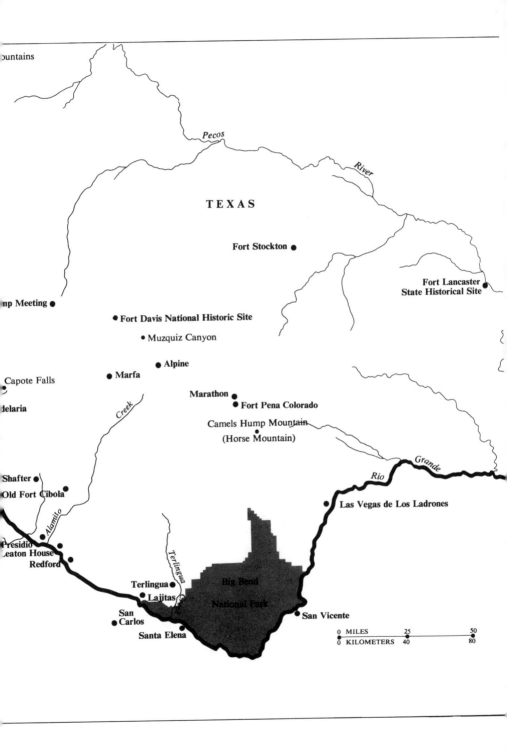

ountains

Pecos

River

TEXAS

Fort Stockton ●

Fort Lancaster
State Historical Site ●

mp Meeting ●

● Fort Davis National Historic Site

● Muzquiz Canyon

● Alpine

Capote Falls

● Marfa

Marathon ●
● Fort Pena Colorado

Camels Hump Mountain
(Horse Mountain)

delaria

Creek

Shafter ●

Old Fort Cibola ●

Alamito

Rio

Grande

● Las Vegas de Los Ladrones

Presidio
eaton House
Redford

Terlingua

Terlingua
● Lajitas

San
● Carlos

Santa Elena

Big Bend

National Park

● San Vicente

0	MILES	25		50
0	KILOMETERS	40		80

Chisos Mountains, the Rio Grande floodplain and the Sierra del Carmen as they stretch into Mexico. The huge stone fireplace in the central room is constructed from large slabs of petrified wood. Four huge ceiling beams (only two remain) radiated from the center point to the four corners.

Old Castolon The Old Castolon Store, located here, is probably one of the oldest buildings in the National Park. It was a border trading post from the days when Castolon was first settled. Founded by Cipriano Hernández about 1900.

Santa Elena Canyon At the end of the Castolon road. The most spectacular of the major canyons of the Big Bend, Santa Elena was one of the last to be floated and documented. The Boundary Survey of 1852 bypassed it, believing that their fragile boats would be wrecked. The first documented trip through the canyon was by surveyor John T. Gano in 1882. U.S. Geological Survey member Dr. Robert T. Hill took the first photographs of the interior of the canyon in 1899.

Sublett Farm House Near the Dorgan residence above the river road between Castolon and Santa Elena Canyon. The Rio Grande floodplain was a fertile area for cultivation of cotton, corn, and other crops. The Sublett Farm House is an adobe structure, of which only the main walls still stand.

*Terlingua Abaja The name in Spanish means "Lower Terlingua." Many ruins remain to suggest the activity that once thrived in this old Mexican village, located several miles north of the unimproved road between Santa Elena Canyon and Maverick. Settled earlier than the mining village of Terlingua, Terlingua Abaja still has its old adobe chapel and cemetery.

Rio Grande Village Area

Daniels Ranch Located in the west picnic grounds area at Rio Grande Village. Original owner was J. M. Graham. The Daniels' Farm Complex dates from about 1920 and illustrates the cotton farming that flourished in the Rio Grande Valley around Boquillas. It was named for John R. Daniels, who owned it when the park was established. Of interest architecturally, the structure is of adobe with a viga and cane ceiling, adobe roof, and flagstone floor.

*Hot Springs Located on the Rio Grande on the two-mile unimproved spur road off the Panther Junction-Rio Grande Village road. Once developed as a health resort and trading post, this is the site of J. O. Langford's original store, motel, and residence. Several hot springs that flow into the Rio Grande near the confluence of Tornillo Creek gave the site its name, and provided a living for Langford and his family for several years. A few small springs still flow but the major hot springs used by Langford have since been silted in by flooding from the Rio Grande. Indian pictographs, kitchen middens, and mortar holes at the foot of the cliffs near the springs testify to occupation by nomadic Indian tribes.

Ore Tramway Line Visible just off the Boquillas Canyon spur road, the tramway line and terminal were used near the turn of the century to transport ore from the Del Carmen silver and lead mine in Mexico, across the Rio Grande, to the terminal on the American side. The mine was closed about 1906.

Senator Berkeley Cottage Located by the river near the group campground at Rio Grande Village. This cottage belonged to State Senator Benjamin F. Berkeley of Alpine, who used it as a vacation residence. He called it Ojos de Boquillas. Today it is a NPS employee residence.

*Ernst Tinaja *Tinaja* is Spanish for a large, earthen storage jar. In the center of the Ernst Canyon, one mile off the Old Ore Road, is a huge natural cistern in the limestone cliffs. It is known as the Ernst Tinaja and is waterfilled the year round.

The Big Bend Region

Alpine The County Seat of Brewster County is located at the junction of Tex. 67 and 118. The community began as a section of the Southern Pacific Railroad and was first called Burgess Springs, then Osborne. To obtain water rights from a local rancher the railroad changed the name to Murphyville. In 1888, when it became the county seat, local citizens changed its name to Alpine. It is still an important rail head for the local ranchers.

Bloys Camp Meeting Begun in 1890, the Bloys Camp Meeting is still celebrated at Skillman's Grove (named for Henry Skillman) in the Davis Mountains, west of Fort Davis on Tex. 166.

Camel Hump (or Horse Mountain) Located on Tex 385 between Marathon and Big Bend National Park, about 8 miles south of Marathon, the mountain got its name from the camels that traipsed through the Big Bend before the Civil War. Lts. Edward L. Hartz and William Echols supplied the name in 1859. Also known as Horse Mountain.

Capote Falls Located on private property off Texas 67 in the Cienega Mountains, the Capote Falls, 175 feet, are the highest falls in Texas. *Capote* is Spanish for Cape.

Chamizal National Memorial This memorial, located on Cordova Island in the Rio Grande south of El Paso, commemorates the peaceful settlement of a 99-year boundary dispute between the United States and Mexico. The Chamizal Treaty was signed in 1963.

Fort Davis National Historic Site Established along the San Antonio to El Paso road in 1854, Fort Davis was meant as a way-station and protective stronghold for troops and travelers in the sparsely settled territory. The post was abandoned in 1891 when there was no longer a need for army protection. Located on Tex. 17 at the north end of the town of Fort Davis.

Fort Lancaster State Historical Site This Federal military outpost was established in 1855 along the old military road from San Antonio to El Paso. It was finally abandoned in 1868, after the frontier had bypassed it. Located 33 miles west of Ozona on U.S. 290.

Fort Pena Colorado Four miles southwest of Marathon in Brewster County, the ruins of this old fort and surrounding grounds are maintained as a county park with picnic and recreational facilities. The fort was established in 1880 to protect the Chihuahua Trail from marauding Mescalero Apaches. It was abandoned in 1893.

Fort Quitman The remains of the fort are located on the Rio Grande off Tex. 192 near the community of Fort Quitman. The military installation was established in 1858 and abandoned in 1877.

Fort Stockton The stone and adobe ruins of this fort remain north of the business district of the town of Fort Stockton on Tex. 290 in Pecos County. Located at Comanche Springs, the fort was built in 1859 to protect the San Antonio—San Diego Mail Route. After the Civil War it was garrisoned by Negro troops. It was abandoned in 1886.

Guadalupe Mountains National Park Located in Hudspeth and Culbertson Counties, this is the newest national park in Texas. It is noted for its wild, rugged landscape, Permian limestone fossils, and Signal Peak of 8,751 feet, the highest in Texas. A campsite and information center are located off Tex. 62 near Pine Springs Canyon.

Hueco Tanks State Park The 738-acre park is located 32 miles northeast of El Paso off Tex. 62. There is the site of the last Indian battle in El Paso County and the large, natural limestone cisterns for which the park is named. The area was long used by Indians as a campsite and their drawings and pictographs cover the surrounding caves and cliffs. The cisterns were also used by wagon trains heading for California and by the Butterfield stagecoaches.

Lajitas Located in southeastern Brewster County on Tex. 170 is Lajitas, which derives its name from the little flat rocks of the Boquillas formation. *Lajitas* means flag stones. The village

223

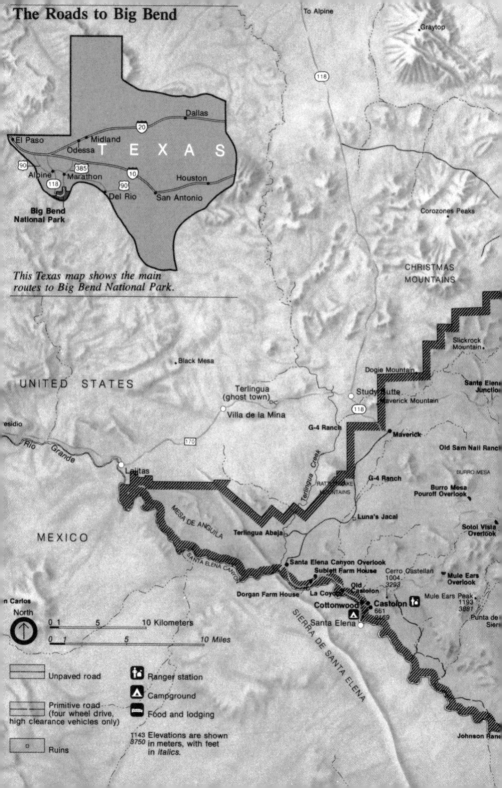

The Roads to Big Bend

T E X A S

To Alpine

Graytop

Dallas

El Paso • Midland
Odessa

90

Alpine
385
Marathon

10

Del Rio

Houston

San Antonio

Big Bend
National Park

*This Texas map shows the main
routes to Big Bend National Park.*

118

CHRISTMAS
MOUNTAINS

Slickrock
Mountain

Dogie Mountain

Santa Elena
Junction

UNITED STATES

Black Mesa

Terlingua
(ghost town)

Study Butte
Maverick Mountain

118

Villa de la Mina

Old Sam Nail Ranch

G-4 Ranch

Maverick

Presidio

170

Rio Grande

Terlingua Creek

RATTLESNAKE
MOUNTAINS

G-4 Ranch

BURRO MESA

Burro Mesa
Pouroff Overlook

Lajitas

Sotol Vista
Overlook

MESA DE ANGUILA

Luna's Jacal

MEXICO

SANTA ELENA CANYON

Terlingua Abaja

Santa Elena Canyon Overlook

Sublett Farm House

Cerro Castellan
1004
3293

Mule Ears
Overlook

n Carlos

Dorgan Farm House

La Coyota

Old
Castolon

Mule Ears Peak
1193
3881

North

Cottonwood

Castolon
661

Santa Elena

SIERRA DE SANTA ELENA

Punta de
Sierr

| 0 1 | 5 | 10 Kilometers |
| 0 1 | 5 | 10 Miles |

Legend

Unpaved road

Primitive road
(four wheel drive,
high clearance vehicles only)

Ruins

Ranger station

Campground

Food and lodging

1143
8750 Elevations are shown
in meters, with feet
in *italics*.

Johnson Ran

is located at the San Carlos ford of the Rio Grande on the Old Comanche Trail.

Ben Leaton House   A State park located a few miles downriver from Presidio enroute to Lajitas. Formerly called Fortin de San Jose. Ben Leaton acquired the title in 1846. Overlooking the floodplain of the Rio Grande, it is a formidable structure and served its owners well through several Indian attacks. Leaton was one of the earliest merchants and ranchers in the Big Bend country. Recently restored by the Texas State Park Service.

Marathon   Probably the site of an Indian culture, settled by white men only after the Civil War. A military subpost was established there in 1879, and the town began in 1882 when the Texas & New Orleans Railroads arrived. Located on Tex. 90 and 385, it is one of the main entrances to Big Bend National Park.

Marfa   Established in 1881 as a water stop on the Texas & New Orleans Railroads, Marfa was named by the wife of the railroad president after the heroine of a Russian novel. Located on Tex. 90 and 67.

Old Fort Cibolo   A private fort located off Tex. 67 near Shafter. Milton Faver built three fortresses in the Big Bend. Remains are located near Big Springs Cibolo, which supplied water for the fort.

Presidio   Located on the Rio Grande on Tex. 67, Presidio is immediately opposite Ojinaga, Mexico, and is an important point of entry to and from Mexico. Originally an outpost of Mexico, called El Presidio del Norte (the fort of the north), the area was awarded to the U.S. in 1848 by the treaty of Guadalupe Hidalgo.

Redford   Located south of Presidio on Tex. 170, Redford is a small farming community on the Rio Grande. The settlement was originally Mexican and called Polvo, which means dust. It is the site of a fort and a customs station.

Presidio San Carlos   Located about 15 miles south of Lajitas, the remains of this presidio are accessible only by foot, horseback, or four-wheel drive vehicle. Established in 1773 and occupied until 1787, this presidio is one of the most vivid ruins in the region. The presidio stands on a high terrace on the east bank of San Carlos Creek. The outside walls are 5 feet high in places; the perimeter walls of the chapel are over 10 feet high.

Presidio San Vicente   Located on a small mesa about 3 miles from the San Vicente crossing of the Rio Grande, this presidio was established in 1773 and abandoned in 1781. The only thing clearly visible today is the outline of the presidio. The upper parts of the adobe walls have melted, concealing the lower parts and any underlying structures. Both this presidio and San Carlos are representative of the defensive alignment along the northern frontier of New Spain in the 1770s.

Shafter   Between the Chinati and Cienega Mountains on Tex. 67 lies Shafter, a mining ghost town. From 1880 to 1940 it was a center for silver mining activities in Presidio County. Abandoned mines, machinery and buildings remain. Shafter is located 20 miles north of Presidio.

Terlingua   Located on Tex. 170 a few miles west of Study Butte outside the west entrance of Big Bend National Park. Today the site of the World Champion Chili Cookoff, the village of Terlingua, during its heyday, was the site of numerous quick-silver mines. The most important was the Chisos Mining Company, responsible for most of the remains that are visible today: the general store, the movie house, the jail house, the chapel, and the two-story house belonging to the mine owner, Howard Perry.

Ysleta Mission   Located 8 miles southeast of El Paso on Tex. 80 lies Ysleta, the oldest permanent settlement in Texas. The community was founded in 1680. The missions, San Antonio de las Tiguas (also called Nuestra Señora del Carmen) and San Miguel del Socorro, were built there in 1682. Both missions have suffered the effects of flood, fire, and time, but their ruins remain.

Following page: Cowboys and their families from Presidio eat lunch around the chuck wagon about 1889.

Bibliographical Essay

There is only a limited amount of information on various aspects of Big Bend National Park for the visitor who wants to know more about it. Former Big Bend Chief Naturalist Roland H. Wauer produced three handbooks that prove useful for driving, hiking, camping, or floating: *Guide to the Backcountry Roads and the River* (Big Bend National Park, Texas, 1970); *Hiker's Guide to the Developed Trails and Primitive Routes* (Big Bend National Park, Texas, 1971); and *Road Guide to the Paved and Improved Dirt Roads* (Big Bend National Park, Texas, 1970). Wauer has also written the best study on birds of the park, *Birds of Big Bend National Park and Vicinity* (Austin and London, 1973). For the botanist, Barton H. Warnock of Sul Ross State University has compiled *Wildflowers of Big Bend Country, Texas* (Alpine, 1970).

To historians the most important material for study of the Big Bend are the manuscript collections in various depositories across the country. The archives of the University of Texas at Austin contains several collections that relate to the Big Bend. General information can be found there in the Big Bend Scrapbook and the Brewster County Scrapbook. Over the years staff members have clipped various newspapers and magazines for material primarily related to the establishment of the national park. Several unpublished manuscripts relating to communities in the region are also in the files, including a typescript of probably the most useful Spanish document on the Big Bend, the diary of Pedro de Rábago y Terán's expedition. The original is in the Archivo General de la Nación, Mexico City. Although most of the information relating to the Texas Rangers is in the Adjutant General's Records of the Archives, Texas State Library, Austin, some material is located in the Adjutant General's Office (Texas) Records Transcripts, of the University of Texas Archives.

Another important source is the National Archives and Records Service, Washington, D.C. Material on the Topographical Engineers' explorations and the army's pacification in the Big Bend, such as letters sent and received by the Topographical Engineers, are also available on National Archives microfilm publications. Information on the bandit raids and subsequent army action can be found in Record Group 94, Office of the Adjutant General Documents File, National Archives. These records include documents from Big Bend residents complaining of conditions, letters from government officials regarding their action, and, finally, Maj. George Langhorne's official report of his "little punitive expedition" into Mexico.

At least five other collections contain important information on the Big Bend. A copy of the fascinating diary kept by Mexican Col. Emilio Langberg on a trip from San Carlos to Old Monclova in 1851 is in the Western Americana Collection at Yale University. Langberg's comments supplement the journals of Americans who traveled through the Big Bend in the 1850s, and provide one of the few Mexican sources for the period. The Western Americana Collection also houses the papers of William H. Emory, who replaced Bartlett as the U.S. Commissioner for the Boundary Survey. Other material on the Boundary Survey is found in the DeGolyer Foundation Library, Southern Methodist University, Dallas, Texas. The George Clinton Gardner Papers provide another opinion on the Green-Chandler exploration of the Big Bend in 1852. The personal papers of Col. Benjamin H. Grierson are located at the Newberry Library in Chicago. Grierson was a significant figure in the conquest of the Indians around the Fort Davis and Big Bend region, conducting several campaigns against Victorio. The personal papers of Walter P. Webb, a consulting historian for the Park Service during the 1930s when the proposed Big Bend National Park was under study, were recently given to the Texas State Library. Another person instrumental in the establishment of the park was Amon G. Carter of Fort Worth. President of the Texas Big Bend Park Association, Carter encouraged others around the State to support the park idea and contribute their money. His papers are available in the files of the Amon G. Carter Foundation, Fort Worth.

Although much historical material is available on the Big Bend country, little is general enough to be of interest to the layman. There are several surveys that might fill that void. Though it was published years ago, Carlysle G. Raht, *The Romance of Davis Mountains and Big Bend Country* (El Paso, 1919), has been the best history of the region for decades. Drawing on published information, personal knowledge of the region, and interviews with residents, Raht provided an easily readable account of the area. The book is out of date, however, for much research has been conducted and much has happened in the Big Bend since it was published.

Several other surveys are also available: Virginia Madison, *The Big Bend Country of Texas* (2d ed. rev. New York, 1968), emphasizes popular tales, folklore, and many incidents that are included because of their flavor or color rather than their authenticity; Ross A. Maxwell, *The Big Bend of the Rio Grande: A Guide to the Rocks, Landscape, Geologic History, and Settlers of the Area of the Big Bend National Park* (Austin, 1968), is more reliable, emphasizing the prehistory and geology of the region; and Clifford B. Casey, *Mirages, Mysteries and Reality, Brewster County, Texas: The Big Bend of the Rio Grande* (Hereford, Texas, 1972), exclusively a history of Brewster County, mostly in the 20th century. The book was issued in such limited numbers that it is no longer available for purchase at most bookstores.

Many of the curious and interesting place names of the Big Bend are discussed in Virginia Madison and Hallie Stillwell, *How Come It's Called That? Place Names in the Big Bend Country* (New York, 1968), but the book must be used with care because of conflicting accounts of how several of the place names originated. Madison and Stillwell seemed to have depended heavily upon oral tradition in many instances.

One of the best sources on the 19th–century history of Presidio County, which at one time included all present-day Brewster County, is John E. Gregg, "The History of Presidio County" (M.A. thesis, University of Texas, Austin, 1933). A resident of the county, Gregg spent years in his research and interviewing. His work was also published in the centennial edition of *Voice of the Mexican Border* (1936).

Very little is available to the layman on the Spanish period in the Big Bend, although there is a great deal of material on the Spaniards in the Southwest, some of which relates to the Big Bend. Perhaps the most useful is Robert S. Weddle, *San Juan Bautista, Gateway to Spanish Texas* (Austin, 1968), which includes a comprehensive account of the Spanish expeditions into the Big Bend that left from San Juan Bautista. A more thorough treatment of the region is found in several chapters of Carlos E. Castañeda, *Our Catholic Heritage in Texas, 1519–1936* (7 vols., Austin, 1936–1950), but the set has long been out of print and is usually available only in specialized libraries. Still more scarce is Victor J. Smith's account of "Early Spanish Exploration in the Big Bend of Texas," *West Texas Historical and Scientific Society Publications*, II (1928).

Almost all of the 16th–century Spanish expeditions that crossed into the Big Bend have received extensive attention from scholars, including translation of their official journals or diaries. Cleve Hallenbeck, *Álvar Núñez Cabeza de Vaca: The Journey and Route of the First European to Cross the Continent of North America, 1534–1536* (Glendale, 1940), contends that Cabeza de Vaca went through the Big Bend, while Carl O. Sauer, *Sixteenth Century North America: The Land and the People as Seen by the Europeans* (Berkeley, Los Angeles, and London, 1971), concludes that he journeyed north of the Big Bend. Later Spanish expedition journals can be found in Herbert E. Bolton, *Spanish Exploration in the Southwest, 1542–1706* (New York, 1967 reprint) and in books published by the Quivira Society: George P. Hammond and Agapito Rey (eds.), *Expedition Into New Mexico Made by Antonio de Espejo, 1582–1583, as Revealed in the Journal of Diego Pérez de Luxán, a Member of the Party* (Los Angeles, 1929); Lawrence Kinnaird (ed.), *The Frontiers of New Spain: Nicholas de LaFora's Description, 1766–1768* (Berkeley, 1958). Rex E. Gerald, *Spanish Presidios of the Late Eighteenth Century in Northern New Spain* (Santa Fe, 1968), has written about the two presidios established in the Big Bend, San Carlos and San Vicente.

Information on the contact between Spaniards and Indians can be found in Alfred B. Thomas, *Teodoro de Croix and the Northern Frontier of New Spain, 1776–1783* (Norman, 1941), Max L. Moorhead, *The Apache Frontier: Jacob Ugarte and Spanish-Indian Relations in Northern New Spain, 1769–1791* (Norman, 1968), and in two articles by Al B. Nelson: "Campaigning in the Big Bend of the Rio Grande, 1787," *Southwestern Historical Quarterly*, XXXIX (Oct., 1935), and "Juan de Ugalde and Picax-ande Ins-tinsle, 1787–1788," *Southwestern Historical Quarterly*, XLIII (Apr., 1940). Among the unpublished sources, James M. Daniel, "The Advance of the Spanish Frontier and the Despoblado" (Ph.D. dissertation, University of Texas, Austin, 1955) is probably the most helpful.

Almost no material is available on the Mexican period in the Big Bend, largely because the territory was practically isolated and left to the Indians until the end of the Mexican War when the United States took possession of it. Anglo-American expeditions soon penetrated the unknown region, led by John Coffee Hays in 1848. Perhaps the most obtainable source on the Hays expedition is James K. Greer, *Colonel Jack Hays, Texas Frontier Leader and California Land Builder* (New York, 1952), which contains a good account of the journey, and Rena Maverick Green (ed.), *Samuel Maverick, Texan: 1803–1870* (San Antonio, 1952), which includes Maverick's diary of the expedition.

The first military expendition into the Big Bend – and the report in which the term "big bend" first appeared in print – was led by Lt. William H. C. Whiting, whose diary is published in Ralph P. Bieber (ed.), *Exploring Southwestern Trails, 1846–1854* (Glendale, 1938), but others were quick to follow. The most easily available account of the Topographical Engineers in the Big Bend is Ronnie C. Tyler (ed.), "Exploring the Rio Grande: Lt. Duff C. Green's Report of 1852," *Arizona and the West,* X (Spring, 1968). It contains the diary that Green, the military commander who accompanied the civilian surveyor through the heart of the Big Bend, submitted after he reached Fort Duncan. The surveyor was M. T. W. Chandler, whose report is printed in a scarce set compiled by William H. Emory, the Chief Surveyor and later Commissioner of the Boundary Survey team, *Report on the United States and Mexican Boundary Survey. . . .* (2 vols.; Washington: Government Printing Office, 1857–1859).

After gold was discovered in California, many men crossed through the Big Bend region en route to the goldfields. Numerous diaries and accounts have been published; among the best are George P. Hammond and Edward H. Howes (eds.), *Overland to California on the Southwestern Trail, 1849: Diary of Robert Eccleston* (Berkeley, 1950); George W. B. Evans, *Mexican Gold Trail: The Journal of a Forty-Niner,* ed. by Glenn S. Dumke (San Marino, 1945), and Robert W. Stephens (ed.), *A Texan in the Gold Rush: The Letters of Robert Hunter, 1849–1851* (Bryan, Texas, 1972).

Trails were soon established through the Big Bend. One of the first pathfinders was the team of Neighbors and Ford, whose story is told in W. Turrentine Jackson, *Wagon Roads West: A Study of Federal Road Surveys and Construction in the Trans-Mississippi West, 1846–1869* (Berkeley, 1952), John S. Ford, *Rip Ford's Texas,* ed. by Stephen B. Oates (Austin, 1963), and Kenneth F. Neighbours, "The Expedition of Major Robert S. Neighbors to El Paso in 1849," *Southwestern Historical Quarterly,* 233

LVIII (July, 1954). The best account of the later teamsters who used the Chihuahua Trail is August Santleben, *A Texas Pioneer: Early Staging and Overland Freighting Days on the Frontiers of Texas and Mexico*, ed. by I. D. Affleck (New York, 1910).

The trail that has attracted the most curiosity, both from those who pioneered in the Big Bend and those who read about it, is the Great Comanche War Trail, which led from West Texas into the Big Bend, then forked before entering Mexico. One of the first studies of it is J. Evetts Haley, "The Great Comanche War Trail," *Panhandle-Plains Historical Review*, XXIII (1950). But the Topographical Engineers mentioned it as a possible location for a fort (Tyler, ed., "Green's Report," and Chandler in Emory, *Report of the Mexican Boundary*), and Judge O. W. Williams recorded the stories that Natividad Luján recalled about it in S. D. Myres (ed.), *Pioneer Surveyor, Frontier Lawyer: The Personal Narrative of O. W. Williams, 1877–1902* (El Paso, 1966). Ralph A. Smith's research on Indian raids into Mexico has led him into detailed study of the trail: "The Comanche Bridge Between Oklahoma and Mexico, 1843–1844," *Chronicles of Oklahoma*, XXXIX (Spring, 1961), and "The Comanche Sun Over Mexico," *West Texas Historical Association Year Book*, LXVI (1970). An archaeological expedition from the University of Texas studied the trail several years ago, but decided that they really did not have enough experience with century-old trails to reach any conclusions. A report on their research is published in T. N. Campbell and William T. Field, "Identification of Comanche Raiding Trails in Trans-Pecos Texas," *West Texas Historical Association Year Book*, XLIV (Oct., 1968).

The Anglo-Americans quickly found that they would have to wrest the territory from the Indians, who had inhabited it for centuries. The Spaniards initially had little difficulty, for they found only the remnants of Puebloan civilizations that were declining by the 16th century. The Mexicans and Anglo-Americans found different Indians in the Big Bend, however, because the more warlike tribes from the plains moved southward during the 19th century. The best information on the Indians themselves remains W. W. Newcomb, *The Indians of Texas: From Prehistoric to Modern Times* (Austin, 1961), but Dorman H. Winfrey and James M.

Day (eds.), *The Indian Papers of Texas and the Southwest, 1825–1916* (5 vols., Austin, 1966), contains a wealth of information. Probably the best material on the Indians of the mid-19th century in the Big Bend and northern Mexico is found in a series of articles published in various journals by Ralph A. Smith, who has spent years searching Mexican as well as United States archives and newspapers for elusive details of unremembered conflicts. The tremendous amount of information he has assembled is revealed in the series of articles in the bibliography. "The Comanche Sun Over Mexico" is perhaps his most penetrating article on the Indians of the Big Bend.

Conquest of the Indians and establishment of United States military control over the Big Bend is told by Barry Scobee, *Fort Davis, Texas, 1583–1960* (El Paso, 1963); Robert M. Utley, *Fort Davis National Historic Site, Texas* (Washington, 1965); William H. Leckie, *The Buffalo Soldiers: A Narrative of the Negro Cavalry in the West* (Norman, 1967); in two articles by Frank M. Temple: "Colonel B. H. Grierson's Victorio Campaign," *West Texas Historical Association Year Book,* XXV (Oct., 1959), and "Colonel B. H. Grierson's Administration of the District of the Pecos," *West Texas Historical Association Year Book,* XXXVIII (Oct., 1962); and Dan L. Thrapp, *Victorio and the Mimbres Apaches* (Norman, 1974).

Accounts of early cattlemen and ranchers can be found in several sources. Many early residents reminisced in the pages of *Voice of the Mexican Border,* a magazine published for several years during the 1930s. Clifford B. Casey, in his report for the National Park Service, *Soldiers, Ranchers and Miners in the Big Bend* (Washington, 1969), included much material on early ranchers and residents of the region. Additional information is included in Casey's *Mirages, Mysteries, and Reality.* Noel L. Keith has recorded the story of *The Brites of Capote* (Fort Worth, 1961), who became benefactors of Texas Christian University to the extent that Brite Divinity School is named for the family. Mrs. O. L. Shipman also wrote of early ranchers in *Taming the Big Bend: A History of the Extreme Western Portion of Texas from Fort Clark to El Paso* (Marfa, 1926). Lewis Nordyke has included accounts of many Big Bend ranchers in his *Great Roundup: The Story of Texas and Southwestern Cowmen* (New York, 1955). A good summary of ranching in the Big Bend is Robert M. Utley, "The Range Cattle Industry in the Big Bend of Texas," *Southwestern Historical Quarterly, LXIX* (April, 1966).

Some ranchers and cowmen chose to tell their own story, such as Will Tom Carpenter, *Lucky 7: A Cowman's Autobiography,* ed. by Elton Miles (Austin, 1957), and Frank Collinson, *Life in the Saddle,* ed. and arr. by Mary W. Clarke (Norman, 1963).

Settlement in the Big Bend is recounted by several who homesteaded land, such as J. O. Langford with Fred Gipson, *Big Bend, A Homesteader's Story* (Austin, 1952), who operated the Hot Springs Bath, and C. A. Hawley, "Life Along the Border," *West Texas Historical and Scientific Society Publications,* XX (1964), who worked for one of the mining companies in Terlingua. The best storyteller of the Big Bend was Judge O. W. Williams of Fort Stockton, whose tales are recorded in Myres (ed.), *Pioneer Surveyor, Frontier Lawyer.* Judge Williams not only wrote his own accounts of the country, but also set down the folklore of significant informants like Luján, an old Mexican who seemed to know all the stories of the Big Bend.

Mining played a large part in development of the region, but little literature has been produced on it. A good study of one company is James M. Day, "The Chisos Quicksilver Bonanza in the Big Bend of Texas," *Southwestern Historical Quarterly,* LXIV (Apr., 1961). Perhaps the most comprehensive is Kathryn B. Walker, "Quicksilver Mining in the Terlingua Area," (M.A. thesis, Sul Ross State College, 1960). But the best account of mining operations and life is C. A. Hawley's, for he lived in Terlingua and worked for the mines for years. His reminiscences in "Life Along the Border" provide an intimate view of mining and the life it created. Casey also has researched the history of mining in the Big Bend and presented it in *Soldiers, Ranchers, and Miners.*

One incident that changed the history of the Big Bend was the coming of the railroad in 1882. The Chihuahua Trail ceased to be so important; isolation was no longer such a major factor. Only one work treats the subject of railroads in Texas, S. G. Reed, *A History of the Texas Railroads and of Transportation Conditions Under Spain and Mexico and the Republic and The State* (Houston, 1941). *From Ox-Teams to Eagles: A History of the Texas and Pacific Railways* (Dallas, n.d.) adds little to the story that Reed tells.

Many colorful characters lived in the Big Bend during its development. One of the best known was E. E. Townsend, who became known as the father of the national park. His biography has been written by Lewis H. Saxton and Clifford B. Casey, "The Life of Everett Ewing Townsend," *West Texas Historical and Scientific Society Publications,* XVII. J. Evetts Haley covers the few years that Jeff Milton spent in the Big Bend in *Jeff Milton, a Good Man with a Gun* (Norman, 1948). Leavitt Corning, Jr., treats Ben Leaton and Milton Faver as thoroughly as possible in *Baronial Forts of the Big Bend* (San Antonio, 1967). Much must go unsaid about these two formidable characters, however, for so little is known about them. James B. Gillett has written his own story in *Six Years With the Texas Rangers, 1875 to 1881* (New Haven, 1925). Much public mention was given the "badmen" of the Big Bend when Robert T. Hill published his account of a float from Presidio to Langtry in "Running the Cañons of the Rio Grande," *Century Illustrated Monthly Magazine,* LXI (Nov., 1900-Apr., 1901). A later account of Hill's expedition is Ronnie C. Tyler, "Robert T. Hill and the Big Bend," *The American West,* X (Sept. 1973).

Material on the bandit era in the Big Bend is plentiful. Some of it contains exaggerations, but two of the best accounts are Clarence C. Clendennen, *Blood on the Border: The United States Army and the Mexican Irregulars* (London, 1969), a work by a scholar who was a member of Pershing's punitive expedition, and Herbert M. Mason, *The Great Pursuit* (New York, 1970). Supplementary sources written by men who went with Major Langhorne into Mexico are James Hopper, "A Little Mexican Expedition," *Collier's,* LVII (July 15, 1916), and Stuart W. Cramer, Jr., "The Punitive Expedition from Boquillas" *U.S. Cavalry Journal,* XXVIII (Oct., 1916). Walter P. Webb, *The Texas Rangers: A Century of Frontier Defense* (Boston, 1935) also contains some material on the Rangers and bandits

Other first-hand accounts of the military participation in the Big Bend are Stacy C. Hinkle, *Wings Over the Border: The Army Air Service Armed Patrol of the United States-Mexico Border, 1919–1921* (El Paso, 1970), and *Wings and Saddles: The Air and Cavalry Punitive Expedition of 1919* (El Paso, 1967). C. D. Wood, owner of the wax factory that was raided at Glenn Springs, told his own story in "The Glenn Springs Raid," *West Texas Historical and Scientific Society Publications,* XIX (1963), and W. D. Smithers, a photographer and journalist who came to the Big Bend in 1916, wrote an account of the bandit raids in *Pancho Villa's Last Hangout – On Both Sides of the Rio Grande in the Big Bend Country* (Alpine, n.d.).

The best surveys of the establishment of the Big Bend National Park are R. M. Wagstaff, "Beginnings of the Big Bend Park," *West Texas Historical Association Year Book,* XLIV (Oct., 1968), Clifford B. Casey, "The Big Bend National Park," *West Texas Historical and Scientific Society Publications,* XIII (1948), and Madison, *Big Bend,* ch. 16. Former Superintendent of the park, L. A. Garrison, wrote "A History of the Proposed Big Bend International Park," which was distributed over a limited area in mimeograph form, but was never published.

I. Primary

A. Manuscripts
- Adjutant General's Office (Texas) Records Transcripts. Archives, University of Texas, Austin.
- Adjutant General's Records. Archives, Texas State Library, Austin.
- "Annual Report for the Fiscal Year 1916 of Major Frederick Funston, U.S. Army, Commanding Southern Department," in Records of the Adjutant General's Office. Record Group 94, National Archives, microfilm publication.
- Big Bend Scrapbook. Archives, University of Texas.
- Bliss, Zenas R. "Reminiscences of Zenas R. Bliss Major General United States Army." Copy in Archives, University of Texas.
- Brewster County Scrapbook. Archives, University of Texas.
- Carter, Amon G., Foundation Files. Fort Worth, Texas.
- Despatches from United States Consuls in Chihuahua, 1826-1906. Roll 1, vol. 1, Aug. 18, 1826–Dec. 31, 1869. National Archives microfilm.
- Emory, William H., Papers. Western Americana Collection, Yale University, New Haven, Conn.
- Gardner, George Clinton, Papers. De Golyer Foundation Library, Southern Methodist University, Dallas, Texas.
- Grierson, Benjamin H., Collection. Newberry Library, Chicago.
- Langberg, Emilio. "Itinerario de la Espedición de San Carlos, Chih. á Monclova Viejo." Copy in Guajardo Collection in Western Americana Collection, Yale University.
- Letters Received by the Topographical Bureau of the War Department, 1824–1865. Microcopy 506, roll 36, I-J, September 1838–December 1854. National Archives.
- Letters Sent by the Topographical Bureau of the War

Department and by Successor Division in the Office of the Chief of Engineers. Vol. II, Oct. 16, 1848–Sept. 15, 1849; microcopy No. 66, Roll 13, National Archives.
• Office of the Adjutant General Document File. Record Group 94, National Archives.
• Rábago y Terán, Pedro de. "Diario de la Campaña executado por el Governador de Coahuila." Typescript in Archives, University of Texas Library.
• Webb, Walter P., Papers. Archives, Texas State Library.

B. Interviews
• W. P. Cameron, Mineral Wells, Texas, July 2, 1970.
• Mr. and Mrs. Hart M. Greenwood, Ciénega Ranch, May 8, 1973.
• Dr. Ross A. Maxwell, Austin, April 6, 1973.
• Dr. Calhoun Harris Monroe, El Paso, November 9, 1971.

C. Maps
• Derotero Topográfico de la espedición que desde San Carlos hasta Piedras Negras II Regreso por la Laguna de Laco a Chihuahua hiso el inspector inter. Colonias Militares de ese estado Coronel Don E. Langberg en el año 1851. Colección de Mapas del Estado de Chihuahua, Sociedad Mexicana de Geográfica y Estadística, México.
• "Map of Southern Part of Presidio County," by John T. Gano. Texas State Land Office, Austin.

D. Government Documents
• "Echols Diary," in *Report of the Secretary of War,* 36th Cong., 2d Sess., Sen. Ex. Doc. No. 1.
• Emory, William H. *Notes of a Military Reconnaissance From Fort Leavenworth, in Missouri, to San Diego, in California.* . . . 30th Cong., 1st Sess., Sen. Ex. Doc. No. 41.
• —————. *Report on the United States and Mexican Boundary Survey.* . . . Washington, 1857–1859. 2 vols.
• Miller, Hunter. Ed. *Treaties and Other International Acts of the United States of America.* Washington, 1937. 8 vols.
• "Reports of Reconnaissances, etc.," in *Report of the Secretary of War.* . . . 31st Cong., 1st Sess., Sen. Ex. Doc. No. 64.
• *Report of the Secretary of War,* 32nd Cong., 1st Sess., Sen. Ex. Doc. No. 1.
• *Report of the Secretary of War,* 36th Cong., 1st Sess., Sen. Ex. Doc. No. 2.
• *Report of the Secretary of War,* 31st Cong., 1st Sess., Sen. Ex. Doc. No. 32.

E. Newspapers
• *Alpine Avalanche.* 1907, 1909, 1911, 1913, 1916, 1951.
• *Arkansas State Gazette.* Little Rock. 1839.
• *Austin Daily Statesman.* 1882.
• *Austin Dispatch.* 1937.

- *Big Spring Herald.* 1941.
- *Corpus Christi Star.* 1848.
- *Daily National Intelligencer.* Washington, D.C. 1848.
- *The Daily Picayune.* New Orleans. 1849–50.
- *Dallas Morning News.* 1937–38, 1941, 1944.
- *Democratic Telegraph and Texas Register.* Houston. 1848.
- *El Paso Daily Times.* 1883, 1886, 1899.
- *Fort Worth Star-Telegram.* 1935, 1942–43, 1955, 1958.
- *Galveston Civilian.* 1871.
- *Houston Chronicle.* 1938.
- *Leslie's Illustrated.* New York City. 1855, 1858.
- *The Morning Star.* Houston. 1841.
- *The New Era.* Marfa. 1908–11.
- *New York Herald.* 1849.
- *Rocky Mountain News.* Denver. 1936.
- *San Angelo Standard-Times.* 1941–42.
- *San Antonio Daily Express.* 1877, 1879–82, 1938.
- *San Antonio Herald.* 1857.
- *San Antonio Ledger.* 1852.
- *San Antonio Light.* 1942.
- *San Saba Weekly News.* 1891.
- *The South-Western American.* Austin. 1851.
- *The Statesman.* Austin. 1881.
- *The Texas Monument.* La Grange. 1851.
- *The Texas Republican.* Marshall. 1849, 1850.
- *Texas State Gazette.* Austin. 1849–51.
- *Victoria Advocate.* 1878.
- *Waco Tribune-Herald.* 1936.
- *The Western Star.* Lebanon, Ohio. 1840.
- *Western Texan.* San Antonio. 1850–52.

F. Books

- Bailey, L. R. Ed. *The A. B. Gray Report.* Los Angeles, 1973.
- Bartlett, John R. *Personal Narrative of Explorations and Incidents in Texas, New Mexico, Sonora and Chihuahua.* New York, 1852. 2 vols.
- Bolton, Herbert E. Ed. *Athanase de Mézières and the Louisiana-Texas Frontier, 1768–1780.* Cleveland, 1914. 2 vols.
- —————————. Ed. *Spanish Exploration in the Southwest, 1542–1706.* New York, 1967 reprint.
- Brinckerhoff, Sidney B., and Faulk, Odie B., Eds. *Lancers for the King: A Study of the Frontier Military System of*

Northern New Spain, with a Translation of the Royal Regulations of 1772. Phoenix, 1965.

• Carpenter, Will Tom. *Lucky 7: A Cowman's Autobiography.* Ed. by Elton Miles. Austin, 1957.

• Chamberlain, Samuel E. *My Confession.* Ed. by Roger Butterfield. New York, 1956.

• Collinson, Frank. *Life in the Saddle.* Ed. and Arr. by Mary Whatley Clarke. Norman, 1963.

• Connelley, William E. Ed. *Doniphan's Expedition and the Conquest of New Mexico and California.* Kansas City, 1907.

• Evans, George W. B. *Mexican Gold Trail: The Journal of a Forty-Niner.* Ed. by Glenn S. Dumke. San Marino, 1945.

• Ford, John S. *Rip Ford's Texas.* Ed. by Stephen B. Oates. Austin, 1963.

• Fulcher, Walter. *The Way I Heard It: Tales of the Big Bend.* Ed. by Elton Miles. Austin, 1959.

• Gillett, James B. *Six Years With the Texas Rangers, 1875 to 1881.* New Haven, 1925.

• González Flores, Enrique, and Almada, Francisco R., Eds. *Informe de Hugo de O'Conor sobre el estado de las Provincias Internas del Norte, 1771-76.* México, 1952.

• Green, Rena Maverick. Ed. *Samuel Maverick, Texan: 1803-1870.* San Antonio, 1952.

• Gregg, Josiah. *Commerce on the Prairies: or the Journal of a Santa Fe Trader.* New York, 1844. 2 vols.

• Hackett, Charles Wilson. Ed. *Historical Documents Relating to New Mexico, Nueva Vizcaya, and Approaches Thereto.* Washington, 1923-1937. 3 vols.

• Hammond, George P., and Howes, Edward H. Eds. *Overland to California on the Southwestern Trail, 1849: Diary of Robert Eccleston.* Berkeley, 1950.

• ―――――――, and Rey, Agapito. Eds. *Expedition Into New Mexico Made by Antonio de Espejo, 1582-1583, as Revealed in the Journal of Diego Pérez de Luxán, a Member of the Party.* Los Angeles, 1929.

• Harris, Benjamin B. *The Gila Trail: The Texas Argonauts and the California Gold Rush.* Ed. by Richard H. Dillon. Norman, 1960.

• Hodge, Frederick W. Ed. *Spanish Explorers in the Southern United States.* New York, 1907.

• Hunter, J. Marvin. *The Boy Captives, Being the True Story of the Experiences and Hardships of Clinton L. Smith and Jeff D. Smith.* Bandera, Texas, 1927.

• Kendall, George W. *Narrative of the Texan Santa Fe Expedition, Comprising a Description of a Tour Through Texas.* New York, 1844. 2 vols.

• Kinnaird, Lawrence. Ed. *The Frontiers of New Spain: Nicholas de LaFora's Description, 1766-1768.* Berkeley, 1957.

• Langford, J. O., with Gipson, Fred. *Big Bend, A Homesteader's Story.* Austin, 1952.

- Leclercq, Jules. *Voyage au Mexique de New-York à Vera-Cruz en suivant les routes de terre.* Paris, 1885.
- Lesley, Lewis B. Ed. *Uncle Sam's Camels: The Journal of May Humphreys Stacey Supplemented by the Report of Edward Fitzgerald Beale, 1857–1858.* Cambridge, 1929.
- Maltby, W. J. *Captain Jeff, or Frontier Life in Texas with the Texas Rangers.* Colorado, Texas, 1906.
- Morfi, Fray Juan Agustín de. *Diario y derrotero (1777–1781).* Ed. by Eugenio del Hoyo and Malcolm D. McLean. Monterrey, 1967.
- Myres, S. D. Ed. *Pioneer Surveyor, Frontier Lawyer: The Personal Narrative of O. W. Williams, 1877–1902.* El Paso, 1966.
- Porras Muñoz, Guillermo. Ed. *Diario y derrotero de lo caminado, visto y obcervado en el discurso de la vista general de precidios, situados en las Provincias Ynternas de Nueva España, que de orden de su magestad executó D. Pedro de Rivera, Brigadier de los Reales Exercitos.* México, 1945.
- Römer, Ferdinand. *Texas, With Particular Reference to German Immigration and the Physical Appearance of the Country.* Trans. by Oswald Mueller. San Antonio, 1935.
- Ross, Marvin C. Ed. *George Catlin: Episodes From Life Among the Indians and Last Rambles.* Norman, 1959.
- Santleben, August. *A Texas Pioneer: Early Staging and Overland Freighting Days on the Frontiers of Texas and Mexico.* Ed. by I. D. Affleck. New York, 1910.
- Scott, Hugh L., *Some Memoirs of a Soldier.* New York and London, 1928.
- Simmons, Marc. Trans. and Ed. *Border Comanches: Seven Spanish Colonial Documents, 1785–1819.* Santa Fe, 1967.
- Stephens, Robert W. Ed. *A Texan in the Gold Rush: The Letters of Robert Hunter, 1849–1851.* Bryan, Texas, 1972.
- Thomas, Alfred B. Trans. and Ed. *After Coronado: Spanish Exploration Northeast of New Mexico, 1696–1727.* Norman, 1935.
- —————————. *Teodoro de Croix and the Northern Frontier of New Spain, 1776–1783.* Norman, 1941.
- Winfrey, Dorman H., and Day, James M. Eds. *The Indian Papers of Texas and the Southwest, 1825–1916.* Austin, 1966. 5 vols.

G. Articles
- Coldwell, Capt. Neal, to Gen. John B. Jones, Fort Davis, July 10, 1880, in *Voice of the Mexican Border,* I (Dec., 1933).

- Cramer, Stuart W. "The Punitive Expedition from Boquillas," *U.S. Cavalry Journal*, XXVIII (Oct., 1916).
- Crimmins, M. L. Ed. "Two Thousand Miles by Boat in the Rio Grande in 1850," *West Texas Historical and Scientific Society Publications*, V, 1933.
- Day, D. T. "Quicksilver in 1894," *U.S. Geological Survey, 16th Annual Report*, Pt. 3.
- Duke, Escal F. Ed. "A Description of the Route from San Antonio to El Paso by Captain Edward S. Meyer," *West Texas Historical Association Year Book*, XLIX (1973).
- Gillett, J. B. "The Old G4 Ranch," *Voice of the Mexican Border*, I (Oct., 1933).
- Haley, J. Evetts. Ed. "A Log of the Texas-California Cattle Trail, 1854," *Southwestern Historical Quarterly*, XXXV (Jan., 1932) and (Apr., 1932), XXXVI (July, 1932).
- Hammond, George P., and Rey, Agapito. Eds. "The Rodríguez Expedition to New Mexico, 1581–1582," *New Mexico Historical Review*, II (July, 1927).
- Hawley, C. A. "Life Along the Border," *West Texas Historical and Scientific Society Publications*, XX, 1964.
- Hill, Robert T. "Running the Cañons of the Rio Grande," *Century Illustrated Monthly Magazine*, LXI (Nov., 1900–Apr., 1901).
- Hopper, James. "A Little Mexican Expedition," *Collier's, the National Weekly*, LVII (July 15, 1916).
- Mecham, J. Lloyd. "The Second Spanish Expedition to New Mexico: An Account of the Chamuscado-Rodríguez Entrada of 1581–1582," *New Mexico Historical Review*, I (July, 1926).
- Meler, T. M., to Roy L. Swift, Cordell, Oklahoma, Aug. 3, 1939, in *American White Water*, XI (Spring, 1966).
- Mitchell, F. A. "The Stampede at Robber's Roost," *Voice of the Mexican Border*, I (Oct., 1933).
- Moore, Mary Lu, and Breene, Delmar L. Trans. and Eds. "The Interior Provinces of New Spain: The Report of Hugo O'Conor, January 30, 1776," *Arizona and the West*, XIII (Autumn, 1971).
- Peril, W. A. "From Texas to the Oregon Line," in J. Marvin Hunter. Ed. *The Trail Drivers of Texas*. 2nd ed. rev. Nashville, 1925.
- Reindrop, Reginald C. Trans. "The Founding of Missions at La Junta de los Rios," *Supplementary Studies of the Texas Catholic Historical Society*, I (Apr., 1938).
- Sanderlin, Walter S. "A Cattle Drive from Texas to California: The Diary of M. H. Erskine, 1854," *Southwestern Historical Quarterly*, LXVII (Jan., 1964).
- Shrode, Maria H. "Overland by Ox-Train in 1870; From Sulphur Springs, Texas, to San Diego, California," *Quarterly of the Historical Society of Southern California*, XXVI (Mar., 1944).
- Simpich, Frederick. "Down the Rio Grande," *National Geographic Magazine*, LXXVI (Oct., 1939).

- Tharp, B. C., and Kielman, Chester V. Eds. "Mary S. Young's Journal of Botanical Explorations in Trans-Pecos Texas, August-September, 1914," *Southwestern Historical Quarterly,* LXV (Jan. and Apr., 1962).
- Townsend, E. E. "Rangers and Indians in the Big Bend Region," *West Texas Historical and Scientific Society Publications,* Bulletin No. 56, 1935.
- Tyler, Ronnie C. Ed. "Exploring the Rio Grande: Lt. Duff C. Green's Report of 1852," *Arizona and the West,* X (Spring, 1968).
- "Up the Trail in 1890 – Experiences of Drive Told by Tom Granger, Ft. Davis," *Alpine Avalanche* (Anniversary Edition), Sept. 14, 1951.
- Wagstaff, R. M. "Beginnings of the Big Bend Park," *West Texas Historical Association Year Book,* LXIV (Oct., 1968).
- Westerlund, Peter. "Reminiscences of a Trip to Pike's Peak and Down the Rio Grande in the Year 1859, at the Time of the Pikes Peak Gold Craze," *Swedish American Historical Society Yearbook,* II (1908).
- Whiting, William H. C. "Journal of William Henry Chase Whiting, 1849," in Ralph P. Bieber. Ed. *Exploring Southwestern Trails, 1846–1854: Philip St. George Cooke, William Henry Chase Whiting, Francois Xavier Aubry.* Glendale, 1938.
- Wood, C. D. "The Glenn Springs Raid," *West Texas Historical and Scientific Society Publications* XIX, (1963).

II. Secondary

A. Books
- Adams, Ramon F. *A Fitting Death for Billy the Kid.* Norman, 1960.
- Bannon, John F. *The Spanish Borderlands Frontier, 1513-1821.* New York, 1970.
- Bender, Averam B. *The March of Empire: Frontier Defense in the Southwest, 1848–1860.* Lawrence, 1952.
- Bobb, Bernard E. *The Viceregency of Antonio María Bucareli in New Spain, 1771–1779.* Austin, 1962.
- Bolton, Herbert E. *Coronado on the Turquois Trail: Knight of Pueblos and Plains.* Albuquerque, 1949.
- Braddy, Haldeen. *Pancho Villa at Columbus: The Raid of 1916.* El Paso, 1965.
- Brown, William E., and Wauer, Roland H. *Historic Resources Management Plan, Big Bend National Park.* Washington, 1968.

● Casey, Clifford B. *Mirages, Mysteries and Reality, Brewster County, Texas: The Big Bend of the Rio Grande.* Hereford, Texas, 1972.

● ―――――. *Soldiers, Ranchers and Miners in the Big Bend.* Washington, 1969.

● Castañeda, Carlos E. *Our Catholic Heritage in Texas, 1519–1936,* Austin, 1936. 7 vols.

● Clendennen, Clarence C. *Blood on the Border: The United States Army and the Mexican Irregulars.* London, 1969.

● Corning, Leavitt, Jr., *Baronial Forts of the Big Bend.* San Antonio, 1967.

● *Corpus Christi: 100 Years.* Corpus Christi, 1952.

● Dobie, J. Frank. *The Longhorns.* Boston, 1941.

● Douglas, William O. *Farewell to Texas: A Vanishing Wilderness.* New York, 1967.

● Faulk, Odie B. *Too Far North–Too Far South.* Los Angeles, 1967.

● Foreman, Grant. *Advancing the Frontier, 1830-1860.* Norman, 1933.

● Fowler, Harlan D. *Camels to California: A Chapter in Western Transportation.* Stanford, 1950.

● *From Ox-Teams to Eagles: A History of the Texas and Pacific Railways.* Dallas, n.d.

● Fuentes Mares, José. *Y México se refugio en el desierto: Luis Terrazas, historia y destino.* México, 1954.

● Geiser, Samuel W. *Men of Science in Texas, 1820–1880.* Dallas, 1959.

● Gerald, Rex E. *Spanish Presidios of the Late Eighteenth Century in Northern New Spain.* Santa Fe, 1968.

● Goetzmann, William H. *Army Exploration in the American West, 1803–1863.* New Haven, 1959.

● ―――――. *Exploration and Empire: The Explorer and the Scientist in the Winning of the American West.* New York, 1967.

● Greer, James K. *Colonel Jack Hays, Texas Frontier Leader and California Land Builder.* New York, 1952.

● Haley, J. Evetts. *Fort Concho and the Texas Frontier.* San Angelo, 1952.

● ―――――. *Jeff Milton, a Good Man with a Gun.* Norman, 1948.

● Hallenbeck, Cleve. *Álvar Núñez Cabeza de Vaca: The Journey and Route of the First European to Cross the Continent of North America, 1534–1536.* Glendale, 1940.

● Hine, Robert V. *Bartlett's West: Drawing the Mexican Boundary.* New Haven, 1968.

● Hinkle, Stacy C. *Wings and Saddles: The Air and Cavalry Punitive Expedition of 1919.* El Paso, 1967.

● ―――――. *Wings Over the Border: The Army Air Service Armed Patrol of the United States-Mexico Border, 1919–1921.* El Paso, 1970.

- Horgan, Paul. *Great River: The Rio Grande in North American History*. New York, 1954. 2 vols.
- Jackson, W. Turrentine. *Wagon Roads West: A Study of Federal Road Surveys and Construction in the Trans-Mississippi West, 1846–1869*. Berkeley, 1952.
- Jones, Billy M. *Health Seekers in the Southwest, 1817-1900*. Norman, 1967.
- Keith, Noel L. *The Brites of Capote*. Fort Worth, 1961.
- Leckie, William H. *The Buffalo Soldiers: A Narrative of the Negro Cavalry in the West*. Norman, 1967.
- Levy, Benjamin. *Hot Springs, Big Bend National Park: Historic Structures Report, Part 1, Historical Data*. Washington, 1968.
- Madison, Virginia. *The Big Bend Country of Texas*. Rev. Ed. New York, 1968.
- —————, and Stillwell, Hallie. *How Come It's Called That? Place Names in the Big Bend Country*. Albuquerque, 1958.
- Martin, George C. *Archaeological Exploration of the Shumla Caves*. San Antonio, 1933.
- Mason, Herbert M. *The Great Pursuit*. New York, 1970.
- Maxwell, Ross A. *The Big Bend of the Rio Grande: A Guide to the Rocks, Landscape, Geologic History, and Settlers of the Area of the Big Bend National Park*. Austin, 1968.
- Merk, Frederick. *Slavery and the Annexation of Texas*. New York, 1972.
- Miles, Elton. "Old Fort Leaton: A Saga of the Big Bend," in Wilson M. Hudson. Ed. *Hunters & Healers: Folklore Tales & Topics*. Austin, 1971.
- Moorhead, Max L. *The Apache Frontier: Jacobo Ugarte and Spanish-Indian Relations in Northern New Spain, 1769–1791*. Norman, 1968.
- Myres, Sandra L. *The Ranch in Spanish Texas*. El Paso, 1969.
- Newcomb, W. W. *The Indians of Texas, From Prehistoric to Modern Times*. Austin, 1961.
- Nordyke, Lewis. *Great Roundup: The Story of Texas and Southwestern Cowmen*. New York, 1955.
- Ogle, Ralph H. *Federal Control of the Western Apaches, 1848–1886*. Albuquerque, 1940.
- Pennsylvania University, Committee of the Society of Alumni, *Biographical Catalogue of the Matriculates of the College. . . . 1749–1893*. Philadelphia, 1894.
- Raht, Carlysle G. *The Romance of Davis Mountains and Big Bend Country*. El Paso, 1919.
- Reed, S. G. *A History of the Texas Railroads and of*

Transportation Conditions Under Spain and Mexico and the Republic and The State. Houston, 1941.

- *Report of the Big Bend Area, Texas.* U.S. Department of the Interior, National Park Service, State Park E C W, Dist. III, Jan., 1935.
- Richardson, Rupert N. *The Comanche Barrier to South Plains Settlement: A Century and a Half of Savage Resistance to the Advancing White Frontier.* Glendale, 1933.
- Sauer, Carl O. *Sixteenth Century North America: The Land and the People as Seen by the Europeans.* Berkeley, 1971.
- Scobee, Barry. *Fort Davis, Texas, 1583–1960.* Fort Davis, Texas, 1963.
- ――――――. *The Steer Branded Murder: The True and Authentic Account of a Frontier Tragedy.* Houston, 1952.
- Shipman, Mrs. O. L. *Taming the Big Bend: A History of the Extreme Western Portion of Texas From Fort Clark to El Paso.* Marfa, 1926.
- Sonnichsen, C. L. *I'll Die Before I'll Run: The Story of the Great Feuds of Texas.* New York, 1951.
- ――――――. *The Mescalero Apaches.* Norman, 1958.
- Thrapp, Dan L. *Victorio and the Mimbres Apaches.* Norman, 1974.
- Utley, Robert M. *Fort Davis National Historic Site, Texas.* Washington, 1965.
- Wauer, Roland H. *Birds of Big Bend National Park and Vicinity.* Austin, 1973.
- ――――――. *Guide to the Backcountry Roads and the River.* Big Bend National Park, Texas, 1970.
- ――――――. *Hiker's Guide to the Developed Trails and Primitive Routes.* Big Bend National Park, Texas, n.d.
- ――――――. *Road Guide to the Paved and Improved Dirt Roads.* Big Bend National Park, Texas, 1970.
- Webb, Walter P. *The Texas Rangers: A Century of Frontier Defense.* Boston, 1935.
- Webb, Walter P. and Carroll, H. Bailey. Eds. *The Handbook of Texas.* Austin, 1952. 2 vols.
- Weddle, Robert S. *San Juan Bautista, Gateway to Spanish Texas.* Austin, 1968.
- Wheat, Carl I. *Mapping the Transmississippi West, 1840-1861.* San Francisco, 1957–1963. 5 vols.
- Wirth, Conrad L. *Boundary Line Report: Big Bend National Park Project, Texas.* Washington, 1935.
- Wormington, H. M. *Prehistoric Indians of the Southwest.* Denver, 1964.

B. Articles

- Bender, A. B. "Opening Routes Across West Texas, 1848–1850," *Southwestern Historical Quarterly,* XXXVII (Oct., 1933).
- Bolton, Herbert E. "The Jumano Indians in Texas, 1650–1771," *Quarterly of the Texas State Historical Association,* XV (July, 1911).

- Campbell, T. N. and Field, William T. "Identification of Comanche Raiding Trails in Trans-Pecos Texas," *West Texas Historical Association Year Book*, XLIV (Oct., 1968).
- Casey, Clifford B. "The Big Bend National Park," *West Texas Historical and Scientific Society Publications*, XIII, 1948.
- —————————. "The Trans-Pecos in Texas History," *West Texas Historical and Scientific Society Publications*, V, 1933.
- Christiansen, Paige W. "Hugo O'Conor's Inspection of Nueva Vizcaya and Coahuila, 1773," *Louisiana Studies*, II (Fall, 1963).
- Clifton, Minnie D. "A History of the Bloys Camp Meeting," *West Texas Historical and Scientific Society Publications*, XII, (1947).
- Connelley, Harry. "Big Bend National Park Project Reality at Last," *West Texas Today* (Sept., 1941).
- Coopwood, Bethel. "The Route of Cabeza de Vaca," *Quarterly of the Texas State Historical Association*, III (Oct., 1899), (Jan. and Apr., 1900).
- Davis, T. C. "The Cross-In Ranch: History and Development of a Pioneer Ranch," *Voice of the Mexican Border*, I (Oct., 1933).
- Day, James M. "The Chisos Quicksilver Bonanza in the Big Bend of Texas," *Southwestern Historical Quarterly*, LXIV (Apr., 1961).
- Dobie, J. Frank. "The Texan Part of Texas," *Nature Magazine*, XVI (Dec., 1930).
- Faulk, Odie B., and Brinckerhoff, Sidney B. "Soldiering at the End of the World," *The American West*, II (Summer, 1966).
- Foree, Kenneth, Jr. "Our New Park on the Rio Grande," *The Saturday Evening Post* (Dec. 2, 1944).
- Gregg, John E. "History of Presidio County," *Voice of the Mexican Border* (Centennial Edition), 1936.
- Haley, J. Evetts. "The Great Comanche War Trail," *Panhandle-Plains Historical Review*, XXIII (1950).
- Hill, Robert T. "The Cinnabar Deposits of the Big Bend Province of Texas," *Engineering and Mining Journal*, LXXIV (Sept. 6, 1902).
- —————————. "The Great Chisos Rift Along the Canyons of the Rio Grande," *American Association, Proceedings*, LXIX (1900).
- Johnson, J. Harlan. "A History of Mercury Mining in the Terlingua District of Texas," *The Mines Magazine* (Sept., 1946).
- Kelley, Charles, Jr., "Factors Involved in the Abandonment of Certain Peripheral Southwestern Settlements," *American Anthropologist*, LIV (July-Sept., 1952).
- —————————. "The Historic Indian Pueblos of La Junta de los Rios," *New Mexico Historical Review*, XXVI (Oct., 1952); (Jan., 1953).

• ————————. "Juan Sabeata and Diffusion in Aboriginal Texas," *American Anthropologist*, LVII (Oct., 1955).

• ————————. "The Route of Antonio de Espejo Down the Pecos River and Across the Texas Trans-Pecos Region of 1583: Its Relation to West Texas Archeology," *West Texas Historical and Scientific Society Publications*, VII, (1937).

• Lammons, Bishop F. "Operation Camel: An Experiment in Animal Transportation in Texas, 1857–1860," *Southwestern Historical Quarterly* LXI, (July, 1957).

• Martin, Mabelle E. "California Emigrant Roads Through Texas," *Southwestern Historical Quarterly*, XXVIII (Apr., 1925).

• Mecham, J. Lloyd. "Antonio de Espejo and His Journey to New Mexico," *Southwestern Historical Quarterly*, XXX (Oct., 1926).

• Mellard, Rudolph. "Early West Texas Cattle and Horse Brands," *Voice of the Mexican Border*, I (Feb.-March, 1934).

• Miles, Elton. "Chisos Ghosts," in Mody C. Boatright, Wilson M. Hudson, and Allen Maxwell. Eds. *Madstones and Twisters*. Dallas, 1958.

• Neighbours, Kenneth F. "The Expedition of Major Robert S. Neighbors to El Paso in 1849," *Southwestern Historical Quarterly*, LVIII (July, 1954).

• Nelson, Al B. "Campaign in the Big Bend of the Rio Grande, 1787," *Southwestern Historical Quarterly*, XXXIX (Oct., 1935).

• ————————. "Juan de Ugalde and Picax-ande Ins-tinsle, 1787–1788," *Southwestern Historical Quarterly*, XLIII (Apr., 1940).

• Park, Joseph R. "Spanish Indian Policy in Northern Mexico, 1765–1810," *Arizona and the West*, IV (Winter, 1962).

• Ponton, Brownie, and McFarland, Bates F. "Alvar Núñez Cabeza de Vaca: A Preliminary Report of His Wanderings in Texas," *Quarterly of the Texas State Historical Association*, I (Jan., 1898).

• Reeve, Frank D. "The Apache Indians in Texas," *Southwestern Historical Quarterly*, L (Oct., 1946).

• Saxton, Lewis H. and Casey, Clifford B. "The Life of Everett Ewing Townsend," *West Texas Historical and Scientific Society Publications*, XVII.

• Schick, Robert. "Wagons to Chihuahua," *The American West*, III (Summer, 1966).

• Schoffelmayer, Victor H. "The Big Bend Area of Texas: A Geographic Wonderland," *Texas Geographic Magazine*, I (May, 1937).

• Schulman, Edmund. "Dendrochronology in Big Bend National Park, Texas," *Tree-Ruling Bulletin*, XVIII (Oct., 1951–Jan., 1952).

• Scobee, Barry. "The First General Cattle Round-Up of the Davis Mountains-Big Bend District," *West Texas Historical and Scientific Society Publications*, III (1930).

• Shipman, Jack. "The Lone Red Murder Yearling of West Texas," *Voice of the Mexican Border*, I (Feb.–March, 1934).

• Skaggs, Jimmy M. "A Study in Business Failures: Frank Collinson in the Big Bend," *Panhandle-Plains Historical Review*, XLIII, 1970.

- Smith, Ralph A. "Apache Plunder Trails Southward, 1831–1840," *New Mexico Historical Review*, XXXVII (Jan., 1962).
- ——... "The Comanche Bridge Between Oklahoma and Mexico, 1843–1844." *Chronicles of Oklahoma*, XXXIX (Spring, 1961).
- ——. "The Comanche Invasion of Mexico in the Fall of 1845," *West Texas Historical Association Year Book*, XXV (Oct., 1959).
- ——. "The Comanche Sun Over Mexico," *West Texas Historical Association Year Book*, LXVI (1970).
- ——. " 'Long' Webster and 'The Vile Industry of Selling Scalps,' " *West Texas Historical Association Year Book*, XXXVII (Oct., 1961).
- ——. "Mexican and Anglo-Saxon Traffic in Scalps, Slaves, and Livestock, 1835–1841," *West Texas Historical Association Year Book*, XXXVI (Oct., 1960).
- ——. "Poor Mexico, So Far From God and So Close to the *Tejanos*," *West Texas Historical Association Year Book*, XLIV (1968).
- ——. "The Scalp Hunters in the Borderlands, 1835–1850," *Arizona and the West*, VI (Spring, 1964).
- Smith, Victor J. "Early Spanish Exploration in the Big Bend of Texas," *West Texas Historical and Scientific Society Publications*, II, 1928.
- Smithers, W. D. "Bandit Raids in the Big Bend Country," in *Pancho Villa's Last Hangout — On Both Sides of the Rio Grande in the Big Bend Country*. Alpine, n.d.
- ——. "Nature's Pharmacy and the Curanderos" and "The Border Trading Posts," *West Texas Historical and Scientific Society Publications*, XVIII, 1961.
- Temple, Frank F. "Colonel B. H. Grierson's Victorio Campaign," *West Texas Historical Association Year Book*, XXV (Oct., 1959).
- ——. "Colonel B. H. Grierson's Administration of the District of the Pecos," *West Texas Historical Association Year Book*, XXXVIII (Oct., 1962).
- ——. "Colonel Grierson in the Southwest," *Panhandle-Plains Historical Review*, XXX (1957).
- Tyler, Ronnie C. "Robert T. Hill and the Big Bend," *The American West*, X (Sept., 1973).
- Utley, Robert M. "Pecos Bill on the Texas Frontier," *The American West*, VI (Jan., 1969).
- ——. "The Range Cattle Industry in the Big Bend of Texas," *Southwestern Historical Quarterly*, LXIX (Apr., 1966).

- Vigness, David M. "Don Hugo O'Conor and New Spain's Northeastern Frontier, 1764–1776," *Journal of the West,* VI (Jan., 1967).
- Webb, Walter P. "The Big Bend of Texas," *Panhandle-Plains Historical Review,* X (1937).
- Wright, Mrs. Joel E. "Early Settling of the Big Bend," *West Texas Historical and Scientific Society Publications,* XIX, 1963.

C. Unpublished Typescripts
- Garrison, L. A. "A History of the Proposed Big Bend International Park," Mimeographed article in the files of the Amon G. Carter Foundation, Fort Worth.
- Raborg, William A. "The Villa Raid on Glenn Springs," Typescript in Sul Ross State University Library, Alpine, Texas.

D. Unpublished Theses
- Daniel, James M. "The Advance of the Spanish Frontier and the Despoblado." Unpublished Ph.D. Dissertation, University of Texas, 1955.
- Gregg, John E. "The History of Presidio County." M. A. Thesis, University of Texas, 1933.
- Hitchcock, Totsy N. "Representative Individuals and Families of the Lower Big Bend Region, 1895–1925." Unpublished M. A. Thesis, Sul Ross State College, 1960.
- Lammons, Bishop F. "Operation Camel: An Experiment in Animal Transportation in the Southwest, 1857–1860." Unpublished M. A. Thesis, Trinity University, 1955.
- Starnes, Gary B. "Juan de Ugalde (1729-1816) and the Provincias Internas of Coahuila and Texas." Unpublished Ph.D. Dissertation, Texas Christian University, 1971.
- Walker, Kathryn B. "Quicksilver Mining in the Terlingua Area." Unpublished M. A. Thesis, Sul Ross State College, 1960.

Following page: A U.S. Army patrol in the Big Bend about 1916.

Notes

The complete entry for all citations can be found in the
bibliography.

Chapter 1

1   Nevill to Z. L. Nevill, in the *Austin Daily Statesman,*
Feb. 25, 1882; Nevill to Adj. Gen. W. H. King, Camp Manske
Cañon, Feb. 4, 1882, copy in Adjutant General's Office (Texas)
Records . . . Transcripts.
2   Goetzmann, *Exploration and Empire: The Explorer and the
Scientist in the Winning of the American West,* 430-66,
489-576; Goetzmann, *Army Exploration in the American West,
1803-1868,* 185-86; Ross (ed.), *George Catlin: Episodes From
Life Among the Indians and Last Rambles,* 174-75; Townsend,
"Rangers and Indians in the Big Bend Region," *West Texas Historical
and Scientific Society Publications,* Bulletin No. 56 (1935), 43-46;
quotation in *El Paso Daily Times,* June 18, 1883.
3   *El Paso Daily Times,* Oct. 31, 1899: Hill, "Running the Cañons
of the Rio Grande," *Century Illustrated Monthly Magazine,* LXI
(Nov., 1900-Apr., 1901), 371-87.
4   The Mexican Boundary Survey team had estimated the depth
of the canyons at much more realistic figures in 1852, but the report
was of limited distribution and virtually unknown to laymen.
El Paso Daily Times, July 13, 1899; Hill, "Running the Cañons of
the Rio Grande," *ibid.,* 371-87.
5   Lieutenant Whiting made reference to the Big Bend in his
journal on March 12, 1849. See "Journal of William Henry Chase
Whiting, 1849," in Bieber (ed.), *Exploring Southwestern Trails,
1846-1854: Philip St. George Cooke, William Henry Chase Whiting,
Francois Xavier Aubry,* 265. Quotations in Echols' Diary, in
Report of the Secretary of War, 36th Cong., 2d Sess., Sen. Ex. Doc.
No. 1, 41. See also letter from O. W. Williams, Fort Stockton,
Texas, Feb. 23, 1901, in Myres (ed.), *Pioneer Surveyor, Frontier
Lawyer: The Personal Narrative of O. W. Williams, 1877-1902,*
222; Casey, *Mirages, Mysteries and Reality, Brewster County,
Texas: The Big Bend of the Rio Grande,* 1-4; and Fulcher,
The Way I Heard It: Tales of the Big Bend, ed. by Elton Miles, xix.
6   Maxwell, *The Big Bend of the Rio Grande: A Guide to the
Rocks, Landscape, Geologic History, and Settlers of the Area of
Big Bend National Park,* 1.
7   Daniel, "The Advance of the Spanish Frontier and the
Despoblado," 1-11; quotation in Jules Leclercq, *Voyage au Mexique
de New-York à Vera-Cruz en suivant les routes de terre,* 15.

8   Hill, "Running the Cañons," 380.
9   Madison and Stillwell, *How Come It's Called That? Place Names in the Big Bend Country*, 53; Emory, *Report on the United States and Mexican Boundary Survey. . . .*, I, Pt. 2, p. 55; Nevill to Z. L. Nevill, in the *Austin Daily Statesman*, Feb. 25, 1882; Hill, "Running the Cañons," 379; quotation in Meler to Roy L. Swift, Cordell, Oklahoma, August 3, 1939, in *American White Water*, XI (Spring, 1966), 32.
10   Hill, "Running the Cañons," 378; Maxwell, *The Big Bend*, 87-91.
11   Pedro de Rábago y Terán, "Diario de la Campaña executado por el Governador de Coahuila." See also Tyler (ed.), "Exploring the Rio Grande: Lt. Duff C. Green's Report of 1852," *Arizona and the West*, X (Spring, 1968), 55; Echols' Diary, 47; Meler to Swift, Cordell, Oklahoma, Aug. 3, 1939; Hill, "Running the Cañons," 381.
12   Madison and Stillwell, *How Come It's Called That?*, 51; Hill, "Running the Cañons," 382; Maxwell, *The Big Bend*, 52-53; Tyler (ed.), "Green's Report," 54.
13   Nevill to Adj. Gen. W. H. King, Camp Manske Canyon, Feb. 4, 1882, copy in Adjutant General's Office (Texas), Records Transcripts; Emilio Langberg, "Itinerario de la Espedición de San Carlos, Chih. à Monclova Viejo," 12.
14   Hackett (ed.), *Historical Documents Relating to New Mexico, Nueva Vizcaya, and Approaches Thereto*, II, 221, 331; Miles, "Chisos Ghosts," in Boatright, Hudson, and Maxwell (eds.), *Madstones and Twisters*, 116-17; Myres (ed.), *Pioneer Surveyor*, 257-64.
15   Miles, "Chisos Ghosts," 107-08; quotation in Maxwell, *The Big Bend*, 79.
16   Madison and Stillwell, *How Come It's Called That?*, 38; Madison, *The Big Bend Country of Texas*, 230.
17   Maxwell, *The Big Bend*, 79.
18   Madison and Stillwell, *How Come It's Called That?*, 29-33, 59.
19   Maxwell, *The Big Bend*, 51, 72.

Chapter 2

1   Leclercq, *Voyage au Mexique*, 33.
2   The most recent consideration of Cabeza de Vaca's route is Sauer, *Sixteenth Century North America: The Land and the People as Seen by the Europeans*, 117-22. See also Ponton and McFarland, "Alvar Núñez Cabeza de Vaca: A Preliminary Report of His Wanderings in Texas," *Quarterly of the Texas State*

Historical Association, I (Jan., 1898), 166-86; Coopwood, "The Route of Cabeza de Vaca," *Quarterly of the Texas State Historical Association,* III (Oct., 1899), 108-40, (Jan.,1900), 177-208, (Apr., 1900), 229-64; and Hallenbeck, *Álvar Núñez Cabeza de Vaca: The Journey and Route of the First European to Cross the Continent of North America, 1534-1536,* 155.

3 Bolton, *Coronado on the Turquois Trail: Knight of Pueblos and Plains,* 23-39, 49-200.

4 For a discussion of the early Spanish *entradas* into the Big Bend, see Castañeda, *Our Catholic Heritage in Texas, 1519-1936,* Vol. I: *The Mission Era: The Finding of Texas, 1519-1693,* 157-94. See also Martin, *Archaeological Exploration of the Shumla Caves;* Bolton, "The Jumano Indians in Texas, 1650-1771," *Quarterly of the Texas State Historical Association,* XV (July, 1911), 68.

5 Bolton (ed.), *Spanish Exploration in the Southwest, 1542-1706,* 137; Mecham, "The Second Spanish Expedition to New Mexico: An Account of the Chamuscado-Rodríguez Entrada of 1581-1582," *New Mexico Historical Review,* I (July, 1926), 266; quotation in Hammond and Rey (trans. and ed.), "The Rodríguez Expedition to New Mexico, 1581-1582," *New Mexico Historical Review,* II (July, 1927), 252.

6 Newcomb, *The Indians of Texas, From Prehistoric to Modern Times,* 230; Wormington, *Prehistoric Indians of the Southwest,* 112-13.

7 Newcomb, *Indians of Texas,* 226-28; Frederic J. Dockstader to Virginia Madison, July 24, 1957, quoted in Madison and Stillwell, *How Come It's Called That?,* 29-30.

8 Hodge (ed.), *Spanish Explorers in the Southern United States,* 103-04; Kelley, "The Historic Indian Pueblos of La Junta de los Rios," *New Mexico Historical Review,* XXVI (Oct., 1952), 257-95, and (Jan., 1953), 20-51; Kelley, "Factors Involved in the Abandonment of Certain Peripheral Southwestern Settlements," *American Anthropologist,* LIV (July-Sept., 1952), 363.

9 Mecham, "Chamuscado-Rodríguez Entrada," 267-70; see also Hammond and Rey (trans. and ed.), "Rodríguez Expedition to New Mexico," 334-62.

10 Mecham, "Antonio de Espejo and His Journey to New Mexico," *Southwestern Historical Quarterly,* XXX (Oct., 1926), 118; Bolton (ed.), *Spanish Exploration,* 161-95; Hammond and Rey (eds.), *Expedition Into New Mexico Made by Antonio de Espejo, 1582-1583, As Revealed in the Journal of Diego Pérez de Luxán, a Member of the Party,* 45-128; Kelley, "The Route of Antonio de Espejo Down the Pecos River and Across the Texas Trans-Pecos Region of 1583; Its Relation to West Texas Archeology," *West Texas Historical and Scientific Society Publications,* VII (1937), 7-25.

11 Bolton (ed.), *Spanish Exploration,* 190; Kelley, "Route of Espejo," 9.

12 Bolton (ed.), *Spanish Exploration,* 200-01.

13 Kelley, "Juan Sabeata and Diffusion in Aboriginal Texas," *American Anthropologist,* LVII (Oct., 1955), 984.

14 Bolton (ed.), *Spanish Exploration,* 314-15.

15 *Ibid.,* 320-43; see also Smith, "Early Spanish Exploration in the Big Bend of Texas," *West Texas Historical and Scientific Society Publications,* II (1928), 59-68; Reindrop (trans.), "The Founding of Missions at La Junta de los Rios," *Supplementary Studies of the Texas Catholic Historical Society,* I (Apr., 1938), 5-28; Castañeda, *Our Catholic Heritage in Texas, 1519-1936:* Vol. III; *The Mission Era: The Missions at Work, 1731-1761,* 197-99.

16 Hammond and Rey (eds.), "The Rodríguez Expedition to New Mexico, 1581-1582," *New Mexico Historical Review,* II (July, 1927), 256; Letter of Oñate, in Bolton (ed.), *Spanish Exploration,* 253.

17 Sonnichsen, *The Mescalero Apaches,* 33.

18 Bannon, *The Spanish Borderlands Frontier, 1813-1821,* 30; *Autos* made by Gen. Juan de Retana, July 19 to July 30, 1693, and "Declaration of Captain Juan de Retana, September 5, 1693," in Hackett (ed.), *Historical Documents,* II, 329-35, 343-49.

19 Daniel, "Advance of the Spanish Frontier," 115-16.

20 Thomas, *After Coronado: Spanish Exploration Northeast of New Mexico, 1696-1727,* 23-24; Newcomb, *Indians of Texas,* 107-09.

21 "Report of Governor Antonio de Oca Sarmiento to the señor viceroy El Parral, March 12, 1667," in Hackett (ed.), *Historical Documents,* II, 91.

22 Daniel, "Advance of the Spanish Frontier," 107-09.

23 Newcomb, *Indians of Texas,* 156-67.

24 Porras Muñoz (ed.), *Diario y derrotero de lo caminado, visto y obcervado en el discurso de la vista general de precidios, situados en las Provincias Ynternas de Nueva España, que de orden de su magestad executó D. Pedro de Rivera, Brigadier de los Reales Exercitos.*

25 Quotations in Weddle, *San Juan Bautista, Gateway to Spanish Texas,* 196-204; see also Castañeda, *Our Catholic Heritage in Texas, 1519-1936,* Vol. II: *The Mission Era: The Winning of Texas, 1693-1731,* 336-46. Colonel Langberg experienced difficulty traveling over the same land years later. See Langberg, "Itinerario de La Espedición."

26 Quoted in Daniel, "Advance of the Spanish Frontier," 170-71.

27 Weddle, *San Juan Bautista,* 206-10. See also Castañeda, *Missions at Work,* 203-07.

28 Quoted in Daniel, "Advance of the Spanish Frontier," 186-87.

29 Weddle, *San Juan Bautista,* 228-29; Daniel, "Advance of the Spanish Frontier," 187, 196-97.

30   All the material on Rábago y Terán's journey is taken from Rábago y Terán, "Diario de la Campaña," with consideration of the judgments made by Daniel, Weddle, and Castañeda, *Missions at Work,* 211-19, regarding location sites mentioned in the journal. See also Kelley, "The Historic Indian Pueblos of La Junta," *New Mexico Historical Review,* XXVI (Oct., 1952), 272-73, 294, (Jan., 1953), 31, 38, 40, 46.

31   Quotations in Rábago y Terán, "Diario de la Campaña," 157-60, 163.

32   Daniel, "Advance of the Spanish Frontier," 186-97; Castañeda, *Missions at Work,* 220-23.

33   Daniel, "Advance of the Spanish Frontier," 203.

34   Kinnaird (ed.), *The Frontier of New Spain: Nicholas de LaFora's Description, 1766-1768,* 12.

35   Brinckerhoff and Faulk (eds.), *Lancers for the King: A Study of the Frontier Military System of Northern New Spain, with a Translation of the Royal Regulations of 1772;* Bobb, *The Viceregency of Antonio María Bucareli in New Spain, 1771-1779,* 131.

36   Flores and Almada (eds.), *Informe de Hugo de O'Conor sobre el estado de las Provincias Internas del Norte, 1771-76,* and Moore and Breene, "The Interior Provinces of New Spain: The Report of Hugo O'Conor, January 30, 1776," *Arizona and the West,* XIII (Autumn, 1971), 265-82. See also Christiansen, "Hugo O'Conor's Inspection of Nueva Vizcaya and Coahuila, 1773," *Louisiana Studies,* II (Fall, 1963), 164-67; and Vigness, "Don Hugo Oconor and New Spain's Northeastern Frontier, 1764-1776," *Journal of the West,* VI (Jan., 1967), 27-40.

37   Gerald, *Spanish Presidios of the Late Eighteenth Century in Northern New Spain,* 12-13, 37-40; Moore and Breene, "Report of O'Conor," 269.

38   Thomas, *Teodoro de Croix, and the Northern Frontier of New Spain, 1776-1783,* 22-24; Faulk and Brinckerhoff, "Soldiering at the End of the World," *The American West,* III (Summer, 1966), 28-37.

39   Thomas, *Teodoro de Croix,* 25, 45-58; Morfi, *Diario y derrotero (1777-1781),* 125, 129.

40   Bolton (ed.), *Athanase de Mézières and the Louisiana-Texas Frontier, 1768-1780,* II, 158; Thomas, *Teodoro de Croix,* 38.

41   Thomas, *Teodoro de Croix,* 43-51; Moorhead, *The Apache Frontier: Jacobo Ugarte and Spanish-Indian Relations in Northern New Spain, 1769-1791,* 120-23.

42   Daniel, "Advance of the Spanish Frontier," 263-67; Starnes, "Juan de Ugalde (1729-1816) and the Provincias Internas of Coahuila and Texas," 44, 57.

43   Nelson, "Campaigning in the Big Bend of the Rio Grande, 1787," *Southwestern Historical Quarterly,* XXXIX (Oct., 1935), 200-27; Nelson, "Juan de Ugalde and Picax-ande Ins-tinsle, 1787-1788," *Southwestern Historical Quarterly,* XLIII (Apr., 1940), 438-64.

44 Wheat, *Mapping the Transmississippi West, 1540-1861*, I, 121-23.
45 Moorhead, *The Apache Frontier*, 221-36.
46 *Ibid.*, 143-69; Starnes, "Juan de Ugalde," 96; Marc Simmons (trans. and ed.), *Border Comanches: Seven Spanish Colonial Documents, 1785-1819*, 14-15, 21-22.
47 Park, "Spanish Indian Policy in Northern Mexico, 1765-1810," *Arizona and the West*, IV (Winter, 1962), 340-41.

Chapter 3

1 Ford, *Rip Ford's Texas*, 68-69, quotation on 107.
2 Gregg, *Commerce on the Prairies: or the Journal of a Santa Fe Trader*, I, 162-65; *The Louisianian*, July 26, 1839, quoted in the *Arkansas State Gazette* (Little Rock), Sept. 4, 1839; Foreman, *Advancing the Frontier, 1830-1860*, 164; Connelley (ed.), *Doniphan's Expedition and the Conquest of New Mexico and California*, 277-82.
3 *Arkansas State Gazette*, Sept. 4, Oct. 9, 1839; Kendall, *Narrative of the Texan Santa Fe Expedition, Comprising a Description of a Tour Through Texas*, II, 120.
4 Gregg, *Commerce on the Prairies*, I, 162-64.
5 Quotations in the *Arkansas State Gazette*, Sept. 4, 1839; *The Western Star* (Lebanon, Ohio), Dec. 11, 1840; *The Morning Star* (Houston), Mar. 27, 1841.
6 Connelley (ed.), *Doniphan's Expedition and the Conquest of New Mexico and California*, 451-52; Gregg, "The History of Presidio County," 45.
7 Greer, *Colonel Jack Hays, Texas Frontier Leader and California Land Builder*, 217-18.
8 Wahm was cared for by some friendly Indians until he made his way back to civilization about a year later. Hays' Report, in the *Democratic Telegraph and Texas Register* (Houston), Dec. 28, 1848; Greer, *Jack Hays*, 391, n. 14; Green (ed.), *Samuel Maverick, Texan: 1803-1870*, 223, 336.
9 *Corpus Christi Star*, Dec. 5, 1848.
10 Hays' Report; Gregg, "History of Presidio County," 45.
11 Hays to William L. Marcy, San Antonio, Dec. 13, 1848, in *Senate Executive Documents*, No. 32, 31st Cong., 1st Sess., 32-33; Greer, *Jack Hays*, 224-25.
12 Hays' Report; Hays to Marcy, San Antonio, Dec. 13, 1848.
13 Ford, *Rip Ford's Texas*, 113-29; Jackson, *Wagon Roads West: A Study of Federal Road Surveys and Construction*

in the Trans-Mississippi West, 1846-1869, 37-39; Neighbours,
"The Expedition of Major Robert S. Neighbors to El Paso in 1849,"
Southwestern Historical Quarterly, LVIII (July, 1954), 36-59.
14   Wheat, *Mapping the Transmississippi West*, III, 64, 68,
274; *Texas State Gazette* (Austin), Nov. 3, 10, 1849, Apr. 27, 1850.
15   Evans, *Mexican Gold Trail: The Journal of a Forty-Niner*,
xv, 60, 76-77.
16   *Democratic Telegraph and Texas Register*, Dec. 28, 1848;
Corpus Christi Star, Sept. 19, Dec. 23, 30, 1848; *Texas State Gazette*,
Dec. 1, 1849.
17   *Corpus Christi Star*, Mar. 17, 24, 31, 1849; *Texas State Gazette*,
Nov. 16, 1850.
18   *Corpus Christi Star*, July 21, 1849; *The Daily Picayune*
(New Orleans), Aug. 21, 1849; *Corpus Christi: 100 Years*,
57; quotation is in *The Daily Picayune*, Aug. 31, 1849. See also
Webb and Carroll (eds.), *The Handbook of Texas*, I, 532.
19   *Texas State Gazette*, Aug. 25, 1849; Hunter to his wife,
Presidio del Norte, June 2, 1849, in Stephens (ed.), *A Texan
in the Gold Rush: The Letters of Robert Hunter 1849-1851*,
13-14.
20   *The Texas Republican* (Marshall), July 13, 1849.
21   *The Texas Republican*, Mar. 28, 1850; *Texas State Gazette*,
Nov. 24, 1849; *The Daily Picayune*, Nov. 13, 1850.
22   Quotation in *Western Texan* (San Antonio), Sept. 10, 1850;
San Antonio Texan, quoted in the *Texas State Gazette*, May 4, 1850;
quote in *Texas State Gazette*, Sept, 20, 1851; quotation in *Western
Texan*, Oct. 2, 1851.
23   Quotation in *Texas State Gazette*, Nov. 24, 1849; quotation
in *The Daily Picayune*, Nov. 13, 1850; quotation in *The Texas
Monument* (La Grange), Feb. 25, 1851; *Galveston Weekly News*,
Aug. 1, 1854; Smith, "Poor Mexico, So Far From God and So
Close to the *Tejanos*," *West Texas Historical Association Year Book*,
XLIV (Oct., 1968), 78; Hammond and Howes (eds.), *Overland
to California on the Southwestern Trail, 1849: Diary of Robert
Eccleston*, 138.
24   Emory, *Report*, I, 86-89.
25   See Campbell and Field, "Identification of Comanche Raiding
Trails in Trans-Pecos Texas," *West Texas Historical Association
Year Book*, XLIV (Oct., 1968), 128-44. O. W. Williams himself
saw the trail. Myres (ed.), *Pioneer Surveyor*, 278-81. Maj. J.
Van Horne to Maj. George Deas, Post opposite El Paso, N.M.,
Nov. 8, 1849, plus enclosures (Langberg to Van Horne, El Paso, Oct.
23, 1849, and Trias to Langberg, Chihuahua, Oct. 10, 1849), in
Winfrey and Day. *The Indian Papers of Texas and the Southwest,
1825-1916*. V, 50-53; Langberg, "Itinerario de la Espedición," 7.
26   For material on the Sol family, see Smith, "The Comanche
Sun Over Mexico," *West Texas Historical Association Year Book*,
LXVI (1970), 25-62. For material on the Comanche Trail, see
Smith, "The Comanche Bridge Between Oklahoma and Mexico,
1843-1844," *Chronicles of Oklahoma*, XXXIX (Spring, 1961), 54-69;

and "Apache Plunder Trails Southward, 1831-1840," *New Mexico Historical Review*, XXXVII (Jan., 1962), 20-42. See also Rogers to Peter H. Bell, San Antonio, Sept. 3, 1851, in Winfrey and Day (eds.), *Indian Papers of Texas*, III, 141; and Neighbors to Elisha M. Pease, San Antonio, Apr. 10, 1854, in V, 171.

27 Quotations are in Fuentes Mares, *Y México se refugio en el desierto: Luis Terrazas, historia y destino*, 144, and Chamberlain, *My Confession*, 270. For material on the raids and on the scalp hunters, see articles by Smith: "Mexican and Anglo-Saxon Traffic in Scalps, Slaves, and Livestock, 1835-1841," *West Texas Historical Association Year Book*, XXXVI (Oct., 1960), 89-115; " 'Long' Webster and 'The Vile Industry of Selling Scalps,' " *West Texas Historical Association Year Book*, XXXVII (Oct., 1961), 99-120; "The Scalp Hunters in the Borderlands, 1835-1850," *Arizona and the West*, VI (Spring, 1964), 5-22; and "Poor Mexico, So Far From God and So Close to the *Tejanos*," *West Texas Historical Association Year Book*, XLIV (Oct., 1968), 78-105. See also Evans, *Mexican Gold Trail*, 84-85.

28 *San Antonio Ledger*, Sept. 2, 1852; *The Texas Republican*, Mar. 28, 1850, Oct. 16, 1852, quoting the *San Antonio Ledger*.

29 Santleben, *A Texas Pioneer: Early Staging and Overland Freighting Days on the Frontiers of Texas and Mexico*, 115, 117, 119.

30 *Ibid.*, 114. *Western Texan*, Sept. 30, Oct. 28, 1852; *The Texas Republican*, Jan. 10, 1850, Apr. 8, 22, 1854, quoting the *Galveston News* and the *Western Texan;* Langberg, "Itinerario de la Espedición," 14.

31 Quotation in *Galveston Weekly News*, Aug. 1, 1854; Santleben, *A Texas Pioneer*, 111.

32 *The Texas Republican*, Jan. 10, 1850; *San Antonio Ledger*, quoted in *The South-Western American* (Austin), June 11, 1851. Miles weaves some even more fantastic tales in "Old Fort Leaton: A Saga of the Big Bend," in Hudson (ed.), *Hunters & Healers: Folklore Tales & Topics*, 88-89.

33 Macmanus to Secretary of State Lewis Cass, Chihuahua, Jan. 28, 1859, in Despatches from United States Consuls in Chihuahua, 1826-1906.

Chapter 4

1 For a summary of Johnston's life, see Webb and Carroll (eds.), *Handbook of Texas*, I, 920.

2 Quotation in Abert to Stephen Markoe, Washington, May 18,

1849, in Letters Sent by the Topographical Bureau of the War Department and by Successor Division in the Office of the Chief of Engineers. See also Emory, *Notes of a Military Reconnaissance From Fort Leavenworth, in Missouri, to San Diego, in California.* . . ., Sen. Ex. Doc. 41, 30th Cong., 1st Sess. El Paso del Norte is present-day Ciudad Juárez. El Paso, Texas, was not founded until 1850 when it was called Franklin. It took the name El Paso when Ciudad Juárez changed its name.

3   Quotation in Abert to Markoe, Washington, May 18, 1849, in Letters Sent. See also Bieber (ed.), *Exploring Southwestern Trails*, 34-35; Raht, *The Romance of Davis Mountains and Big Bend Country*, 127. Someone on the expedition wrote long letters to the *New York Herald* reporting their progress and difficulties. See July 13, 1849.

4   "Reports of Reconnaissances, etc.," *in Report of the Secretary of War.* . . ., 31st Cong., 1st Sess., Sen. Ex. Doc. 64, 49.

5   *Ibid.,* 27; *Report of the Secretary of War,* 32d Cong., 1st Sess., Sen. Ex. Doc. 1, 112; Green quoted in Merk, *Slavery and the Annexation of Texas,* 162.

6   Crimmins (ed.), "Two Thousand Miles by Boat in the Rio Grande in 1850," *West Texas Historical and Scientific Society Publications,* V (1933), 44-45. See also Horgan, *Great River: The Rio Grande in North American History,* II, 808-09; Johnston to W. F. Smith, San Antonio, April 9, 1850, Johnston to Abert, San Antonio, January 7, 1851, Johnston to Abert, San Antonio, September 11, 1850, and Smith to Johnston, San Antonio, January 6, 1851, in Letters Received by the Topographical Bureau of the War Department, 1824-1865.

7   W. F. Smith to Johnston, San Antonio, October 26, 1850, and Johnston to Abert, San Antonio, January 7, 1851, in Letters Received.

8   Quotations are in Johnston to Abert, Sept. 11, 1850, and Johnston to "General," Jan. 6, 1851, in *ibid.*

9   Goetzmann, *Army Explorations in the American West,* ch. 5; Faulk, *Too Far North − Too Far South,* ch. 6.

10   Gardner to Sarah, El Paso, Nov. 27, 1851, Gardner to father, Camp opposite Presidio del Norte, July 10, 1852, and Gardner to father, Frontera near El Paso, Mar. 27, 1852, all in George Clinton Gardner Papers; Langberg, "Itinerario de la Espedición," 4.

11   Gardner to Alida, Camp on the Rio Grande above Presidio del Norte, July 29, 1852, in Gardner Papers.

12   Duff C. Green to Emory, Camp opposite Presidio del Norte, Aug. 30, 1852, Emory to Bartlett, on road near first crossing of San Pedro River, Sept. 18, 1852, in William H. Emory Papers; Geiser, *Men of Science in Texas, 1820-1880;* Pennsylvania University, Committee of the Society of Alumni, *Biographical Catalogue of the Matriculates of the College.* . . . 1749-1893, 107; Gardner to father, Frontera near El Paso, Feb. 6, 1852, in Gardner Papers. Chandler later served as a meteorological observer for the Smithsonian Institution at the Falls of the Saint Croix, Wisconsin,

and finally died in Brazil in 1868 while in the service of the Brazilian government.

13   Emory to Chandler, Presidio del Norte, August 8, 1852, and Emory to Green, Presidio del Norte, August 30, 1852, in Emory Papers. See Langberg's map, "Derotero Topográfico de la espedición que desde San Carlos hasta Piedras Negras II regreso por la Laguna de Laco a Chihuahua hiso el inspector inter. Colonias Militares de ese estado Coronel Don E. Langberg en el año 1851," in the Colección de Mapas del Estado de Chihuahua.

14   The best work on the artists of the survey is Hine, *Bartlett's West: Drawing the Mexican Boundary*. See also Tyler (ed.), "Green's Report," 51; Emory to Charles Radziminski, Camp opposite Presidio del Norte, August 28, 1852, and Emory to Green, Camp opposite Presidio del Norte, August 30, 1852, in Emory Papers.

15   Tyler (ed.), "Green's Report," 52; Lt. Dixon S. Miles to Emory, Fort Fillmore, August 13, 1852, and Emory to Green, Camp opposite Presidio del Norte, Aug. 30, 1852, in Emory Papers; *San Antonio Ledger*, Sept. 2, 23, 1852; Bartlett, *Personal Narrative of Explorations and Incidents in Texas, New Mexico, Sonora and Chihuahua*, II, 396-97.

16   Chandler, "San Vicente to Presidio del Norte," in Emory, *Report*, I, 80, quotation in Tyler (ed.), "Green's Report," 54.

17   Chandler, "San Vicente," 81; quotation in Tyler (ed.), "Green's Report," 54.

18   For information on the Indian trail and crossing, see Haley, *Fort Concho and the Texas Frontier*, ch. 1; Smith, "Comanche Bridge Between Oklahoma and Mexico," 54-56; "The Comanche Invasion of Mexico in the Fall of 1845," *West Texas Historical Association Year Book*, XXV (Oct., 1959), 4-5. See also Chandler, "San Vicente," 81; Tyler (ed.), "Green's Report," 54-55.

19   Thompson to Chandler, Camp near San Carlos, October 1, 1852, in Emory Papers; Wauer, *Guide to the Backcountry Roads and the River*, 27.

20   Chandler, "San Vicente," 82.

21   *Ibid.;* Tyler (ed.), "Green's Report," 55-56.

22   Tyler (ed.), "Green's Report," 56; Chandler, "San Vicente," 83.

23   Chandler, "San Vicente," 83.

24   *Ibid.*, 83-84; Emory to Chandler, Presidio del Norte, Aug. 8, 1852, in Emory Papers; Langberg, "Itinerario de la Espedición," 9.

25   Chandler, "San Vicente," 84; Tyler (ed.), "Green's Report," 56.

26 Tyler (ed.), "Green's Report," 57.

27 Chandler, "San Vicente," 84-85.

28 Quotations in Chandler to Emory, Camp on Rio Grande, Nov. 4, 1852, in Emory Papers; quotes in Tyler (ed.), "Green's Report," 57-58; Chandler, "San Vicente," 85.

29 Green to Chandler, Camp on Rio Grande, Nov. 3, 1852, Schott to Emory, Fort Duncan, n. d., Parry to Chandler, Camp on Rio Grande, Nov. 4, 1852, all in Emory Papers.

30 Chandler to Emory, Camp on Rio Grande, Nov. 4, 1852, in Emory Papers; Tyler (ed.), "Green's Report," 58.

31 Schott to Emory, Camp on Rio San Felipe, Oct. 1, 1852, Charles Radziminski to Emory, Saltillo, Dec. 10, 1852, in Emory Papers; Tyler (ed.), "Green's Report," 59-60.

32 The description of Michler's survey comes entirely from his report, in Emory, *Report*, I, 74-79.

33 Miller (ed.), *Treaties and Other International Acts of the United States of America*, V, 217; Abert to Seymour, Washington, Mar. 2, 1852, in Letters Sent.

34 Bailey (ed.), *The A. B. Gray Report.*

35 Scobee, *Fort Davis, Texas 1583-1960*, 5-8; Utley, *Fort Davis National Historic Site, Texas*, 5-7; Brooke to Gen. Winfield Scott, San Antonio, May 28, 1850, in Winfrey and Day (eds.), *Indian Papers of Texas*, III, 120.

36 Bliss, "Reminiscences of Zenas R. Bliss Major General United States Army," I, 153, 175. See also Webb and Carroll (eds.), *Handbook of Texas*, I, 175.

37 Lesley (ed.), *Uncle Sam's Camels: The Journal of May Humphreys Stacey Supplemented by the Report of Edward Fitzgerald Beale (1857-1858)*, 4-12. See also the *San Antonio Herald.* Jan. 31, 1857; Fowler, *Camels to California: A Chapter in Western Transportation*, 32-45.

38 Lesley (ed.), *Uncle Sam's Camels*, 6-7, 13; Jackson, *Wagon Roads West*, 245-46, 249.

39 Lesley (ed.), *Uncle Sam's Camels*, 45-46; Diary of Lieutenant Hartz in *Report of the Secretary of War*, 36th Cong., 1st. Sess., Sen. Ex. Doc. No. 2, 422-41. The account of the 1859 expedition is taken entirely from Hartz.

40 The account of the 1860 expedition is taken from Echols' journal, 33-50.

Chapter 5

1 Langford, *Big Bend, A Homesteader's Story*, 4; Hawley, "Life Along the Border," *West Texas Historical and Scientific Society Publications*, XX (1964); Myres, *Pioneer Surveyor*, 238.

2 Utley, *Fort Davis*, 113; Schick, "Wagons to Chihuahua," *The American West*, III (Summer, 1966), 74; quotation in Moye to Sec. of State William H. Seward, Chihuahua, June 3, 1867, in Chihuahua Consular Despatches.

3 Schick, "Wagons to Chihuahua," 76.

4   *Ibid.,* 77-78.

5   *Ibid.,* 77-79, 87-88.

6   Moorhead, *Chihuahua Trail,* 198-99.

7   *Galveston Civilian,* April 9, 1871; quotation in *The Statesman* (Austin), Dec. 2, 1881; Thrapp, *Victorio and the Mimbres Apaches,* 218-19.

8   Information on the Indian campaigns is taken from Scobee, *Fort Davis,* 37-145; Utley, *Fort Davis,* 17-47; Utley, "Pecos Bill on the Texas Frontier," *The American West,* VI (Jan., 1969), 4-13, 61-62; and Leckie, *The Buffalo Soldiers: A Narrative of the Negro Cavalry in the West,* chs. 4, 6, 8. See also Winfrey and Day (eds.), *Indian Papers of Texas,* IV, 215, 330; Duke (ed.), "A Description of the Route from San Antonio to El Paso by Captain Edward S. Meyer," *West Texas Historical Association Year Book,* XLIX (1973), 139.

9   Sonnichsen, *Mescalero Apaches,* 71-72, 158; Winfrey and Day (eds.), *Indian Papers of Texas,* IV, 387, 394, 398; Twiggs to Col. L. Thomas, San Antonio, June 16, 1857, and Aug. 24, 1858, in V, 204, 260-61; Hunter, *The Boy Captives, Being the True Story of the Experiences and Hardships of Clinton L. Smith and Jeff D. Smith,* 146; Ogle, *Federal Control of the Western Apaches, 1848-1886,* in *Publications in History,* IX (July, 1940), 183.

10   See Marcy and Neighbors to Gov. Bell, Fort Belknap, Sept. 30, 1854, in Winfrey and Day (eds.), *Indian Papers of Texas,* III, 190; quotation in Newcomb, *Indians of Texas,* 333.

11   Richardson, *The Comanche Barrier to South Plains Settlement: A Century and a Half of Savage Resistance to the Advancing White Frontier,* 172-77, 375-76; Sonnichsen, *Mescalero Apaches,* 58, 60-61, 161.

12   Quotations in *San Antonio Daily Express,* June 15, 26, 1877. See also July 4, 1879, Dec. 1, 1880. Col. Edward Hatch quoted in Sonnichsen, *Mescalero Apaches,* 185, n. 1.

13   Sonnichsen, *Mescalero Apaches,* 164-72; Thrapp, *Victorio,* 220-67.

14   See, for example, the reports of 1879 (manuscripts in the Grierson Collection, Newberry Library, Chicago). I am indebted to Frank M. Temple, of Lubbock, Texas, for use of transcripts of the Grierson material that he made while completing his study of the colonel. See Temple, "Colonel B. H. Grierson's Victorio Campaign," *West Texas Historical Association Year Book,* XXV (Oct., 1959), 99-111; "Colonel B. H. Grierson's Administration of the District of the Pecos," *West Texas Historical Association Year Book,* XXXVIII (Oct., 1962), 85-96; Thrapp, *Victorio,* 284.

15   Sonnichsen, *Mescalero Apaches,* 173-84; Thrapp, *Victorio,* 286-88.
16   Sonnichsen, *Mescalero Apaches,* 188; Rister, *The Southwestern Frontier, 1865-1881,* 203-17; Maltby, *Captain Jeff, or Frontier Life in Texas with the Texas Rangers,* 95; *San Antonio Daily Express,* Sept. 15, 1881; Jan. 29, 1882; Thrapp, *Victorio,* 293-307.
17   *San Antonio Daily Express,* Aug. 11, 1881.
18   *Daily Statesman* (Austin), Oct. 25, 1881; *San Antonio Daily Express,* Sept. 17, 1881, May 4, 1882. See also Reed, *A History of the Texas Railroads and of Transportation Conditions Under Spain and Mexico and the Republic and The State,* 191, 197; *From Ox-Teams to Eagles: A History of the Texas and Pacific Railways,* 29-30; Casey, *Mirages, Mysteries and Reality,* 22.
19   Myres, *The Ranch in Spanish Texas, 1691-1800,* 18.
20   Casey, *Soldiers, Ranchers and Miners in the Big Bend,* 142.
21   *Ibid.,* 146, 148; Utley, "The Range Cattle Industry in the Big Bend of Texas," *Southwestern Historical Quarterly,* LXIX (Apr., 1966), 421; quotation in Gillett, "The Old G4 Ranch," *Voice of the Mexican Border,* I (Oct., 1933), 82.
22   Casey, "The Trans-Pecos in Texas History," *West Texas Historical and Scientific Society Publications,* V (1933), 12.
23   Corning, *Baronial Forts of the Big Bend,* 44, 53-55; Bliss, "Reminiscenses," I, 263-64; Gregg, "History of Presidio County," *Voice of the Mexican Border,* 23, 41; interview with Mr. and Mrs. Hart M. Greenwood, Ciénaga Ranch, May 8, 1973.
24   Gregg, "History of Presidio County," *Voice of the Mexican Border,* 22; Bliss, "Reminiscences," I, 175, 260; *San Antonio Daily Express,* June 15, 1877, 2; Scobee, *Fort Davis,* 23-24, 41-43.
25   Utley, "Range Cattle Industry," 427; Bliss, "Reminiscences," I, 171.
26   *San Antonio Daily Express,* June 15, 1877, May 4, 1882, June 23, 1882; Davis, "The Cross-In Ranch: History and Development of a Pioneer Ranch," *Voice of the Mexican Border,* I (Oct., 1933), 76-77.
27   *San Antonio Daily Express,* May 4, 1882, June 23, 1882; interview with Mr. and Mrs. Hart M. Greenwood.
28   Keith, *The Brites of Capote,* 3-6.
29   Casey, *Soldiers, Ranchers and Miners,* 150-51. See also "Map of Southern Part of Presidio County" by John T. Gano in Texas State Land Office, Austin.
30   Gillett, "The Old G4 Ranch," 82-83. See also Gillett, *Six Years With The Texas Rangers, 1875 to 1881,* 238-39.
31   Shipman, *Taming the Big Bend: A History of the Extreme Western Portion of Texas From Fort Clark to El Paso,* 115-19; Nordyke, *Great Roundup: The Story of Texas and Southwestern Cowmen,* 83, quotations on 84, 202-03.
32   Peril "From Texas to the Oregon Line," in Hunter (ed.), *The Trail Drivers of Texas,* 411-12; Utley, "Range Cattle Industry," 426.

33 Carpenter, *Lucky 7: A Cowman's Autobiography*, 111-16.
34 *Daily Statesman*, Feb. 12, 1882. For further information on Rudabaugh see Adams, *A Fitting Death for Billy the Kid*, 31-32, 127, 157, 160, 186, 197, 216-17, 296.
35 Utley, "Range Cattle Industry," 436; Raht, *Romance of Davis Mountains and Big Bend Country*, 377; Gregg, "History of Presidio County," *Voice of the Mexican Border*, 41; Nevill to Capt. Neal Coldwell, Camp Manske Cañon, Dec. 12, 1881, in Adjutant General's Records.
36 Utley, "Range Cattle Industry," 428; Mellard, "Early West Texas Cattle and Horse Brands," *Voice of the Mexican Border*, I (Feb.-Mar., 1934), 289-90.
37 Madison, *Big Bend Country*, 139-42; Mitchell, "The Stampede at Robber's Roost," *Voice of the Mexican Border*, I (Oct., 1933), 90.
38 "Up the Trail in 1890 – Experiences of Drive Told by Tom Granger, Ft. Davis," *Alpine Avalanche*, Sept. 14, 1951, 22.
39 Wright, "Early Settling of the Big Bend," *West Texas Historical and Scientific Society Publications*, XIX (1963), 61; *El Paso Daily Times*, May 27, 1886; Scobee, "The First General Cattle Round-Up of the Davis Mountains-Big Bend District," *West Texas Historical and Scientific Society Publications*, III (1930), 45-47.
40 Quotations in both Collinson, *Life in the Saddle*, 207, 214, and Skaggs, "A Study in Business Failure: Frank Collinson in the Big Bend," *Panhandle-Plains Historical Review*, XLIII (1970), 12, 14, 16.
41 Utley, "Range Cattle Industry," 439-40; *The New Era* (Marfa), Jan. 7, 1911.
42 Dobie, *The Longhorns*, 61-64; Scobee, *The Steer Branded Murder: The True and Authentic Account of a Frontier Tragedy*; Shipman, "The Lone Red Murder Yearling of West Texas," *Voice of the Mexican Border*, I (Feb.-Mar., 1934), 271-73.
43 Hitchcock, "Representative Individuals and Families of the Lower Big Bend Region, 1895-1925," 4-5.
44 *Victoria Advocate*, Sept. 28, 1878.
45 Madison, *Big Bend Country*, 169-70.
46 *El Paso Daily Times*, May 30, 1886.
47 Madison, *Big Bend Country*, 169-71; *The New Era*, June 18, 1910.
48 *El Paso Daily Times*, May 30, 1886; Maxwell, *The Big Bend*, 117; Myres (ed.), *Pioneer Surveyor*, 233-34.
49 *The New Era*, Aug, 14, 1909.

50   Wauer, *Backcountry Roads and the River,* 11-12; Wauer, *Hiker's Guide to the Developed Trails and Primitive Routes,* 22, 24.

51   Römer, *Texas, With Particular Reference to German Immigration and the Physical Appearance of the Country,* 268; Johnson, "A History of Mercury Mining in the Terlingua District of Texas," *The Mines Magazine* (Sept., 1946), 390; Walker, "Quicksilver Mining in the Terlingua Area," 22-23.

52   Day, "Quicksilver in 1894," *U.S. Geological Survey, 16th Annual Report,* Pt. 3, 601; Hawley, "Life Along the Border," 19.

53   Hawley, "Life Along the Border," 43-45; Walker, "Quicksilver Mining in the Terlingua Area," 28, 42.

54   Hawley, "Life Along the Border," 15, 17, 20, 51; *The New Era,* Feb. 15, 1908.

55   Day, "The Chisos Quicksilver Bonanza in the Big Bend of Texas," *Southwestern Historical Quarterly,* LXIV (Apr., 1961), 429; Walker, "Quicksilver Mining in the Terlingua Area," 37; Myres (ed.), *Pioneer Surveyor,* 227-29 .

56   Day, "Chisos Quicksilver Bonanza," 433-34; *Alpine Avalanche,* Mar. 31, 1910.

57   Walker, "Quicksilver Mining in the Terlingua Area,", 45.

58   Casey, *Soldiers, Ranchers and Miners,* 217-19.

59   *Ibid.,* 228-31; Wauer, *Guide to the Backcountry Roads,* 17.

60   *Alpine Avalanche,* Apr. 5, 1907; Casey, *Mirages, Mysteries and Reality,* 106-07.

61   *The New Era,* Mar. 7, 1908, Apr. 3, May 22, 1909, Nov. 19, 1910; *Alpine Avalanche,* Oct. 14, 1909; Casey, *Mirages, Mysteries and Reality,* 121; Jones, *Health Seekers in the Southwest, 1817-1900,* 103-04.

62   *Alpine Avalanche,* Nov. 2, 1911.

63   *The New Era,* Apr. 29, 1911; *Alpine Avalanche,* Oct. 26, 1911, Nov. 2, 1911.

64   Smithers, "Nature's Pharmacy and the Curanderos" and "The Border Trading Posts," *West Texas Historical and Scientific Society Publications,* XVIII, 42, 45, 49.

65   Clifton, "A History of the Bloys Camp Meeting," *West Texas Historical and Scientific Society Publications,* XII (1947).

66   Hawley, "Life Along the Border," 47; Sonnichsen, *I'll Die Before I'll Run: The Story of the Great Feuds of Texas,* 86.

67   Hawley, "Life Along the Border," 9, 12, 15, 52; quotation in Smithers, "Bandit Raids in the Big Bend Country," in *Pancho Villa's Last Hangout – On Both Sides of the Rio Grande in the Big Bend Country,* 79; *The New Era,* July 18, 1908, 1; quotation in Hinkle, *Wings and Saddles: The Air and Cavalry Punitive Expedition of 1919,* 32-33.

68   *Alpine Avalanche,* Oct. 21, Dec. 2, 1909.

69   Hawley, "Life Along the Border," 82-85.

70   Hitchcock, "Families of the Lower Big Bend," 13-14, 22, 54-55; Haley, *Jeff Milton, a Good Man with a Gun,* 66-92.

71   Saxton and Casey. "The Life of Everett Ewing Townsend," *West Texas Historical and Scientific Society Publications*, XVII, 37-40.

Chapter 6

1   Hill, "Running the Cañons," 372; Haley, *Jeff Milton,* 58.

2   Capt. Neal Coldwell to Gen. John B. Jones, Fort Davis, July 10, 1880, in *Voice of the Mexican Border*, I (Dec., 1933), 174-76; Gillespie to Coldwell, Fort Davis, Jan, 10, 1882, in Adjutant General's Records; *San Antonio Daily Express, Aug.* 9, 1879 (quotation), Aug. 11, 1881, Feb. 25, 1882; Adams, *Billy the Kid,* 4, 80, 88, 133, 240; Robert M. Utley, *Billy the Kid, a Short and Violent Life,* 3; Utley, *Lone Star Justice: The First Century of the Texas Rangers,* 209- 12; Clayton W. Williams, *Texas' Last Frontier: Fort Stockton and the Trans-Pecos, 1861-1895,* 251-52.

3   For information on the Chinese laborers, see Edward J. M. Rhoads, "The Chinese in Texas," *Southwestern Historical Quarterly,* LXXXI (July 1977), 8-10; and Utley, *Lone Star Justice,* 209-12.

4   *San Saba Weekly News,* Oct. 30, 1891; and "ATEN, EDWIN DUNLAP," The Handbook of Texas Online, <http://www.tsha.utexas.edu/handbook/online/articles/view/AA/fat10.html> [Accessed Wed. Mar. 26 22:01:59 US/Central 2003]; Utley, *Lone Star Justice,* 229-30.

5   Madison, *Big Bend County,* 47-48.

6   Saxton and Casey, "Everett Ewing Townsend," 53-54; Hill, "Running the Cañons," 371, 376.

7   "Annual Report for the Fiscal Year 1916 of Major Frederick Funston, U.S. Army, Commanding Southern Department," in Records of the Adjutant General's Office, 1, 42; Hawley, "Life Along the Border," 74-75.

8   Second Asst. Sec. of State Alvey A. Adee to Sec. of War Jacob Dickinson, Washington, Nov. 19, 1910, in Office of the Adjutant General Documents File, 1716354, Box 6314, Doc. No. 1716354; *The New Era,* Jan. 28, 1911: Hawley, "Life Along the Border," 74.

9   *The New Era,* Feb. 4, 1911.

10   Statement of Francisco and Dario Sánchez, in Office of the Adjutant General Documents File, 1716354, Box 6316, Doc. No. 1716354/A-784.

11   *Ibid.,* Feb. 11, 1911.

12   Captain Barton to Adjutant General, Department of Texas, Candelaria, June 8, 1911, in Office of the Adjutant General Documents File, 1716354, Box 6316, Doc No. A-771.

13   Duncan to Adjutant General, San Antonio, March 9, 1912, in

Office of the Adjutant General Document, File, 1716354, Box 6807, Doc. No. 1875135/A-143; Langford, *Big Bend,* 140-44.

14   Langford, *Big Bend,* 150-51.

15   See *Alpine Avalanche,* Feb. 20, 1913; Smithers, "Bandit Raids," 65, 67; Webb, *The Texas Rangers: A Century of Frontier Defense,* 498.

16   Landrum to Sheppard, Boquillas, Texas, March 4, 1913, and Brig. Gen. Tasker H. Bliss to Adj. Gen. George Andrews, Fort Sam Houston, Mar. 24, 1913, in Office of the Adjutant General Documents File, 2008188, Box 7128, Doc. No. 2019224; *Alpine Avalanche,* Feb. 20, 27, 1913.

17   Barnhardt to Commanding General Southern Department, Marfa, May 22, 1915, in Office of the Adjutant General Documents File 2212358, Box 7644, Doc. No. 2292205.

18   Wilson to Garrison, Cornish, N.H., July 12, 1915, Garrison to Wilson, Washington, July 22, 1915, Doc. No. 2264551-E; Ferguson to Funston, Austin, June 25, 1915, and Funston to Ferguson, Fort Sam Houston, July 1, 1915, Doc. No. 2264551-D; quotation in Garrison to Wilson, Washington, Mar. 2, 1915, Bliss to Chief of Staff, Washington, June 22, 1915, and Garrison to Wilson, Washington, June 22, 1915, Doc. No. 2264551-C: all in Office of the Adjutant General Documents File 2212358, Box 7644.

19   See Glenn Justice, *Little Known History of The Texas Big Bend: Documented Chronicles from Cabeza de Vaca to the Era of Pancho Villa,* 110-11. See also Braddy, *Pancho Villa at Columbus: The Raid of 1916,* 1, 15-16; "Annual Report of Major General Funston," 19; Clendennen, *Blood on the Border: The United States Army and the Mexican Irregulars,* chs. 9 and 10.

20   Smith to Baker, Washington, Mar. 23, 1916, in Office of the Adjutant General Documents File, 2377632, Box 8143, Doc. No. 2383978.

21   *Alpine Avalanche,* May 11, 1916; Wood, "The Glenn Springs Raid," *West Texas Historical and Scientific Society Publications,* XIX (1963), 65-71; Raht, *Romance of Davis Mountains and Big Bend,* 350-58; Maxwell, *The Big Bend,* 61-67; Mason, *The Great Pursuit,* ch. 10: Smithers, "Bandit Raids," 71-74.

22   Barnum to Adjutant General, Fort Sam Houston, May 7, 1916, in Office of the Adjutant General Documents File, 2398805, Box 8132, Doc. No. 1361.

23   Smithers, "Bandit Raids," 72.

24   *Ibid.;* Maxwell, *The Big Bend,* 67.

25   Copy of Carranza to Eliseo Arrandondo, Mexico, May 8, 1916, Doc. No. 2399537; Scott and Funston to Secretary of War, El Paso, May 7 and 8, 1916, Docs. No. 13 and 16, all in Office of the Adjutant General Documents File, 2398805, Box 8132; Arthur R. Gómez, *A Most Singular Country: A History of Occupation in the Big Bend,* 147.

26   James Hopper, "A Little Mexican Expedition," *Collier's, the National Weekly,* LVII (July 15, 1916), 6; Langhorne to Col. F. W. Sibley, Deemer's Store, May 22, 1916, in Office of the Adjutant General Documents File, 2398805, Box 8132, Doc. No. 2398805-V; Mason, *Great Pursuit,* 186.

27   Langhorne to Sibley, Deemer's Store, May 22, 1916; Cramer, "The Punitive Expedition from Boquillas," *U.S. Cavalry Journal,* XXVIII (Oct., 1916), 211-12.

28   Hopper, "Little Mexican Expedition," 22; Langhorne to Sibley, Deemer's Store, May 22, 1916; Cramer, "Punitive Expedition from Boquillas," 213; the *Alpine Avalanche,* May 18, 1916.

29   Hopper, "Little Mexican Expedition," 22.

30   Langhorne to Sibley, Deemer's Store, May 22, 1916; quotation in Cramer, "Punitive Expedition from Boquillas," 213.

31   Cramer, "Punitive Expedition from Boquillas," 214.

32   *Ibid.,* 217-18.

33   *Ibid.,* 219-20.

34   *Ibid.,* 223; Funston to Adjutant General, Fort Sam Houston, May 20, 1910, in Office of the Adjutant General Documents File 2398805, Box 8132.

35   Cramer, "Punitive Expedition from Boquillas," 223-24.

36   Smithers, "Bandit Raids," 74; Rahorg, "The Villa Raid on Glenn Springs."

37   Clendennen, *Blood on the Border,* 287, 289-90.

38   Scott, *Some Memoirs of a Soldier,* 527-28.

39   Interview with W. P. Cameron, Mineral Wells, July 2, 1970.

40   Interview with Dr. Calhoun H. Monroe, El Paso, Nov. 9, 1971.

41   Smithers, "Bandit Raids," 67, 69, 71; Webb, *The Texas Rangers,* 502-03; and Hawley, "Life Along the Border," 65 (quote). A different and fuller version of the Porvenir massacre is told in Justice, *Little Known History of the Texas Big Bend,* 148-58.

42   The story of the raid on the Nevill ranch is told in Justice, *Little Known History of the Texas Big Bend,* 159-64.

43   Smithers, "Bandit Raids," 74-79; Webb, *The Texas Rangers,* 499-504.

44   Casey, *Soldiers, Ranchers and Miners,* 47-51, 57-58; interview with Mr. and Mrs. Hart M. Greenwood.

45   Hinkle, *Wings Over the Border: The Army Air Service Armed Patrol of the United States-Mexico Border, 1919-1921,* 10-12.

46   Hinkle, *Wings and Saddles,* 8-10, 12-22, 28-38, 55-65, contains a thorough account of the ransom of the flyers.

Chapter 7

1   Interview with Ross A. Maxwell, Austin, April 6, 1973; Saxton and Casey, "Everett Ewing Townsend," v.

2   August 12, 1916 is the date on the postcard pictured in a *Fort Worth Star-Telegram* story, Apr. 5, 1958, Sec. 5, 16.

3   Schoffelmayer, "The Big Bend Area of Texas: A Geographic Wonderland," *Texas Geographic Magazine,* 1 (May, 1937), 1; *Dallas Morning News,* Oct. 12, 19, 23, 1937; Connelly, "Big Bend National Park Project Reality at Last," *West Texas Today* (Sept., 1941).

4   Dobie, "The Texan Part of Texas," *Nature Magazine*, XVI (Dec., 1930), 343-46, 393, 395; Wagstaff, "Beginnings of the Big Bend Park," *West Texas Historical Association Year Book*, XLIV (Oct., 1968), 3-4, 6.

5   Wagstaff, "Beginnings of the Big Bend Park," 7, 9, 11.

6   *Ibid.*, 11-12.

7   *Ibid.*, 12, 14.

8   Foree, "Our New Park on the Rio Grande," *The Saturday Evening Post*, Dec. 2, 1944, 106; Madison, *The Big Bend*, 231-32; Townsend to Lewis, Nov. 25, 1933, copy in Brewster County Scrapbook.

9   Interview with Maxwell; Madison, *The Big Bend*, 233-34.

10   *Report on the Big Bend Area, Texas*. U.S. Department of the Interior, National Park Service, January 1935.

11   Casey, *Soldiers, Ranchers and Miners*, 188; *Fort Worth Star-Telegram*, June 24, 1935.

12   Garrison, "A History of the Proposed Big Bend International Park"; *Fort Worth Star-Telegram*, June 24, 1935.

13   *Rocky Mountain News* (Denver), Feb. 26, 1936.

14   Interview with Maxwell; *Waco Tribune Herald*, June 28, 1936.

15   *Austin Dispatch*, Apr. 19, 1937; *Dallas Morning News*, May 11, 1937; *Houston Chronicle*, Art Gravure Section, Feb. 27, 1938.

16   Because of the uncertainty of establishing the park and because the Park Service insisted that the project be completed immediately, Webb never finished the history of the Big Bend that he had proposed. Instead, he submitted an account of his trip through Santa Elena Canyon that remains unpublished. See Webb to Herbert Maier, Feb. 3, 1938, and "Materials Prepared as a Basis for a Guide to Points of Interest in the Proposed Big Bend National Park," in the Walter P. Webb Papers.

17   Skaggs to Webb, McCamey, Texas, June 10, 1937, in Webb Papers; interview with Maxwell.

18   Maier to Record, Oklahoma City, July 13, 1937, in Carter Foundation files; Madison, *The Big Bend*, 235.

19   Minutes of the Meeting of the Executive Board Texas Big Bend Park Association, and Mayes to Morelock to Carter, May 9, Alpine, in Carter Foundation files.

20   Audit of the TBBPA in Carter Foundation files; *Fort Worth Star-Telegram*, Sept. 13, 1942, Sec. 1, 5; *Dallas Morning News*, Sept. 15, 1939.

21   Memo from Harry Connelly to Carter, Fort Worth, Dec. 6, 1941, and radio script, Feb. 16, 1941, in Carter Foundation files; *San Antonio Express*, July 19, 1938, Mar. 5, 1941; *San Angelo Standard-Times*, Apr. 11, 1941; Madison, *The Big Bend*, 236; Saxton and Casey, "Everett Ewing Townsend," 61; *Big Spring Herald*, Mar. 5, 1941.

22   Interview with Mr. and Mrs. Hart M. Greenwood.

23   *Dallas Morning News*, Aug. 9, 16, 1941. Casey, *Soldiers, Ranchers and Miners*, 189, 250-51; Madison, *Big Bend*, 237-38; *San Antonio Light*, Mar. 1, 1942; *San Angelo Standard-Times*, Feb. 27, 1942.

24   *Fort Worth Star-Telegram,* Sept. 6, 1943; Garrison, "Big Bend International Park."
25   Madison, *Big Bend,* 239-40; *Dallas Morning News,* June 7, 1944, Sec. 1, 2; Wauer, *Birds of Big Bend National Park and Vicinity.*
26   Interview with Maxwell.
27   Garrison, "Big Bend International Park." *Fort Worth Star-Telegram,* Nov. 21, 1955, 1. Madison, *Big Bend,* 251-52. Another excellent summary of the establishment of the national park is Casey, "The Big Bend National Park," *West Texas Historical and Scientific Society Publications,* XIII (1948), 26-42.

Historic Sites

1   Madison and Stillwell, *How Come It's Called That?,* 5-7.
2   *Ibid.,* 4, 6-7, 51, 57-58, 74; Maxwell, *The Big Bend,* 4, 83.

This factory near Candelaria produced wax from the candelilla plant. It was photographed about 1918.

Index

Live Oak Creek, 55
Llanero Indians, 45
Llano Estacado, 101
Llano River, 54
López, Francisco, 23, 25
López, Nicholás, 26
Lost Mine Peak, 19
Lost Mine trails, 211
Love, John, 77, 100
Lozoya, Jesús, 207
Lujan, Natividad, 14

M

McCutcheon, Beau, 134
McCutcheon, Jim, 134
McKay, Douglas, 207
McKenzie, ——, 137
McKinney Springs, 105, 147
McMahon, James, 148
Macmanus, George L., 72
Madison rapids, 97
Mague, 64–66
Maier, Herbert, 202
Maltby, W. J., 119
Mangas Coloradas, 117
Manless, George W., 138–39
Mano, 86–87
Mapimí, Chihuahua, 10, 32, 36
Maps of Big Bend, 6, 38, 39, 46–47, 48, 54–55, 57, 78–79, 101, 170
Marathon, Tex., 5, 127, 128, 133, 147, 152, 154, 155, 162, 167, 169, 175, 195, 218–19
Maravillas Canyon, 95–96, 100
Maravillas Creek, 128, 131
Marcy, Randolph B., 115
Marcy, William L., 76
Marfa and Mariposa Mining Company, 139, 142, 143, 144
Marfa National Bank, 183, 184
Marfa, Tex., 5, 111, 112, 124, 125, 126, 136–37, 139, 142, 147, 154, 160, 177, 178, 179, 181, 183, 184, 186, 200, 201
Mariscal Canyon (Little San Vicente Canyon), 2, 13, 35, 48, 65, 77, 90–95, 101, 192
Mariscal Mine, 110, 144–45
Mariscal Mining Company, 145
Mariscal Mountain, 13, 18, 90, 144

Matlack, Leonard F., 181, 184
Maverick Mountain, 8–9
Maverick, Samuel, 54
Maxwell, Ross A., 5, 15, 19, 197–98, 199, 205–06
Means, John Z., 128
Meler, T. M., 11, 148
Melnotte, ——, 71
Menard County, Tex., 26, 42, 129
Mendoza, Juan Domínguez de, 25–26, 51
Mercury, See quicksilver
Merfelder, Nick, 151
Merritt, Wesley, 114
Mesa de Anguila, 2, 10, 18, 88, 108
Mesa de los Fresnos, 35
Mescalero Apache Indians, 29, 38, 45, 48, 63, 68, 90, 114, 115, 117
Mexican Boundary Survey, 71
Mexican Revolution (1911), 159–61, 187
Mexican War (1846–1848), 51, 53, 69, 70, 75, 76, 104, 121
Meyer, Edward S., 114
Michler, Nathaniel, 59, 77, 97–100
Michler Survey, 97–100
Midland, Tex., 191
Miller, Sam, 123
Miller, T. J., 147
Milton, Jeff, 155
Mineral Wells, Tex., 175, 177
Mining in Big Bend, 135–45, 200
"Mirror twins," 87
Mission 66, 207, 210
Mitchell, F. A., 132
Mitchell, W. F., 134
Monclova, Coahuila, 10, 25, 32, 33, 35, 36, 37, 42, 101
Monclova Vieja, 45
Monier, John, 111
Monterrey, Nuevo León, 111, 113
Morelock, Dr. H. W., 202, 203, 206
Morfi, Juan Agustín de, 43
Mowinkle, J. E., 203
Moye, Charles, 111, 112
Mule Ears Peaks, 36
Mulhem, Charles, 123
Murderer's Canyon, 11
Murphy, Daniel, 123
Murrah, J. E., 187

281

PICTURE CREDITS

The National Park Service and the Amon Carter Museum gratefully acknowledge the generosity of Mr. Bank Langmore, Dallas, Texas, in contributing his splendid photographs of the Big Bend region to both the exhibition and this book. Many other individuals and institutions contributed illustrations, as listed below, and thanks is due them also.

- Alabama Department of Archives and History: 85.
- David Muench: 12.
- American Antiquarian Society: 46–47.
- Amon Carter Museum of Western Art: 107, 153 (top right), 182, 210.
- Arizona Historical Society: 81 (Bartlett).
- Clifford Casey, Alpine, Tex.: 31, 169, 170, 212.
- From William E. Connelley, *Doniphan's Expedition* . . . (1907), 277: 53.
- Charles Crabtree Collection, Fort Worth, Texas: 254, 273.
- Emory's *Report:* 65, 66, 87, 88, 91, 96.
- El Paso Public Library: 3 (Nevill).
- *Fort Worth Star Telegram.* April 5, 1958: 191 (left).
- Mr. and Mrs. Hart Greenwood, Marfa, Texas: 130, 228.
- Junior Historians, Marfa, Texas: 122, 125 (top left), 140, 160, 200 (top).
- Bank Langmore: 8–9, 16–17, 50, 74, 110, 156, 188, 208–09.
- Library of Congress: 78 (Johnston), 80 (Whiting), 81 (Emory), 119 (Shafter).
- Ministerior del Ejército, Madrid, Spain: 39–41.
- Missouri Historical Society: 68.
- National Archives: 78–79, 116 (Victorio), 119 (Grierson), 176 (top) 183.
- Western History Collections, University of Oklahoma Library: 53 (Hays), 69.
- University of Rochester: 101, 102–03.
- Rochester Historical Society: 92–93.
- Sul Ross State University Library, Alpine, Texas: 159, 176 (bottom two).
- Ron C. Tyler: 20
- Barker Texas History Collection, University of Texas, Austin: 124–25 and 125 (top right).
- Hunter Collection, Harry Ransom Humanities Research Center, University of Texas, Austin, 113.
- W. D. Smithers Collection, Harry Ransom Humanities Research Center, University of Texas, Austin: 34, 116, 124, 128, 129, 135, 140 (right), 141, 143, 146, 148, 150, 151, 152, 152–53, 165, 166, 167, 171, 175, 178, 179, 181, 185, 186, 191 (Townsend), 195, 199, 200, 201, 207.
- U.S. Geological Survey, Denver: 3, 4, 7, 136, 194, 204.
- Wells Fargo Bank, History Room, San Francisco: 108.